W9-AXE-599

Pool Techniques and Tricks

A Firefly Book

Published by Firefly Books Ltd. 2011

Copyright © 2011 Les Éditions de l'Homme
Translation © 2011 Firefly Books Ltd.

All rights reserved. No part of this publication may be reproduced, stored in a retrieval system, or transmitted in any form or by any means, electronic, mechanical, photocopying, recording or otherwise, without the prior written permission of the Publisher.

First printing

Publisher Cataloging-in-Publication Data (U.S.)
Morin, Pierre.
    Pool techniques and tricks / Pierre Morin.
Originally published: Quebec: Sogides, 2010.
[258] p. : photos. ; cm.
Includes index.
Summary: A guide to playing pool including advice from players, vocabulary, rules, equipment, basic techniques and various strategies, clear diagrams, and more than 100 professional trick shots.
ISBN-13: 978-1-55407-938-4 (pbk.)
1. Pool (Game). I. Title.
794.7330922   dc22   GV891.A3M675 2011

Library and Archives Canada Cataloguing in Publication
Morin, Pierre, 1946 June 29-
    Pool techniques and tricks / Pierre Morin.
Translation of: Techniques et trucs de billard.
ISBN 978-1-55407-938-4
    1. Billiards. I. Titre.
GV891.M67313 2011   794.72   C2011-902757-7

Published in the United States by
Firefly Books (U.S.) Inc.
P.O. Box 1338, Ellicott Station
Buffalo, New York 14205

Published in Canada by
Firefly Books Ltd.
66 Leek Crescent
Richmond Hill, Ontario L4B 1H1

Printed in China

Pierre Morin

Pool Techniques and Tricks

FIREFLY BOOKS

TABLE OF CONTENTS

PART I
The Techniques

PART II
The Tricks

INTRODUCTION

Billiards is the supreme art of anticipation. It is not a game but a complete artistic sport that requires, in addition to being in good physical condition, the logical reasoning of a chess player and the touch of a concert pianist.

Albert Einstein

When I started playing pool at the age of 13, there were no competent instructors in my area that could teach me the rudiments of this game that fascinated me so much. There was no pool on television, in contrast to today. Therefore, I decided to get a book on the topic so that I could learn quickly and correctly. Unfortunately, whether you believe it or not, there were no books on pool in French! There were a few, rare books in French on the market, but they all dealt with pocketless billiards, a game played in Europe using only three balls. I was disappointed; however, to fix the situation, I promised myself that I would write a book at some point in

the future and I even announced my intentions to family and friends. Everyone took my words with a grain of salt, for, since I was a teenager, they thought that this project would be forgotten. However, over the years, people would ask me to find a book in French on the fundamentals of pool. Regrettably, I always had to inform them that this didn't exist, whether in Quebec or elsewhere. As I remained a fervent fan of this game, I started to buy books in English on the topic. I became increasingly convinced that publishing this type of guide in French would be useful. At the time, much like today, actually, I could have been happy translating a book by

Mosconi, Mizerak or Crane. I believe, however, that these works, despite the celebrity of their authors, can't completely satisfy the average amateur. Most of the time, the professionals began playing at the age of 5 and are so familiar with the game that they forget some of the critical, basic rules. Even if some of them have published excellent books, none of them can claim to know everything about the game. Each one has his strengths and his weaknesses. I thought it would be better to publish an original work that emphasizes the particular aspects of the different types of games played here. It took several years to fulfill this dream; in 1978 I was the first to publish a book on pool in French, *Techniques de billard*, which was a huge success. Since then, I've published two other books, *100 trucs de billard* in 1982 and *Le livre du billard* in 1999.

The first two books haven't been available for quite some time now, and I'm sometimes asked where my 1982 book on tricks can be found. Therefore, there's a real need for a book to be published explaining the tricks that are regularly seen in professional competitions on television. And, to be able to do the tricks, you first have to learn and assimilate the basic techniques! In pool as in other sports, the caliber of the game constantly improves, creating changes in technique, which has evolved somewhat in the last 30 years: amateurs have adopted new games, particularly eight-ball and nine-ball, which involves a change in dynamics and strategy from

several points of view. Therefore, I placed more emphasis on the new techniques, such as the jump shot, which is very popular in the game of nine-ball.

For an experienced amateur pool player such as myself, with a respectable library on the topic (more than 300 books and approximately 1,000 magazines and journals, mostly in English), it's an inexhaustible subject. Indeed, there are multiple aspects to this game, whether you think of its origins, its evolution, its history, its champions or its techniques. If you reflect at greater length on this game, its evolution is fascinating, and it represents the evolution of society that we see pass before our eyes. For example, since gender equality is a reality in almost all fields, including sports, pool is now as popular among women as it is among men.

Of course, the context has completely changed. The places to practice are completely different. Luxurious rooms, outfitted in the style of the day, have 20, 30 or 40 tables, sometimes even more, and have become the meeting place of choice for teenagers and young adults. The old biases against this recreational activity have disappeared, and we now see pool scenes in movies, soap operas, television commercials and newspapers. It's become very fashionable to play pool. At the turn of the millennium, surveys showed that this sport was extremely popular. While we almost never used to see any tournaments on television, the sports channels now show entire pool competitions and billiard tricks. It's finally possible, practically every day, to see the best players compete. Throughout the Western world, women have assumed their place in the world of pool as in many other fields, and they're grouped together in one organization that promotes their interests. Their professional competitions are very structured and, today, female champions have as many prizes and sponsorships as their male counterparts.

Another new, equally remarkable trend: the globalization of pool. The influence of American society being what it is, we now play pool not only in North America, but also in Asia and Europe, in particular Germany, France, the Netherlands, Belgium, Switzerland, England and Scandinavia, as well as Australia, Japan, China, South Korea and the Philippines. An international organization oversees and approves world competitions. Several professionals from other countries have been participating for several years in many tournaments held in the United States and throughout the world. The invasion of foreign players isn't just symbolic, for they win many major tournaments. Moreover, in 1997, for the first time in the history of pool, two non-Americans, Jose Parica from the Philippines for the men and Allison Fisher of Great Britain for the women, won the title of Player of the Year in the United States. Fisher also won in 1996. All female recipients of this title since then have not been American; on the men's side, non-Americans have won every year since 2007. In 2006, a 14.1 world championship was reintroduced in the United States. A type of game invented by the Americans 100 years ago, it was completely dominated by Americans until the last championship held in 1990. It's now the Europeans who are being crowned the champions, whether it's the Germans in 2006 and 2007, the Dutch in 2008, or, a major event in the history of pool, the French in 2009!

Another remarkable change, this time closer to home: in Canada, pool is in the process of replacing snooker. The release of the film *The Hustler* in 1961, with Paul Newman and Jackie Gleason, caused a wild craze for pool in America and marked the start of the decline of snooker in favor of its American counterpart. Hollywood did it again in 1986 when it released the sequel to *The Hustler*, *The Color of Money*, with Tom Cruise and Paul Newman, who won an Oscar for his role as the veteran pool player making a spectacular comeback to the game, which increased the popularity of pool throughout the world. Even in the United Kingdom, the stronghold of snooker, pool is making inroads that were still unimaginable just a few years ago. It's not surprising that the prestigious American magazine *Billiards Digest* wrote, at the turn of the millennium, "American Pool tables are replacing snooker tables (at a ratio of about three-to-one) in clubs all over Britain, and the American game is gaining in popularity against staid, old snooker … As many as 3,000 American Pool tables are currently in place in the UK, and the number is climbing. Billiard manufacturers and distributors estimate that the American Pool market in the UK has experienced 100 percent growth in each of the last four years. That is what younger people want to play when they go into the clubs." Since then, the situation has only become more acute, and pool is now as popular as snooker in the United Kingdom!

Of course, snooker is still very popular in Canada. Many players play both games, like Paul Potier who was the Canadian pool champion in 2000. The same is the case for John Horsfall, who won the Canadian pool championship in 2002. Both are over 50 now, but the new generation's younger champions prefer pool, like current Canadian pool champion Chris Orme (from the Toronto area), who also competes frequently (and sometime wins) in professional pool tournaments in the United States. To win the crown in 2010, he had to defeat in playoff the previous champion for 2008 and 2009, Alain Martel from Montreal, a very tough opponent. There are also several proficient females playing pool in our country. In 2010, the Canadian woman champion was Naomi Williams, who beat in playoff the champion of the previous year, Brittany Bryant.

Another major change can be found in the regulations for different types of pool games. In the past, it was total anarchy when it came to the rules, with everyone advocating his own and claiming to be an expert. In fact, in Quebec there were as many rules as there were pool halls, as we used to say. It was ridiculous, a well-established custom that saw the owner of a hall inherently invested with the power to decree the rules that applied there. Since you don't become an expert just by opening a pool hall, there was a proliferation of confusing, and sometimes contradictory, laws and dictates. Normally, one of the first duties of a law should be to simplify the lives of those who have to obey it. Not only were the rules imposed at the time extremely complicated, but they also made the game much more difficult than the one played by professionals. Fortunately, different factors sped up the change in behavior in this area. After several decades of battles, one uniform set of regulations was announced. Around 2000, nearly all the organizations promoting pool, both locally and internationally, adopted a set of so-called "standard" rules concerning the different types of pool, of which the most popular are eight-ball and nine-ball. They were drafted, then made public. Today, they're accepted and applied by almost all players and in all major competitions, not only in Quebec, but also around the world.

Pool is a fascinating game. It's a hobby that is accessible to all, regardless of age and gender. In fact, it is the best family pastime. Pool has some unique advantages. Anyone who plays hockey or football has to "retire" at the age of 40 or even earlier, while this is the age when we most need a hobby. This disadvantage doesn't exist in pool.

Photo: © Billiards Digest

Not only is billiards accessible to women and men of all ages, but also, in some instances, the physically challenged can take part. In the U.S., tournaments reserved for wheelchair players are held regularly. In this photo, we see Scott Simonetti, who took up billiards again after his left hand and left foot were amputated following a serious Staphylococcus aureus infection in 2009. Despite being young and in good health, Simonetti fell victim to this terrible bacterium. A friend who manufactures cues created a type of prosthesis that has a support at the end of the cue that he attaches to his left arm using Velcro. Scott demonstrated extraordinary courage and took up most of his former activities. Even though he acknowledges that the caliber of his game has decreased, he considers himself lucky to still be alive.

You can play it until you're 100. In fact, Willie Hoppe set the record for longevity in all sports when he won his last world title at the age of 65. More recently, the famous Belgian Raymond Ceulemans won his last world championship in 2001 at the age of 64, playing three-cushion billiards. It was the 21st time that he had won this title! We need to emphasize, however, that, in general, it's no different in pool than in any other sport: champions reach their peak between 25 and 30 years of age. Certainly, since pool is less physically demanding, most can still achieve great results for decades, but admittedly, sharpness diminishes, beginning in the 40s. Your motions aren't as fluid, your eyesight diminishes, the tension surrounding competitions becomes less tolerable and your motivation is no longer the same.

Aside from the fact that many families have a pool table at home, over the last few years pool tables have also become available in public places, such as discos, pubs and restaurants. Since games played on these tables largely depend on using coins (eight-ball), they don't always help enthusiasts to improve their game, for this type of environment doesn't promote a high level of play. We're witnessing a curious phenomenon: girls are now playing as much as boys, and young people have adopted discos and bars equipped with pool tables in order to socialize without ever wanting to become champions. Even if the number of enthusiasts today is higher than ever, the proportion of expert players remains minimal. Therefore, it's easy to predict that the future of pool in our country and elsewhere in the world is extremely promising.

The trend in family and commercial tables motivated manufacturers, sellers and owners to promote the game by organizing tournaments, leagues, demonstrations and competitions. Increasingly, pool is finally getting its fair share of publicity in the vast world of sports. Despite this improvement, there's still a long way to go before pool will be on an equal footing with other individual professional sports like golf and tennis, especially with respect to the prizes awarded to champions. Thus, in 2009, when Frenchman Stephan Cohen won the world 14.1 championship in the United States, he earned a prize of $10,000, or 100 times less than what he would have earned if he had played golf or tennis! It's very disappointing for people who spend much time and effort mastering this discipline and who reach the pinnacle of their sport.

It's a myth to think that pool professionals lead the life of a prince with the winnings they earn from their success in North America. It costs a fortune to register, travel, stay overnight and eat in order to play in major tournaments, without any guarantee they'll have reasonable winnings, so that few have the financial resources necessary to participate regularly. You can count on the fingers of one hand the number of people who succeed in living (modestly) on their success in this field. And to get there, a professional has to win several tournaments each year, which is not an easy thing to do, especially if you consider that there are few large-scale competitions, and that the world of professional pool has no organizational structure. Even the great American professional and champion Johnny Archer, who at the age of 40 was elected to the Billiard Congress of America (BCA) Hall of Fame in 2009, was forced, over the last few years of his career, to financially invest in a pool hall because the earnings he won from his success at pool were not enough to live on! In addition, there's no pension and therefore no security. The famous champion Ralph Greenleaf, a veritable legend in pool circles, who dominated the sport in the 1920s and 1930s, died in poverty in 1950. Only in 1987 was a tombstone placed on his grave, thanks to fundraising organized by his admirers. The situation since hasn't improved much.

Interestingly, American women professional players are more organized than their male counterparts, for they have had an association for more than 20 years: the Women's Professional Billiards Association (WPBA), which was able to attract major business sponsors, so that they can now win amounts as high as those paid to the men. Curiously, in the United Kingdom, it's the opposite. Male snooker champions can win major prizes, while their female counterparts can only participate in a few minor tournaments offering small prizes. This is what caused several talented UK female players to move to the United States. The first was Allison Fisher in 1995, followed a few years later by Karen Corr and Kelly Fisher (no relation), who are classified in the upper ranks of the American women's professional section. Currently, the two best female players are Jasmin Ouschan of Austria and Ga Young Kim of China.

This illustrates the ups and downs of professional sports, pool being no exception to the rule. You'll have a lot of fun playing pool and you'll spend some pleasant moments with family or friends, for it's an ideal game for socializing in a relaxed atmosphere. But if you want to become a champion, know that you'll have to spend a lot of money and time. The great pool champion Robert Byrne, an American engineer and author of several books on the subject, describes the situation well: "Readers really serious about mastering the game should drop out of school, quit their jobs and get a divorce." Unfortunately, there's a lot of truth in this joke.

In Canada, because of the major temperature shifts, all outdoor sports (such as skiing, golf, baseball, football and tennis) are subject to the seasons, so that playing these sports is limited to as little as five months of the year. From this point of view, pool offers a distinct advantage, since you can play it all year round and, moreover, in your own home. No heavy, expensive equipment to transport, no long distances to travel, no need to make a reservation or pay a fee.

It's generally believed that, to play pool, you have to have good eyesight. False. Good eyesight is certainly an asset, but you can play pool without having the eyes of a lynx. Some years, Dave Trush was considered legally blind by the Illinois Department of Transportation and he couldn't hold a driver's license. However, at the same time, he was ranked second in the annual tournament in Peoria, Illinois. This proves that perfect vision is not essential to playing pool. Many professionals wear glasses and are very good players. You may have seen the UK champion on television a few years ago, wearing huge glasses that seemed to be fitted backwards in their frames, do well in major competitions. It was the Irishman Dennis Taylor, who won several major snooker tournaments in the 1980s, including the world title in 1985, and who is recognized for his funny impersonations of his fellow players.

In fact, pool, when played seriously, is a game that is as scientific as chess or bridge but that requires extraordinary skill. As the eloquent words of the great scientist Albert Einstein, quoted in the epigraph, show, it's the ideal entertainment for mathematical minds. At the heart of the game are two very different physical realities: the circle and the straight line. Balls that are as round as possible, a playing surface that is as horizontal as you can find, and a cue that is perfectly straight: this is all that's needed to have a good game of pool. Don't be afraid of getting bored, for the number of situations is almost infinite. An eminent American professor of mathematics, Dr. Frank G. Dickenson, calculated that there are approximately 63,000 trillion possible ways to pocket a ball during a regular game. What individual sport offers as many possibilities? Even if you play your entire life, it's almost impossible to find yourself in the same situation twice. When I published these figures for the first time in my first book, I received a letter a few months later from a famous American author and pool historian, Clem Trainer (who died in 1995), who stressed that Dr. Dickenson had redone his calculations, and that the new result was only 62,000 trillion possible different situations. Clearly, these mathematicians are good!

Another feature to highlight: pool is probably the only individual sport in the world where you can lose the game without taking a single shot. In tennis, golf, boxing and chess, or in any other sport or game, each player takes their turn and can also influence their opponent's game. This isn't the case in pool, since a player continues to play as long as they don't miss their goal. As a result, an expert can finish the match without ever letting their opponent get near the table. This is what happened during the 1963 world tournament in New York, when Georges Chénier from Montreal racked up a series of 150 points. The only time he allowed his opponent, Irving Crane, to get up from his chair was when he shook Georges's hand!

Whether you are an occasional amateur or a pool virtuoso, it pays to know the techniques of this exciting game. This book doesn't pretend to cover every aspect, as this would require several lengthy treatises. The goal is simply to present all the basic principles. Without proper technique, you're condemned to remaining a mediocre player. There's no miracle method. In all sports, you need to know the essential theory before moving on to practice. Of course, you can learn on your own. Before 1980 in Quebec, circumstances were such that pool enthusiasts were forced to be self-taught, and they couldn't benefit from professional advice or from the learning found in publications (which were non-existent) on the subject. These gaps force the amateur to follow a long and laborious apprenticeship: what can be learned in a week with the help of a professional can take six months when you're learning on your own. If you don't have the chance to meet with good players on a regular basis, this book will make up for the lack of teachers and become your reference guide. You won't become a champion in a few weeks, but you'll certainly improve, as you'll know the basic principles.

THE WORLD CHAMPIONS

POOL

14.1

For several decades, 14.1 was considered the ultimate scientific game used to determine who the world champion would be. Its primary distinctive feature was the fact that the player continues to play as long as they don't miss a shot. As a result, they could potentially make an unlimited number of shots, depending on their ability. In other games, the game ends when the player pockets a ball determined in advance, for example, the eight- or the nine-ball. Or, in rotation pool, the maximum number of balls that can be pocket-ed is 15, the only restriction being that they have to be pocketed in precise order beginning with the lower-numbered balls, and a win is earned when the total of the numbers on the balls pocketed exceeds the total of the numbers on the balls remaining on the table. In 14.1 professional competitions, competitors may sometimes win the game without giving their opponent a chance to play. Since the 1940s, the world championship format has been 150 points and, with every or almost every championship, the participants were able to score a run of 150. The world record (in a demonstration) was 526, achieved in 1954 by the legendary Willie Mosconi; in 1963, at the world championship held in New York, the Quebecker Georges Chénier beat Irving Crane with a run of 150 points, an extraordinary feat under the circumstances, as his opponent was then one of the best players in the world. Johnny Archer played a run of 201 points during a tournament (U.S. Open) in 1991, and Thorsten Hohmann recorded a 174 at the world championship in 2006. In 1989, the prestigious U.S. Open (a 14.1 game) was won for the first time by a European, Oliver Ortmann, a German then aged 22, who, to everyone's surprise, beat the legendary Steve Mizerak in the final. During the awards ceremony, the new champion stated: "There are many good players in Europe, but we are all young, between

20 and 25 years old. We still have much to learn, but I think in five years or so we will be even with the Americans." He won the same tournament again in 1993, but then it was discontinued until 2000, when it was again won by ... a German, Ralf Souquet. After experiencing a golden age during the first half of the 20th century, 14.1 became much less popular over the years until the world championships ended in 1990. But the purists (especially the Europeans) were infatuated with this type of pool, so much so that the world championship was reinstated in the United States in 2006, with the difference being that the matches now run 200 points (instead of 150). Below is a list of the world title holders since this time:

2006: Thorsten Hohmann, Germany
2007: Oliver Ortmann, Germany
2008: Niels Feijen, Netherlands
2009: Stephan Cohen, France
2010 : Oliver Ortmann, Germany

PLAYER OF THE YEAR

The gradual replacement throughout the 1980s of 14.1 by nine-ball as a game to determine the world champion in pool caused a major upset: it was the end of the time when the same player could monopolize the championship for several years. Aside from the fact that chance plays an important role in this, a game of nine-ball is so short that it is not possible to really measure the superiority of one player over another. It would be unfair to determine the best player based on a single tournament, regardless of whether it's called a "world championship." Indeed, in nine-ball, contrary to 14.1, a participant can benefit from luck and win a tournament without being the best. This is why, instead of referring to a world championship, since 1980 we've been referring to the "Player of the Year." He or she is chosen based on the overall performance of each of the professionals participating in most of the major tournaments throughout the year, somewhat similar to current practice in tennis or golf. At the end of each season, a panel of experts made up of analysts, columnists and journalists meets to review the statistics and performance of the best players over the last 12 months and to determine which one dominated the game and thus deserves the ultimate reward. Below is a list of the people who have received this badge of honor since 2000:

	MEN	WOMEN
2000	Earl Strickland	Allison Fisher
2001	Corey Deuel	Karen Corr
2002	F. Bustamente	Allison Fisher
2003	Johnny Archer	Allison Fisher
2004	Johnny Archer	Allison Fisher
2005	Wu Chia-Ching	Allison Fisher
2006	Ralf Souquet	Allison Fisher
2007	Shane Van Boening	Allison Fisher
2008	Mika Immonen	Kelly Fisher
2009	Mika Immonen	Jasmin Ouschan
2010	Darren Appleton	Ga Young Kim

WORLD CHAMPIONS OF SNOOKER

2000	Mark Williams
2001	Ronnie O'Sullivan
2002	Peter Ebdon
2003	Mark Williams
2004	Ronnie O'Sullivan
2005	Shaun Murphy
2006	Graeme Dott
2007	John Higgins
2008	Ronnie O'Sullivan
2009	John Higgins
2010	Neil Robertson

Photo: © Larry Busacca, *Billiards Digest*

Luc Salvas was the only Quebecker to be the subject of an in-depth article (6 pages) of the prestigious American magazine Billiards Digest. *It was in the January 2005 issue.*

PROFILE OF CHAMPIONS

LUC SALVAS

Originally from Sorel, Luc began playing pool at the age of 5. At 13 years of age, he began to compete in regional tournaments and he won more than 50, playing eight-ball and straight pool, as well as snooker. He certainly has an amazing talent, but what really set him apart was the speed with which he would make the shot. Thus, in snooker, he finished a series of 104 points in three minutes! Luc is recognized as one of the most dramatic players on the world stage because of his ultra-quick style. Everywhere he goes, he lights up the crowds. He literally runs around the table, making his opponents dizzy and distracting them. When he began competing, sometimes fans would come down from the stands to tell him to slow down, thinking they were doing him a favor. "I've already tried to play slower but I can't do it," he answers ingenuously. His flamboyant style was noticed by a major worldwide distributor of pool equipment, who recruited him to his team of pros to put on demonstrations around the world. The representative for Quebec traveled to China, where 400 million viewers watched him deliver a rare defeat to the American pool ace, Earl Strickland (whom he also defeated in competition). "I'm one of the most dramatic players in the world because of my great speed, and that's why I've been called Machine-Gun Luc," he gleefully announced. That he is as skillful as his opponents, who are champions, while playing three times as fast as they do remains a mystery to which only he knows the secret.

For more than 20 years, Luc has been regularly participating in professional championships in the United States and Europe, and he's had some stunning successes. In 1990, when he began, he played against the famous Steve Mizerak in a tournament as part of the Pro Billiards Tour in Toronto and he delivered a crushing defeat with a score of 11 to 5; Mizerak left the arena like a zombie and he asked, "Who was that guy? My God, before I knew it, before I realized I was in the game, he had me 7 to 0." Even the very strong Finn Mika Immonen recognized his talent. "The first time I saw Luc play, I thought he was kidding. I could not believe someone could shoot that fast and still play well. But he does. And I can tell you that he takes a lot of players out of their game, throws them off balance." During his career, Luc has won an unbelievable number of tournaments (approximately 100), not only in Quebec, but also throughout Canada, the United States and elsewhere in the world in five types of games: snooker, 14.1, eight-ball, nine-ball and ten-ball. His greatest wins were recorded between 2000 and 2004. When he began to play on the international scene, his ambition was to become one of the 10 best players in the world. He surpassed his goal when he was ranked sixth in the world in 2004, his career best. In addition, in 2004, he was awarded the title Pool World Master in the Netherlands for his tournament successes, and he was also declared Billiard Trick Shot Artist. He has won against the greatest: Earl Strickland, Johnny Archer, Mika Immonen, Thorsten Hohmann, Buddy Hall, Jim Rempe, Steve Mizerak and Dennis Hatch, among others. Tournament promoters grab him because he puts on a stunning performance and he's the darling of the spectators. In 2006, a world speed championship—the international Speed Pool Challenge—was inaugurated, which takes place every year in Las Vegas. To add to the pressure on the players, the entire prize is awarded solely to the winner. That was no problem for our good friend Luc, who won the first challenge and carried off the impressive prize of $50,000. Then, he won this championship again in 2009 and 2010—both victories were broadcasted on ESPN. Luc Salvas has a lot of determination and doesn't back away from any opponent, whatever the stakes. He's one of the most spectacular players Quebec has ever produced.

STEPHAN COHEN

Frenchman Stephan Cohen caused quite a stir in August 2009 when he won the 14.1 world championship held in a suburb of New York. He

Photo: © Jonathan Smith, *Billiards Digest*

surprised everyone, beginning with himself. Almost no one had heard of him at the start of the tournament. Originally from Nice and 38 years old, Cohen had some success in Europe, holding, among other things, a personal record at 344 consecutive balls, but the American organization AzBilliards placed him 308th in world rankings! He was a surprise right from the start, in the preliminary competitions, when he won the first five matches, accumulating a total of 500 points against 188 for his opponents, and at one stage winning a run of 97 points. Despite this performance, Cohen believed his chances of winning were so slim that he bought his airline ticket for the return flight to France for the last day of the tournament, even before the grand finale. He won the semifinal, eliminating the famous pro Johnny Archer (with a score of 200

to 149) during a rather lackluster match that lasted more than four hours! Cohen was probably the first traveler in history to be happy to delay his flight, scheduled for the same time as the end of the tournament. His final match (200 points) against the very strong Mika Immonen (2009 player of the year) began badly for him, since the Finn gained a huge lead of 145 to 14. But Cohen knew how to remain calm and bravely fought back to take the game with a score of 200 to 181. This victory was so incredible that the American magazine *Billiards Digest* awarded him the title of The Most Remarkable Performance of 2009 in the male category. He was the first Frenchman to win a pool championship in the United States, instantly becoming a celebrity in the world of pool in France.

JASMIN OUSCHAN

Still a young woman (she was born on January 10, 1986), the talented Jasmin Ouschan has already beaten many records that were believed to be impossible to beat. This extraordinary athlete was born in Austria to parents who ran a pool hall in the city of Klagenfurt. She is proud to remind people that she started playing when she was 3 and that she began to compete in European tournaments at the age of 10. Since then, her star has continued to rise. After winning almost all the trophies available in amateur tournaments in Europe, she started to move into

Photo: © Jonathan Smith, *Billiards Digest*

professional circles in 2002. It would take too long to list all the titles that she's won: she was European female champion at nine-ball and 14.1 in 2005 and at eight-ball in 2006. Since then, she's been ranked among the best female players in the world, and reached first place in women's rankings in 2008. Ouschan replaced Allison Fisher, who had dominated the sport since 1996. She also began winning even more spectacular victories. Having reached the top in eight-ball and nine-ball, she wanted to test her skills at 14.1, but, since there's no world championship for women in this discipline, she decided to try her luck among her male colleagues. At her first competition in 2006, she created a sensation by establishing a new female record with a run of 85 consecutive balls in a match during which she inflicted a humiliating defeat on one of

the American hopefuls, John Schmidt! She finished in fifth place in 2006 and in ninth place in 2007. But her performance was even more extraordinary in 2008: she set a new female record with a run of 90 points (as well as another 84), and she is also ranked third and, along the way, beat two of the tournament's great favorites, the German Oliver Ortmann (he was world champion at this same event the previous year) with a score of 200 to 133, and the Finn, Mika Immonen, with a score of 200 to 174. It was the first time that a woman had the upper hand against the greats in pool in a world championship. Even though she didn't participate in 2009 because of a schedul-ing conflict and the fact that the World Pool-Billiard Association withdrew its sanction be-cause the organizers unilaterally decreased the amount of the prizes, she was still crowned female player of the year! She's the only woman in history to compete successfully in pool on an equal footing with the men, which is always a dramatic event for the fans. And her career is only beginning! Let's hope that her example will motivate other women to follow the same path, which would make pool the first sport where men and women would develop together on an equal basis. Many observers believe that this would be a great asset for pool in terms of gaining popularity with television audiences, thus allowing pool champions to access prizes that are as astronomical as those offered in golf and tennis.

THORSTEN HOHMANN

Born in Germany in 1979, Hohmann did not begin playing pool until the age of 12. But he immediately developed an obsession for the game and began training six to eight hours a day, seven days a week. "For four years, I practically didn't see the light of day," he says about this period. He earned his first major title in 2003 when he won the WPA world championship in nine-ball. The following year, under the guardianship of an important promoter, he became a permanent resident of the United States in order to participate on the American professional circuit. He won the 14.1 European championship in 2005 when matches consisted of 125 points. He attained the unequaled achievement of a run of 125 points in three consecutive matches and maintained an incomparable average of 50 balls throughout the entire tournament! In addition, in 2005, he was named the best-dressed player in the world of pool. The following year, in 2006, he registered in the 14.1 world championship (the first since 1990), held in East Brunswick, a suburb of New York. Not only did he win the title, but he also set a new record by shooting 174 consecutive balls. He was nick-named "The Hitman" for his nerves of steel. A few weeks later, he landed another major title that got his name in the record books for pool, and his name will remain there for a very long time. This victory in the eight-ball world championship earned him the highest prize ever offered in a pool tournament: $350,000. The famous American magazine *Pool & Billiard* named him player of year in 2006. And his career is far from over, since he'll continue to shine in the world of pool.

NIELS FEIJEN

While almost all pool champions are themselves the children of pool hall owners, and began playing at the age of 5 or 6, the career of this great Dutch master began in a less orthodox manner. Born in 1977, Feijen fell in love with snooker when he was 11 years old after watching it on television. But he didn't start playing seriously until he was 16. At 17, after playing pool, he quit snooker for good. Since then, he's become hooked on pool, for he finds the game a lot more dramatic and exciting. He's

Photo: © Jonathan Smith, *Billiards Digest*

Photo: © *Billiards Digest*

quickly climbing the ranks in competitions in the Netherlands and throughout Europe. Moreover, he was European champion (14.1) five times. Even though his home port is The Hague, his participation in the most important championships takes him to all the continents. He's won a phenomenal number of tournaments throughout the world and is so strong that he was nicknamed "The Terminator." However, as with the other European champions, what interests him the most is the country they consider the Mecca of pool: the legendary United States. His greatest victory came in 2008 when he won the 14.1 world championship in New Jersey—which brought together the 64 best players in the world—crushing his opponent, Franciso Bustamente of the Philippines, in the final with a score of 200 to 11. He's only just begun to impress.

OLIVER ORTMANN

Born in 1967 in Gelsenkirchen in northern Germany, Oliver gained a taste for the game at a very young age, playing on a pool table set up in his parents' pub. It was love at first sight. He became a veritable maniac, training more than eight hours a day, thereby depriving his parents of the chance to make some money off the pool table which was constantly being used by their son. "For me, pool was like a drug," he remembers, "and I could never play enough." At that time in Europe, pool was in its infancy. Therefore, no one paid attention to this young, unknown European aged 22 when he registered for the prestigious U.S. Open in Chicago in 1989. However, when he made it to the final, people started to wonder who this guy was who was beating all the champions. Most were convinced that the famous Mizerak would chew him up and spit him out!

Photo: © Jonathan Smith, *Billiards Digest*

That was no problem: to everyone's surprise, Ortmann won a close game with a score of 200 to 180, becoming the youngest player in history to win the prestigious tournament. "I still can't believe it," he said after his victory, "No one at home will ever believe me. They will ask me where I bought the trophy!" To the chagrin of all his American detractors, he proved that it wasn't a stroke of luck when he won the same tournament again in 1993. He was five-time 14.1 European champion between 1986 and 2006, before winning the world championship in East Brunswick, a suburb of New York, in 2007. His best run in this competition was 131 consecutive balls. He's rightly considered one of the best players in the world and justly deserves his nikname "The Machine."

MIKA IMMONEN

Mika was born in 1972 in Finland. Introduced to pool at a very young age, he began to compete in tournaments during his teenage years, joining the professional ranks around 1995 and winning his first pro tournament in 2000. Next, he won his first major title, the nine-ball world championship, in 2001. Since then, he has participated in all the world championships around the world and was nicknamed "The Iceman" because of his nerves of steel. He watches what he eats and does a lot of physical exercise, confirming that his good physical condition helps him

Photo : © Mason King, *Billiards Digest*

remain calm and perform. However, even though he always ranked well, he hadn't won first place often, which was becoming increasingly frustrating for him. Until 2008, that is. The tide turned and he rode on a wave of prestigious victories, one after another. His success was even greater in 2009, the year in which he won five out of six of the most lucrative tournaments in the world, including the ten-ball championship in Japan. He was named Player of the Year in 2008 and 2009, and was recently awarded the title Player of the Decade 2000–2010. He claims that a pool champion generally reaches his peak between the ages of 35 and 50, but he maintaines that, because of his good physical condition, he intends to play well until 55. This story isn't over yet.

PART I

THE TECHNIQUES

STANDARDS AND EQUIPMENT

THE TABLE

A large variety of pool tables, varying in price, size and quality, can be found on the market. They all have one thing in common: the length is twice the width. The biggest tables are snooker tables, for which the regulation dimensions are 6 x 12 ft. (1.83 x 3.66 m), although in the United States, they are only 5 x 10 ft.(1.52 x 3.05 m). Another peculiarity of snooker tables is that the ends of the cushions, on each side of the pockets, are rounded, and the openings are smaller.

As for pool tables, their dimensions vary. They might also be 3 x 6 ft. (0.91 x 1.83 m), or $3^{1}/_2$ x 7 ft. (1.07 x 2.13 m), or 4 x 8 ft. (1.22 x 2.44 m),

or even 4 $^{1}/_2$ x 9 ft. (1.37 x 2.74 m). In professional competitions, the regulation size is $4^{1}/_2$ x 9 ft. These measurements are taken along the top of the cushion, starting where it meets the fabric. As a result, the playing surface is slightly smaller than that of the table, since the width of the rubber cushion has to be subtracted. The surface of a 4 x 8 ft. table is not, therefore, 48 x 96 in. (1.22 x 2.44 m), but rather 46 x 92 in. (1.17 x 2.34 m); and that of a $4^{1}/_2$ x 9 ft. table is 50 x 100 in. (1.27 x 2.54 m). The same principle applies to all the other sizes.

The height of American tables is 31–32 in.

(79–81 cm), while English tables are 33$^1/_2$ in. (85 cm) high.

The price of a pool table can vary between $1,000 and $10,000, or more. Of course, the quality is based on the price paid. Why such a big difference? Many factors have an impact on the price. The first thing to consider when buying is the type of bottom (or bed). The ideal material is slate. Some manufacturers claim they have discovered equivalent synthetic products, but experience has shown that the results are better with slate. It doesn't bend or warp, and it helps the balls roll better.

From a commercial standpoint, there are four major categories of pool tables: toy tables, residential tables, commercial tables and professional tables.

The cost of toy tables is less than $600. They often measure less than 3$^1/_2$ x 7 ft. (1.07 x 2.13 m). Their main disadvantage: the synthetic material used for the bottom (plywood, Formica, etc.), which, in the long run, warps, bends or curves such that it becomes impossible to level the table. In addition, the elasticity of the cushions is clearly inadequate. Buying a table like this isn't recommended, as you'll get tired of it within a few weeks and scrap it. Rather than lose a few hundred dollars in the short term, you would do better to buy a good quality table right from the start that you'll enjoy for many years. At any rate, a good pool table never loses its value.

If you want to play pool solely for your own pleasure, without ever wanting to become a champion but still wanting to enjoy it, buy a residential table. In 2010, this type of table was selling for $1,000 to $3,000. At that price, you have to specify a slate bottom and cushions with a high degree of elasticity. This table is recommended for amateurs: it looks good and it meets the standards.

Halfway between the residential table and the professional table is the commercial table, the kind we see in bars and pubs. Often, its dimensions are 3$^1/_2$ x 7 ft. (1.07 x 2.13 m), but there are others that range from 3 x 6 ft. (0.91 x 1.83 m) to 4 x 8 ft. (1.22 x 2.44 m). Its main features: the slate is a single piece and the elasticity of the cushions is poor or uneven. In addition, to get the balls back, you have to insert the required amount of money in a side slide and activate the return mechanism, so that only short games are played, such as eight-ball, nine-ball, or rotation. These games, even if they're interesting, don't help determine the strength of the players because chance plays too great a role. If you want a table for personal use, don't buy a commercial table because it won't give you the enjoyment a residential or a professional table will. Moreover, most of the time, commercial tables don't meet the standards.

Lastly, for those who are ambitious and who want to make pool their main hobby, a professional table is highly recommended. Even if it costs more than the other types of tables, it's a good investment because, far from depreciating, it will gain in value over the years.

The professional table is massive, weighing at least 1,000 lb. (450 kg). The bottom is made of real slate imported from Italy, with a minimum thickness of 1 in. (2.5 cm). Despite its weight, slate is a very fragile material. On a well-built table, this is not a problem, but shipping it requires taking a lot of precautions. For this reason, the slate is divided into three sections, which makes it easier to move and reduces the risk of breaking it. On a good-quality table, the fit between the different pieces is perfect, so that the seams, once the fabric is installed, are invisible.

A tricky question: which is the best table on the market today? Forty or fifty years ago, people would have answered without hesitation: Brunswick. However, since the 1970s, the phenomenal growth in the number of buyers of residential tables has caused a lot of manufacturers to spring up and the foreseeable consequences have followed: major competition, lower prices and ... lower quality. This has resulted in a company like Brunswick having to introduce a larger selection of models to be able to compete and to satisfy all budgets. Unfortunately, quality suffers a lot because of this. It's a little like an automaker that produces all kinds of models, from the "soapbox" to the roaring sports car.

In short, in pool as in other areas, remember the old, popular saying: you get what you pay for. Personally, I've always preferred our buying policy in Canada, i.e., competitive pricing. We have one of the best manufacturers in North America right here in Quebec. A dynamo, Michel Lemyre has spent many years consolidating his business. His ultra high-performance factory is located in Laval and employs several dozen workers. He set up a major distribution network in the other Canadian provinces and in several U.S. states. His tables compare favorably with all the others and, moreover, are often offered at a lower price. His high-end table (Black Crown) is the top of the line at a very reasonable price. Don't forget that Michel Lemyre has been the biggest sponsor of pool tournaments in Quebec for 30 years. We encourage those who encourage us.

If you're buying a used table, the first thing to check is the slate. Naturally, if the stone is broken, the table loses its value. Don't be impressed by the quality of the cloth or the appearance of the table; check if the stone is in good condition. It should be intact and straight.

THE CUSHIONS

We don't always appreciate the quality of today's materials. Consider the quality of the rubber used to make the cushions of a pool table, for example, a quality that ensures a consistent re-bound. It wasn't always like that. The game was invented in the 11th century and rubber wasn't imported from India until 1835. This revolutionary discovery was complemented by the discovery in 1839 of the vulcanization process by Goodyear. Prior to that, all kinds of materials were tried: leather, multiple layers of cloth, fabric stuffed with cotton, braided hair, cork combined with other flexible products and even, around 1855, inflated rubber tires (that had to be reinflated every day using a pump)! Even with rubber, there were still other problems to solve: a glue was needed that could adequately attach the rubber to the cushion, which took more time to develop.

The flexibility of the cushions (or strips of rubber) are another feature of professional tables. In the United States, the cushions usually have a spine and are pointy. Snooker-table cushions used in English Canada are flat: they're square or L-shaped. In all instances, the rubber must have the same elasticity throughout to ensure control of the ball and positioning. To check if the cushions respond well, throw the ball hard across the width of the table and count the number of times it rebounds from one side to the other. With square cushions, the number of rebounds should exceed six; on pointy cushions, four to five. Obviously, the cushion has to be firmly attached to the frame of the table to create one solid piece, for a cushion that is not completely attached is less effective. Remember that in the long run the cushions will tend to harden or lose their elasticity if the table is placed in a damp place.

If the balls jump up when they hit the cushions, this means the cushions are too low in relation to the size of the balls. In this case, raise the cushions or switch the balls for smaller ones.

THE CLOTH

Bob Cannafax was three-cushion billiards world champion in 1917, 1919, 1924 and 1925. One day in the 1920s, when he was to put on a demonstration, he arrived at the agreed-to location the day before to practice. Seeing the cloth was worn out, he asked the owner to install a new one. When the owner refused, Cannafax pulled a penknife from his pocket and slit the baize from one end to the other, then announced: "Now you'll change it." Such a radical attitude would probably not be tolerated today. Moreover, Cannafax was suspended for several months because of his deed. Nonetheless, this anecdote shows the importance professionals place on the quality of the cloth, an essential element in the way the balls perform.

In all pool games, special spins have to be used from time to time (discussed later) to control or modify the trajectory of the balls. The intensity of the spin lies largely in the quality of the cloth. The best ones are made of wool and come from England. Over the last few years, American-made cloth can be found at more affordable prices (75% wool and 25% nylon), and its performance is satisfactory. Today, there's a choice of 25 colors of cloth, making it possible to match the color of your decor. However, even if you have the best cloth there is, if it's poorly installed, you'll get the worst results. It's vitally important that the cloth be appropriately stretched, i.e. neither too tightly nor too loosely. The more the baize is stretched, the faster the balls will roll. However, the tension of the cloth is not the only factor that affects speed.

The room's temperature is also a determining factor: the balls roll faster and farther in a dry location than in a humid one. In fact, humidity is harmful to pool tables, for it hardens the cushions, slows the balls as they roll on the cloth, and risks warping the table's structure. As far as is possible, install your table in a dry location. To avoid premature wear and tear of the cloth, buy a cover that you can use to drape over the table after each use to protect the cloth against accidents, damage, dirt and dust.

Finally, even if it's in mint condition, the table must be level. There's nothing more frustrating than playing on a slanted surface: you lose all confidence and you can't concentrate on your shots because you'll always be afraid that the trajectory transmitted to the ball will change due to the slant of the table. Professionals always refuse to play a game on a table that isn't level. It would be like asking players in the National Hockey League to play on in-line skates. They wouldn't be able to perform at one-tenth of their normal ability.

LIGHTING

A few years before his death, Georges Chénier successfully defended his title as North American snooker champion for the 22nd consecutive year during a competition held in Toronto. In the days leading up to the tournament, he brought in electricians several times to change the lighting conditions. Chénier didn't want to see any shadows on the table or inside the pocket openings.

Indeed, the light must be uniformly diffused over the entire surface of the table. If the corners or the ends are darker than the center, or if the balls throw off a bigger shadow, then the lighting is inadequate or inappropriate. Sellers of specialized pool accessories offer excellent lighting systems, including Tiffany-style lamps. The best light is provided by two fluorescent tubes hung approximately 4 ft. (1.22 m) above the table. In addition to improving your performance, good lighting will help you avoid visual fatigue, which shouldn't be ignored. Take care when installing your system to include lamp shades or reflectors so that the light is concentrated over the table and doesn't dazzle either players or spectators.

THE BALLS

The gleaming pyramid of 15 numbered balls, organized in this shape at the start of each frame, is, for some, the image that most represents pool. Except in a few specific instances, for example in eight-ball where the 8-ball is placed in the center, or rotation where the 1-ball is placed at the apex, in most games, the balls are organized randomly in the shape of a pyramid. Have you already thought about the many ways to rack the balls in a triangle, taking into account that each ball bears a different number? In his *Encyclopedia of Billiards* published in 1993, Mike Shamos confirms that there are 6,227,020,800 different ways to organize the balls. Astounding, isn't it? Therefore, it's highly likely that you'll never rack the balls the same way twice in your life! Today, perfectly shiny, round, high-performance balls made of phenolic resin are used, but this wasn't always the case.

Let's take a moment to visit the long road traveled to get to this point.

It seems that the first ivory balls appeared around 1627, but they weren't commonly used before 1820. Wooden balls were mostly used. Contrary to popular opinion, ivory isn't the ideal material to make balls. Since it's a rare and therefore costly material, thought was given to another appropriate material in the 1860s. A major manufacturer of tables in New York offered a $10,000 reward (an enormous amount at the time) to the person who discovered a chemical composition that would match the standards of ivory in terms of density and elasticity. This search for a new material intensified following an embargo on ivory pool balls during the American Civil War. It was an American, John Wesley Hyatt, to whom we owe the discovery in 1868 of a manufacturing process that would revolutionize the billiard-ball industry. This chemist was the first to use a new product (a mixture of nitrocellulose and alcohol that hardened as it dried) that he called celluloid and that he patented in 1870. The resulting balls literally made a huge impact. As they were partly made of nitrocellulose, they had two major disadvantages: they caused sparks to fly when they struck each other with force, and even worse, they also produced an explosion like a gunshot. Many people complained, including the owner of a saloon. He didn't mind about the noise itself, but whenever it happened, all his customers jumped and pulled out their revolvers. It took several years of research and fine-tuning to come up with the result we know today. This is why, at least as far as three-cushion pool is concerned, ivory continued to be used until well after 1900. It seems that Hyatt never received the promised reward, but it is a small consolation that he was elected to the Billiard Congress of America (BCA) Hall of Fame in 1971, long after his death. In a twist of fate, most balls used today in North America are not made in the United States, but in Belgium, by a company called Saluc, a huge company that has eliminated all its European competitors over the last 20 years. This company alone produces tens of thousands of balls every day, generally under the name Aramith, and it sells them around the world.

According to the standards, a billiard ball must be perfectly round, with a margin of error close to $5/1000$ in. (0.125 mm), but manufacturers exceed this requirement and aim for a margin of $1/1000$ in. (0.025 mm). A regulation pool ball must measure $2^1/4$ in. (57 mm) in diameter and weigh $5^1/2 -$ 6 oz. (156–170 g). Snooker balls measure $2^1/8$ in. (54 mm) in diameter and weigh between 5– $5^1/2$ oz. (142–156 g). In carom billiards (a game played mostly in Europe, see page 103) balls weight between $7^3/4 - 8^1/2$ oz. (220–241 g) and are bigger than pool balls, measuring 2.4–2.44 in. (61.6–62 mm) in diameter. For

over 40 years nows, the English snooker balls have been sold in Canada and the U.S., and today, snooker equipment in North American is generally identical to that in the UK. Here's a good tip: you may buy balls of the highest quality, but you'll be unhappy if you don't clean them after using them for extended periods of time. Use a damp cloth (you can buy products made specifically for this from suppliers of pool accessories) and rub them frequently and carefully to get the most out of them.

REGULATION POCKET SIZE

The book of official regulations of the Billiard Congress of America specifies the regulation dimensions of pool table openings. These measurements must be taken where the cushions come to a point on each side of the pocket. For a table that is 4 x 8 ft. (1.22 x 2.44 m) or $4^1/2$ x 9 ft. (1.37 x 2.74 m), the corner openings must be 5 in. (127 mm) wide, give or take $1/8$ in. (3.2 mm). The center pockets must be $5^1/2$ in. (140 mm) wide, give or take $1/4$ in. (3.2 mm).

In the case of snooker tables, North American specifications are as follows: the corner openings must measure $3^1/2$ in. (89 mm), give or take $1/8$ in. (3.2 mm). The center openings must measure 103–110 mm ($4^1/16 - 4^5/16$ in.), or approximately 108 mm ($4^1/4$ in.). These standards only apply in North America, for it's more difficult to play on English snooker tables. Indeed, openings for snooker tables in North America are 6–9 mm ($^1/_4$–$^3/_8$ in.) larger than those found on snooker tables elsewhere in the world. In addition, the slope of the stone on North American tables is roughly 1 in. (25 mm) closer to the playing surface, which makes it possible to pocket a ball along the cushion, something that is practically impossible on English tables.

THE CHALK

Today, a left or a right sidespin is so inherent to pool that few amateurs ask themselves about the origins of this discovery. No one agrees on the subject: some analysts attribute it to the Frenchman Mingaud, others to Englishman Jack Carr. Historians tell a funny story about the latter. Having discovered the sidespin in 1820, and conscious of the huge potential of his discovery, Carr kept the secret to himself. Asked by the amateurs who attended his demonstrations about the extraordinary spins that he was able to achieve, Carr attributed his skill to a piece of chalk that he had just invented. He began to sell these little cubes of chalk at a high price, with everyone wanting to benefit from this amazing invention. Unfortunately for him, an amateur who couldn't find him to get his chalk bought

1

another type of chalk and figured out the trick. The deception ended quickly, but Carr was already rich. He continued to travel and to do demonstrations in Spain and France.

Today, the chalk is still sold in the shape of a cube, most often the color blue. There are other colors that can be matched to the color of the cloth so that the chalk powder is less visible. For the chalk to be effective, it shouldn't be too powdery or too grainy. The best brand, recognized worldwide and even recommended by English professionals, is National Tournament, which is made in the United States. Don't buy blue chalk made in Asian countries because it's completely inadequate, despite its appearance. Also, avoid storing the chalk in a damp place where it will crumble and become less effective.

Apply a light layer of blue chalk to the cue before each shot, just like the professionals do. This is the best way to avoid making a bad shot. See Diagram 1 to learn how to apply the chalk without damaging the tip (the ferrule). A basic point of etiquette: when you place the chalk cube on the edge of the table, place it with the top facing up to avoid dirtying everything.

THE POOL CUE

Of all the myths surrounding pool, for a long time the most persistent and false one concerned the weight and diameter of pool cues. It was generally accepted that the thinner the cue (the narrower the tip), the better the results. Nothing could be farther from the truth. This false belief stems once again from people confusing snooker with pool. These two games are completely different, and the ideal cues for each game have different specifications. Today, fortunately, amateurs are much more aware of the need to have the appropriate cue for pool. The length, weight and dimensions of your cue will depend on how you intend to use it.

In snooker, the ideal cue should weigh 16–18 oz. (454 –10 g) and measure approximately 59 in. (1.5 m). The diameter at the thinnest end should be 9–11 mm. In the case of pool, the balls are bigger, so the cue has to be heavier, weighing roughly 19 or 20 oz. (539 or 567 g). The length of the cue is 58 in. (1.47 m) and the diameter of the tip is 12–14 mm, or ideally 13 mm. Moreover, almost all American professionals use a pool cue that is 58 in. (1.47 m) in length, 20 oz. (567 g) in weight, and 13 mm in diameter. Europeans use shorter cues that are 1.37–1.42 m (4 1/2 – 4 2/3 ft.) in length.

A good way to know if your cue is too thin is to listen carefully to the sound it makes when you play. If your shot makes a cracking sound, or if your cue resonates a lot, it's too thin for the way you're using it. A suitable cue makes a short, muted sound, with no resonance.

Diagram 1
Left: a worn-out chalk risks damaging the ferrule over time. The chalk must never rub the ferrule, only the cue tip.
Right: used properly, the chalk only touches the tip.

2

Left: A 12.5 mm cue. The one on the right is a snooker cue; the narrowing below the ferrule indicates that the chalk was applied incorrectly.

Obviously, the cue has to be perfectly straight: this is the first thing to check when buying one. There's no point trying to play with a curved cue, as the results will be poor. To ensure the cue is straight, a lot of amateurs roll it by laying it flat on the pool table, and if the roll is uneven and there are gaps, they think the cue is warped. Beware of this test because it's very deceptive. The best way to tell if your cue is straight is to look along its length by holding the widest end near your eye, in the same way a carpenter checks to see if a beam is straight or not. If this test reveals a bend, it's better to get rid of the warped cue, since it's practically impossible to straighten it.

To keep your cue straight, always store it upright in a dry place. Never leave a cue leaning against a wall in a corner for several hours or several days: this will permanently warp the cue. If you have to take the cue with you in the car, try to ensure it spends as little time as pos-sible there because temperature changes are bad for the wood, which is inclined to warp. Even if the cue is made using wood that is specifically dried and treated, don't risk it, and handle the cue with care. To clean the cue, simply rub it with a cloth moistened with an aerosol furniture polish. Never use sandpaper to smoothen it: this habit should be banned. If you regularly sand your cue, you'll end up with a toothpick in a few months!

Today, most amateurs have their own cue divided into two sections: the shaft (the thinnest end) and the butt (the thickest end). You'll often notice that the shaft isn't var-nished: this isn't a manu-facturing oversight, but something that is perfectly normal. If you find that the shaft isn't smooth enough, coat it with floor wax paste,

tip
ferrule

shaft

joint

butt

bumper

Diagram 2
The different parts of a pool cue.

then polish it with a dry cloth. Furthermore, if your cue doesn't slide well under your hand, don't hesitate to dust it with talcum powder (baby powder), found in all pool halls. This is the best way to counteract any moisture problem caused by the skin that prevents the cue from sliding properly.

There's an infinite variety of pool cues on the market, with prices ranging from $100 to $1500 and higher, if you're in the market for something extravagant. Beware of gimmicks such as aluminum, graphite or fiberglass cues, or those outfitted with exotic sculptures or a screw-on tip (the disk made of leather or a similar material, at the end of the cue). These are nothing more than show. All professionals around the world use wooden cues, to which the tip is glued. Follow their example. Over the long run, it's better to own your own cue. This way you're always sure to have the same feeling in your arms when you play. Expect to pay at least $100 for a good-quality pool cue. The end of the shaft below the tip must be uniformly tapered for 12–15 in. (30–38 cm) so that the back-and-forth movement of the cue doesn't cause the bridge to narrow as you prepare to take the shot. If the diameter of the shaft increases too quickly from the tip down, the effect will be like narrowing the bridge, thereby hindering movement.

In the 1980s, because pool professionals

Photo: © Billie Billing

In all professional tournaments, organizers place a small table and two chairs (one on each side) for two players near each pool table where games are being played. On the small table are chalk cubes, towels, a pitcher and two glasses of water, as well as a small box of powder for the players to use. An amusing incident occurred during the American Masters Tournament in Arlington, Virginia, in 1969. The famous Luther Lassiter, who had been 14.1 world champion many times during the 1960s, was sitting at the small table waiting for his opponent, Danny DiLiberto, to miss a shot. When DiLiberto did miss a shot, Lassiter jumped up from his chair and, wanting to put some powder on his hand, grabbed the glass of water by mistake and generously sprinkled water on his hands and his pants!

developed a new jumping technique now used by all champions, a new type of cue, called a jump cue, appeared on the scene. We know that it's possible to make the cue ball jump, even using a normal cue, but this jump will be much higher if you use the jump cue. You can even make the cue ball jump right over the ball in its path! In nine-ball, in particular, where you lose the game if you don't make contact with the lowest-numbered ball three times in a row, it becomes extremely important to be able to make contact with the object ball (the one bearing the lowest number) even if you don't have direct access. This is why you have to know and master the jump shot. (This technique will be described in greater detail in the section entitled *"Massé Shots and Jump Shots,"* page 84.) If you are a pasionate follower of nine-ball, it may be worthwhile to buy a jump cue. In fact, using this kind of cue has become so commonplace that the organization overseeing the rules and regulations of billiards, the BCA, had to impose rules on the dimensions of this very specific instrument. Since 1998, the rule book specifies that the cue must be at least 40 in. (1 m) long and have a maximum diameter of 14 mm at its narrowest end. It has to be said that the use of a jump cue isn't always allowed. Thus, in banning the jump shot, Great Britain also banned the use of the jump cue in snooker. Even in the United States, a pool paradise, the use of this type of instrument is not unanimously accepted. For example, the United States Pool Players Association (USPPA) banned the use of the jump cue in its competitions under the pretext that this was a travesty of the game: not only does the proliferation of this kind of cue misrepresent the skills needed to get around obstacles, the USPPA claimed, but it also damages the cloth and the entire table. As a result, many pool-hall owners prohibit the use of this type of cue in their establishments.

For most of the regulars at eight-ball and nine-ball tournaments, a break cue is required. Indeed, at the highest level of competition, whether amateur or professional, it's generally acknowledged that the most important shot is the break at the beginning of each game. It's not unheard of for a player at this level to redo the break frame after frame. Scattering the balls well from the start is a major priority! On the other hand, if you pocket the white ball on the break, you risk losing the game, even if you're playing against an average player. Remember that it's the break that often determines who will control the game and who will win. If you pocket a ball on the break and the white ball is positioned strategically for the next shot, you're definitely in the driver's seat, because you'll determine the dynamics of the frame. Therefore, if you participate regularly in major competitions, you need to think about buying a break cue. First, it's the best way to protect your regular cue because the

A 40 in. (1 m) long jump cue.

force used to perform the break is very hard on your cue, especially on the tip, which risks wearing out too soon, becoming crushed or even breaking or coming unstuck. Buy a break cue with specifications that don't exceed the maximum allowed by the rules of the BCA, i.e. 25 oz. (710 g) in weight and 14 mm in diameter. What's your ideal weight? Opinions are divided on this point. The great champion, Mike Sigel, a member of the BCA Hall of Fame, uses a regular cue weighing 20 oz. (562 g), but his break cue weighs 18 oz. (510 g). Other famous pros use their regular cue to break, including former world champion Nick Varner, as well as the very strong Shane Van Boening, even if they admit that this

causes the tip to weaken and wear out prematurely. In truth, you need to know how to set your priorities when deciding what your goals are with respect to the break. On this topic, experts have determined that it's better to use a lighter cue, approximately 18–20 oz. (510–562 g), which represents a fair compromise between power, on the one hand, and accuracy and control, on the other. Remember that the rules of the BCA restrict the number of cues that a player can bring to a competition to three. You'll be fine if you bring your usual cue, a jump cue and a break cue. However, many manufacturers produce a hybrid cue that can be disassembled: it helps if a cue divides and, by removing one section, it can be shortened and used as a jump cue.

THE TIP

It's usually the small things that matter. Therefore, the tip is the most important part of your pool equipment. A miscue at a critical moment can mean losing the frame. Therefore, it's worth it to pay more and to choose a top-quality tip. Always ensure that it's completely level when installed and use sandpaper to round the sides. This is about the only instance where you can use sandpaper in pool. Ensure the tip is the same size as your cue, i.e., not bigger or smaller.

A mushroom tip (where the sides exceed the ferrule) or angles that are too straight will cause a miscue (see Diagram 3). If it's installed by someone competent, the tip can last a long time without the need for maintenance. If at any point you have the impression that the chalk is no longer sticking to your tip, simply hold a sheet of sandpaper in your hand, point the tip of your cue against the sandpaper in your hand and twist it two or three times. This way, you'll remove all the old chalk from the tip without damaging it.

If your tip often comes unstuck, it's probably because you didn't remove all the old glue before replacing it. Ensure that the two surfaces are straight and clean, and use a good glue, and your tip will hold so firmly that you'll have to use a penknife to remove it once it's worn out.

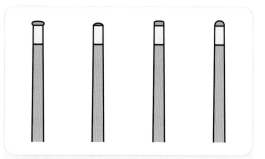

Diagram 3
Miscues are often caused by an inadequate tip. Here, the tip on the left is a mushroom and can be fixed by sanding the edges until they line up with the ferrule. The second tip is much too thin and has to be changed. The third one has angles that are too sharp, which can be easily corrected so that it looks like the fourth one. This represents the ideal tip, thick and rounded, with sides that perfectly match the ferrule.

THE STANCE

The position of the body once you're ready to take the shot is very important. It would be wrong to say that there's only one way to stand in the moments leading up to a shot. Moreover, the professionals don't agree on this point and each one advocates his or her own playing style. Willie Hoppe, who was one of the best players of all time, had a unique style. Indeed, any stance is good if it's stable and natural. However, experience has shown that there are some constants when it comes to the ideal position.

First of all, the body must be positioned so that the face is directly over the cue and facing the object ball. The shoulders must be an extension of the cue as much as possible. You must stand firmly so that your stance is stable and solid. If you lose your balance with the slightest push, this means that your posture isn't solid. To ensure maximum stability, distribute your body weight evenly over your legs. The following three photos show the steps to follow to achieve a playing stance.

Should your feet be perpendicular, parallel or diagonal to the table? Naturally, the answer to this question varies according to where the cue ball is located on the table. Look at photos 4 to 6 to understand how to place your feet. Don't spread your legs too far apart: there should be no more than 2 ft. (60 cm) separating your ankles. Photos 7, 8 and 9 show how not to stand.

First, stand in front of the table.

Next, turn about one-eighth of a turn to the right.

Simply lean forward to reach the last stage.

In this photo, the legs are too far apart.

In this photo, you can see the mistake that many beginners make who bend their knees too much instead of bending forward at the hips.

This photo shows an unstable stance.

According to the American style, the chin is positioned approximately 6 in. (15 cm) above the cue.

Snooker professionals lean so far forward that their chin almost touches the cue.

How far forward should you lean to play? It all depends on the height of the player. Avoid standing too straight or leaning too far forward. Ideally, the chin should be positioned about 6 in. (15 cm) above the cue. This is the most popular style among American professionals, but the British lean so far forward that their chin almost touches the cue. This may be due to the fact that English snooker tables are higher (and larger) than pool tables. Georges Chénier's style more closely resembled that of the Americans, even though he excelled at both pool and snooker.

Whatever the case, to achieve this posture, lean farther forward from the hips and try not to bend your knees, or bend them as little as possible. This is the most common mistake made by beginners: they tend to bend their knees instead of leaning forward. Try to avoid this mistake.

Another common error among beginners is "stabbing" the table with their cue. When you get ready to take the shot, your cue should be horizontal, or parallel to the table. Many beginners have the habit of raising the butt of their cue as if they wanted to stab the table. Not only do they risk causing a miscue, but they might also tear the cloth. Watch this part of your game, especially if you're just starting out.

If, when you lean forward and are ready to take

This stance is ideal for photographers, but it shows an error: the player is not leaning forward enough.

In this photo, you'll notice an error in the way the cue is held, as the butt is too high.

This is the right way to hold the cue: parallel, or almost parallel, to the table.

the shot, you change your mind and decide to change balls, take the time to stand up straight, put some chalk on the tip and move to another spot so that your body is in the right position with respect to your new goal. In other words, even if the new ball is only a few inches away from the ball you were originally targeting, take the time to assume a new stance based on the position of the ball you want to pocket. Make every effort for each of these shots, for it's the only way to excel at pool.

HOW TO HOLD AND MOVE THE CUE

To check if your cue is balanced, place it horizontally on your left index finger, as shown in photo 15. Once you've found the point of bal-ance, grip the butt of the cue approximately 6 in. (15 cm) behind this point, or almost half-way between the point of balance and the widest end (photo 16). You're now holding your cue at the right spot for about 95% of all shots. Sometimes you may have to hold it closer to the end, for example, when the cue ball is far away. However, avoid stretching out too far and don't hesitate to use the rake if the position of the balls prevents you from playing comfortably.

Hold your cue using at least three fingers in addition to the thumb: the index finger, the middle finger and the ring finger. As for the baby finger, a lot of players also use it to grip the butt, along with the rest of the hand; others hold it slightly to the side. Whatever your choice, don't hold the cue too tightly, as this could cause your movements to stiffen and hinder the flexibility of your shot. Also, don't hold it with your fingertips (photo 17); rather, grasp it completely.

When you're in a playing stance, the right hand, your head and the bridge (formed by the left hand) must be in a straight line as an extension of each other. This is essential for aiming. Like the hunter who places his gun near his eye to see the direction in which the gun is pointed, the cue must be directly beneath your eyes to

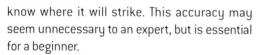

It's a bad habit to hold the cue with your fingertips. Refer to photo 20 where you'll see the proper way to hold the cue.

know where it will strike. This accuracy may seem unnecessary to an expert, but is essential for a beginner.

In the moments just before the shot, the forearm holding the cue must be absolutely

In this photo, it's impossible to aim, since the cue doesn't match the player's field of vision. Compare this photo to photos 10 and 11 and you'll understand better.

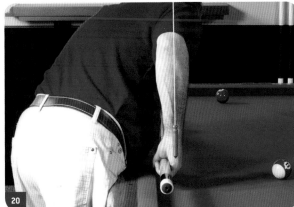

The wrist is turned too far to the inside.

The wrist is turned too far to the outside.

vertical on all sides, as shown in photos 19 and 20. Even the wrist must be perfectly in line with the forearm. Some people hold their wrist turned to the inside (photo 21) while others hold it turned to the outside (photo 22), depending on what they learned, but the best position is still the one shown in photos 19 and 20. A lot of great players, including the now-deceased Willie Hoppe, play with the wrist turned to the outside. This difference can be explained by the fact that the player started playing at a young age when he was hardly taller than the top of the table and he had to lift his forearm and his wrist to hit the balls. He more or less simply kept this habit.

The wrist and forearm must do most of the work. The elbow and the shoulder should move as little as possible.

While it's true that all the principles mentioned in the description of pool technique are critical, the way in which a shot is made is very important. This part of the game often separates the mediocre player from the expert. It's wrong to use the whole arm, elbow and shoulder to push the cue forward, as the wrist is usually enough. It's been mentioned several times that the style of professionals can vary in many ways, but they all make the shot the same way, gently and with flexibility.

The force used to make the shot must be restrained. You could say there are five degrees of movement in the playing style: very gentle, gentle, somewhat moderate, moderate and hard. The main charactertistic of the champions lies in their slow, gentle and flexible style. Most balls are to be pocketed gently. Don't play hard unless absolutely necessary—for example, to break the balls or to strike a ball at 90°. Even then, it must always be a controlled force that doesn't exceed the point where the cue ball could shoot off the table. In addition, it's impossible to know where the cue ball will stop if it travels far or if it does several turns of the table. Don't be impressed by those supposed champions who pocket balls too forcefully or by using special spins. They're nothing more than terrible amateurs. A really good player never plays with such force.

Preparatory shots (a process called "filing") are also important. Like a golfer who imitates the movement two or three times before hitting the ball, the pool player should repeat the movement at least three times before hitting the cue ball. During this movement, the forearm and wrist behave a little like a clock pendulum that swings back and forth at a constant pace. This back-and-forth motion is indispensable and offers a lot of advantages: it promotes concentration, makes it easier to take aim and helps avoid missing an easy shot because you're in too much of a hurry. We often hear about players who wonder why they make the hardest shots but miss the easiest shots. The reason is simple: they take the easy shots too quickly without even taking the time to line them up. On the other hand, for a complicated shot, all players carefully study the situation and play diligently. When he won the greatest honor in the United States, the U.S. Open, in 1975, Dallas West announced to journalists to explain his win, "For some time now, I've strived to slow down my speed. I stopped rushing and, since then, my game has vastly improved." Follow his example and you'll notice considerable progress.

THE BRIDGE

For the person playing pool for the first time in his or her life, the most difficult thing is to create a stable support to hold the cue using the left

Photo: © Billiards Digest

You lament the fact that you have trouble grasping your cue correctly, or you find that your bridge isn't stable? Take heart in thinking about this brave man who became an expert pool player despite his serious handicap: George H. Sutton had both arms cut off 3 in. (7.5 cm) below the elbow during a tragic accident that occurred in an industrial sawmill when he was 8 years old. This didn't prevent him from getting his medical degree and from becoming a pool virtuoso. Other men and women deprived of their arms have managed, through practice and perseverence, to use their feet to write, paint or play a musical instrument, but Sutton is the only one to have succeeded in mastering the game of pool using his stumps and what remained of his arms. Pool was initially a pastime, then he played as a professional, crisscrossing his native United Stated to demonstrate his prowess, which he did for 35 years. In 1904, traveling aboard the ocean liner Le Lorraine, he even spent eight months in France (where he was called the "handless professor"), where he demonstrated his expertise mainly at the Café Olympia in Paris. He died in 1938 at the age of 68. What an example of courage!

24

An open bridge.

hand. This is what is referred to as the bridge. Pool regulars are so familiar with this part of the game that they aren't always aware of how difficult it is for a beginner to form a stable bridge. If taught well at the start, the beginner will soon achieve the proper technique, but only after a few hours. Since the bridge is the essential element of all shots, it's well worth the effort to stop

and learn the proper technique. It's important to correct your mistakes from the start, otherwise, you run the risk of developing bad habits that you won't be able to break.

Generally, bridges can be classified in two large categories: open bridges and closed bridges. The bridge is open when the cue is simply pressed against the space located between the thumb and the index finger with no finger on top (photo 24). You could also call it an English bridge, for it's the support adopted by British professionals. In contrast, all American professionals use the closed bridge, with the index finger over the cue, which is pressed against the thumb and the first joint of the middle finger.

25

Close your left hand and hold the fist as shown.

26

Extend the index finger and hold the thumb against the middle finger.

27

Fold the tip of the index finger over the thumb to form a kind of loop.

Look at photographs 25 to 31 to understand how this works.

At first glance, the open bridge seems easier to form, since all you have to do is place your left hand (the right hand for left-handed people) on the cloth, slightly raising the hollow in your hand so that only your fingertips and the outside of your hand are resting on the table. It's difficult to explain why British professionals prefer this type of bridge, contrary to Americans. In reality, snooker players have to use this type of bridge because of the considerable length of the table, which requires a sight line that is as clear as possible for distant shots. Since nothing hinders the view of the cue when the bridge is open, it seems

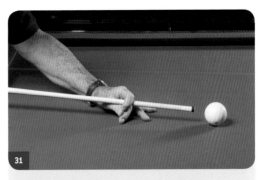

31

Lastly, lower your hand on the table so that the tips of the three fingers and the outside of the hand serve as a support.

this makes it easier to aim at a target.

On the other hand, the closed bridge is much easier to use than it appears. Refer to photos 25 to 31 and the accompanying explanations, which demonstrates the various stages in its formation.

In the case of the closed bridge, the loop formed by the index finger must be large enough

28

At this point, the last three fingers are still folded into the palm.

29

Extend the last three fingers completely.

30

Push the end of the pool cue through the opening between the thumb and the index finger.

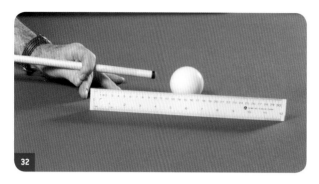

to allow the cue to slide through it easily. Since the two types of bridge are equally valid, you'll be able to adopt the one that suits you the best. Remember the two most important things: firmness and stability. On this topic, ensure that the end of your cue is never more than 6–8 in. (15–20 cm) from your bridge (photo 32). For backspin strokes, the distance should be no more than 4–5 in. (10–13 cm); if you want to move the cue ball a little, the distance should be even less. In other words, the farther the hand

Don't lean too far forward.

forming the bridge is located from the cue ball, the harder it is to aim at and hit properly. In addition, a bridge that is too far away can lead to a miscue. Ensure that the distance between the bridge and the tip is as short as possible. If you can't do it, don't hesitate to use a rake instead of leaning forward too far (photo 33). Get accustomed to using the rake, or replacement bridge, and refer to photos 42 to 44 to understand how to use this instrument.

Forming the ideal bridge assumes that the space beyond the cue ball is sufficiently clear that you can place your whole hand down. Sometimes, there is so little space between the ball and the cushion, or between it and other balls, that it becomes impossible to use the conventional bridge. The player must then improvise, creating an nonstandard support and, without moving the other balls, providing a stable support for his cue. In this regard, one picture is worth a thousand words: refer to the photographs to get a more accurate idea of the different kinds of bridges that are needed in specific situations.

The bridge on the cushion (photo 34), the most common, is the one used when the cue ball is sitting 6 in. (15 cm) or less from the cushion. In this case, lean the four fingers of your left hand on the cushion, with the thumb completely inside your hand, and slide the cue between the index finger and the middle finger still on the cushion. This support provides maximum safety, for the cue can't deviate up or down or to the

side. It's the thumb that guides the cue from within the hand.

If the cue ball is frozen to the cushion (photo 35) or near it, within 2 in. (5 cm), you use the same bridge, except if you have to move your left hand from the cushion to the outside of the table while the cue continues to rest on the cushion.

Under the same circumstances you can also use the open bridge by simply placing the cue in the V-shaped space between the thumb and the index finger (photo 36). In fact, the open bridge can be used in almost all situations. Therefore, the choice between the different types of supports is a personal one. Choose the one that seems most natural to you.

There is another version of the bridge on the cushion when the cue ball and the ball that you want to pocket are both lying along the same

cushion, so that the cue has to be placed almost parallel to the cushion (photos 37 and 38). In this instance, the palm of the left hand rests on the cushion, while the cue is inserted between the index finger and the middle finger with the thumb folded inside the hand. If, however, to pocket the desired ball you absolutely have to hold the cue parallel to the cushion (e.g., if the cue ball and the object ball are frozen to the same cushion), you can use the closed bridge by adapting it to the situation, as shown in photo 39.

The cushions may not be the only thing preventing you from forming the usual bridge. Indeed, other balls sometimes fill the space that the bridge would use, thus creating an obstacle that you have to overcome to pocket the next ball.

In this situation, you must raise the left hand by pushing on the tips of the three last fingers, the index finger itself placed against the middle finger (photo 40). This nonstandard support could be called a "tripod." This is a case where you have no other option but to use the V-shaped bridge, with the cue placed in the hollow located between the thumb and the index finger.

When the cue ball is too far away from the cushion yet still accessible without having to use the rake, you'll use the open, V-shaped bridge (photo 41).

Often, the shape of the conventional bridge that a left-handed person can master is impossible for the right-handed player, who has to use the rake, which is a handicap. You, as well as

In this photo, the bridge is held incorrectly: the player, who doesn't have the benefit of something stable to support his arm, risks unconsciously moving the bridge just as he strikes with the cue.

This is the correct way to use the bridge. When supported on the table, it won't move as the cue moves.

Here's a trick that might prove very useful: to have more room, place one bridge on top of the other, as shown in the inset.

everyone else, will occasionally miss a fairly easy ball by leaning too far forward rather than using the rake. Once you've lost a few frames because of this, you'll understand how useful this tool is when it becomes impossible to play otherwise. Don't do what one amateur did in Melbourne, Australia, in December 1978, as he was playing a heated game in his garage against one of his friends and was suddenly faced with a shot impossible to make by playing normally. The ball was placed in such a way that he couldn't reach it without using the rake. Because he evidently hated using it, Raymond Priestly climbed to the ceiling and hung by his feet from a beam. He had cause to regret it: he slipped, cracked his skull on the cement floor and died in hospital. If you're fairly persistent, try to get accustomed to using the cue with the left hand as much as the right hand. People who are naturally ambidextrous are rare. But almost all professionals have become ambidextrous by dint of practice and perseverance. Playing with both hands is a valuable asset that will often help you avoid having to use the replacement bridge. Try to get used to it.

HOW TO AIM

It's a self-evident truth that, when placed on a horizontal surface, a sphere that is pushed on one side will be projected in the opposite direction. This basic principle of physics applies constantly in pool, for each time a ball is pocketed, it's because it first received a push in the direction of the pocket in question. Even if this principle may seem simple, it's a lot more difficult to actually execute. If a pool enthusiast completely mastered this part of the game, he would be a perfect player. Such a phenomenon has never existed and will never exist. It's easy to think of how to aim at the cue ball with the cue, but the situation becomes more complicated when it comes to projecting another ball to a specific location using the cue ball.

You must first learn to line yourself up with the cue to hit the ball in the center. The first drill involves placing the cue ball on the head spot and aiming at the center diamond on the bottom rail.

Position the ball as shown in Diagram 4 and play perpendicularly to the cushion farthest away. If you aim at the center of the ball, it should rebound directly onto the tip of your cue, to the same spot where you struck it. You have to first master this shot before moving on to the next step.

The following drill involves pocketing a ball placed close to, and in a straight line with, the pocket. Where should the cue ball contact the object ball? The object ball must be hit at the

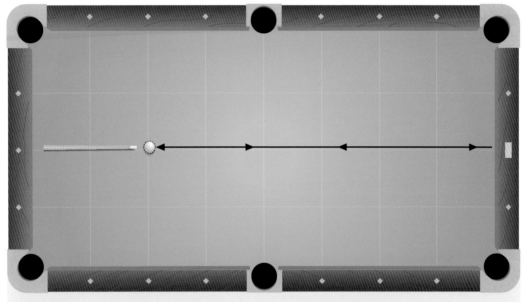

Diagram 4 *The cue ball hit right in the center must return along the exact same trajectory.*

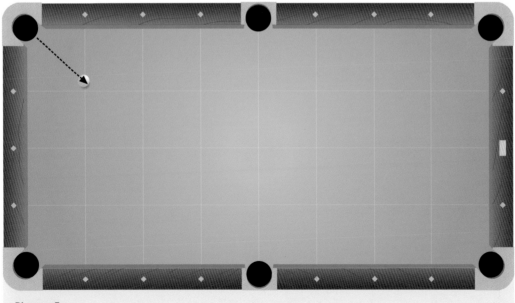

Diagram 5

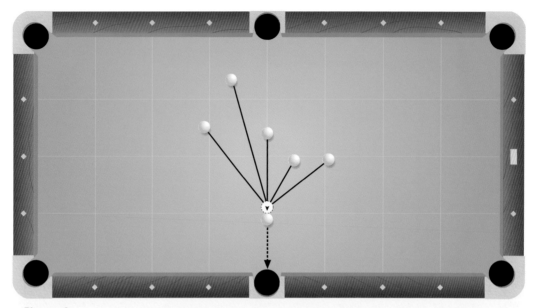

Diagram 6

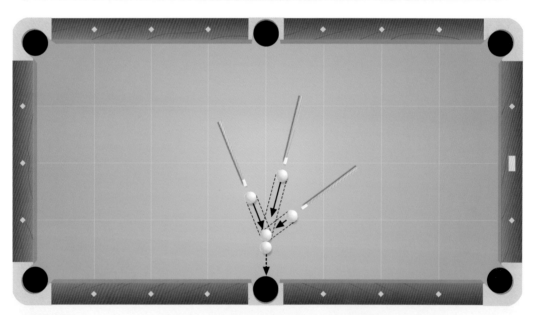

Diagram 7

45

The target.

point directly opposite the direction in which you want to send the ball. You can find this spot by tracing an imaginary line from the pocket, through the center of the object ball to the focal point. (See Diagram 5.)

This is the target that you should hit to send the ball to the desired spot. Notice that the point of contact is determined based on the ball targeted, and not on the cue ball on the table. (See Diagram 6.)

You can see that the point of contact remains the same, whatever the position of the cue ball: there's only one place where the object ball must be hit. Only the angle (at which the cue ball hits the other ball) varies. To pocket this kind of ball, contact must take place in a straight line with the pocket targeted, and this straight line must pass through the center of the two balls. (See Diagram 7.)

At the moment of contact, the cue ball, the object ball and the pocket targeted must be perfectly lined up. This diagram also shows that the focal point, at that moment when the player is getting ready to take the shot, is the imaginary central point of the cue ball when it's

struck. Indeed, keep in mind that the balls strike each other on their sides and not in the center. The absolute center of the balls is on the inside, while they hit each other at a point on their outside curve. Therefore, you have to take into account that the diameter of the balls is $2^{1}/_{4}$ in. (58 mm), compared with the tiny point of contact (less than 1 mm^2). Imagine the trajectory that the cue ball will travel and the spot that it will occupy at the moment of impact with the object ball.

Before leaning forward to play, first use your imagination to determine exactly what the target

46

Aim at the target.

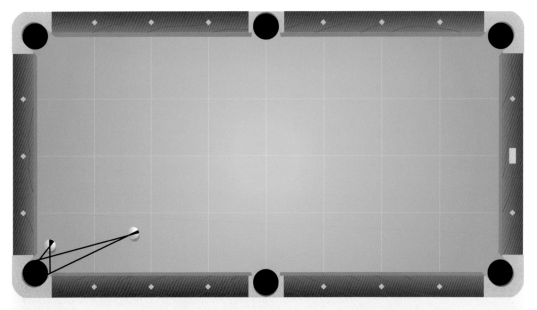

Diagram 8

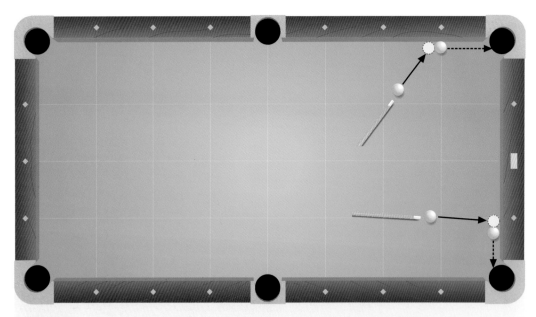

Diagram 9

is. Then, assume the playing stance and form a bridge. Look carefully at the focal point, then check if the contact with the cue will definitely be in the center of the cue ball. Imitate a few preparatory shots, looking carefully at the cue ball and the object ball until the trajectory is clearly visible in your mind. Finally, at the last moment, focus on the object ball at the point where contact is to take place and make your shot.

Don't be intimidated by this lengthy, detailed description, for, in fact, the entire process happens instinctively and naturally. Some shots are easier to make than others; for example, when the ball is close to the pocket. Nonetheless, don't pounce on a ball that you think is easy to hit, for experience has shown that all shots require the same attention and the same application. It is true, however, that the farther away the object ball is from the pocket, the harder it is to pocket it.

Since the pocket opening is approximately two-and-a-half times larger than the diameter of the ball, there is a margin of error, shown in Diagram 8 by the darker section on the balls. However, you can see that the margin of error is smaller for the ball farther away from the pocket than the one that is closer.

Now you'll know that, in general, when many options become available, you have to choose the easiest ball, the one that is normally the closest to the pocket. Don't complicate things unnecessarily, as the simplest solution is almost always the better one.

For balls frozen to the cushion, you simply have to ensure that the cue ball hits the cushion and the object ball at the same time (Diagram 9). There are other shots that require particular types of alignment, including combination, carom, curve, bricole and ricochet shots. They'll be discussed in greater detail later.

THE SPIN

The way the cue ball behaves once it's struck directly in the center is completely normal and predictable: the trajectory is a straight line and the rebound off the cushions or the other balls occurs logically. But, despite its apparent ease, the shot with no spin is not as easy to do as you might think. All you need to do is hit the ball a little off-center to change its path. Any serious player has to be able to do a center shot and completely master it to be able to execute, among other things, the kick shots, those types of bank shots in which the cue ball makes contact with a cushion before hitting the ball, that we'll talk about later. Diagram 4 (see page 59) explains and illustrates a good way to check

whether you've mastered the shot without a spin. Repeat this drill often.

Two types of obstacles can hinder the way the cue ball rolls on the pool table: the cushion and the other balls. What the amateur doesn't know is that the rebound of the cue ball after the shot can be changed by the spin.

The spin (which is also called "English") is the rotation of the cue ball around itself, a rotation that changes the normal trajectory. A word of warning: it's useless to think of using the spin if you haven't first mastered the basic shot without a spin. In theory, a perfect player should always hit the cue ball directly in the center. Yet, since there's no such thing as perfection, professionals

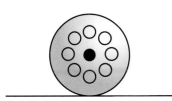

Diagram 10 *On this ball viewed from the front, you can see the nine possible points of contact.*

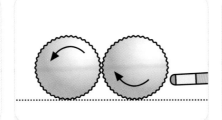

Diagram 11

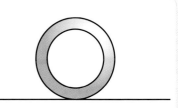

Diagram 12 *On this ball viewed from the front, the shaded area indicates where it would be dangerous to play a spin, increasing the risk of a miscue.*

assert that 80% of all shots should be performed without a spin. This percentage assumes that the player has mastered the play, which is not the case for most amateurs. In fact, you have to aim at using the least amount of spin possible because of the risk of performing a miscue and, moreover, the difficulty in controlling the ball's trajectory once it's been hit.

On the other hand, the average amateur must often resort to the spin to counterbalance errors in positioning and to prepare the next shot. Therefore, he can benefit from understanding this important aspect of pool, which can increase the available options tenfold.

Since the surface of the ball is a lot larger than the surface of the tip of the cue, the number of possible points of contact is also greater. What an amateur often doesn't know is that the trajectory of the cue ball can be changed considerably depending on whether the point of contact of the cue ball is located in the center, low, high, to the left, to the right, or even more precisely, low to the left, low to the right, high to the left or high to the right.

To understand the process of spin, you have to know that the balls rolling on the table behave in some ways like a cogwheel. It isn't solely for aesthetic reasons that pool tables are covered with an expensive cloth. It's mostly to allow the balls to have a good grip on the baize while ensuring maximum spin. The best cloths come from England and are made of wool. They are so tightly woven that you can't see the weft. At the touch of the hand, you only feel the silky down. This cloth is made of thousands of fibers that form many tiny bumps to which the outside film of the balls grips.

The balls behave like cogwheels in relation to the other balls and the baize (see Diagram 11). As a result, if, as an example, you strike the cue ball on the right side, the spin will be transferred to the left of the object ball, but to a lesser degree.

To trigger the spin, all you have to do is strike the cue ball somewhere other than the center. But be careful: don't overdo the spin, be reasonable and never play more than the width of the tip to the outside of center. Otherwise, the result will often end up being a miscue.

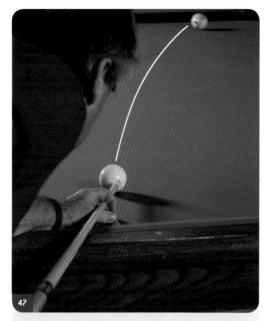

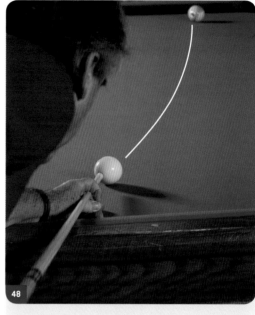

Right spin.

Left spin.

If you strike the ball in the center, it will roll normally. But often if you strike the ball on the side, above or below, you'll transmit momentum to it causing it to rotate around itself, or spin. The spin changes the path of the cue ball at two different moments: before and after the strike. Before the strike, the spin is in some ways suspended and the ball, loaded with spin, slides or skids along the cloth, a little like a bowling ball rolling down the lane.

For the left and the right sidespin, accuracy is required: even if the spin is suspended, it causes the trajectory of the cue ball to shift ever so slightly, so that you may not even notice it at first. But with experience, you'll be able to anticipate its importance with certainty. You'll note that the cue ball, struck on the right by the cue, will tend to veer to the right (and to the left if it's struck on the left).

Photos 47 and 48 exaggerate the curve that you have to take into account when you're lining up the shot. This is another reason why you generally have to play with no spin. The sidespin, in particular, always makes pocketing the object ball more difficult.

It's the impact (against the cushion or against another ball) that triggers the spin in a decisive manner: at the moment when it occurs and right after, the cue ball stops skidding and is pushed in the direction determined by the rotation of the spin.

If you have the chance to see good players at work, you'll sometimes notice the erratic behavior of the cue ball. Since you now understand

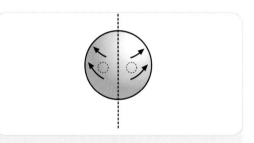

Diagram 13 Cue ball viewed from the front. When the cue ball is struck on the side, the rotation of this ball on itself takes place along an imaginary vertical axis.

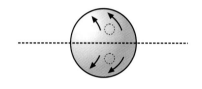

Diagram 14 Cue ball viewed from the front. When the cue ball is struck on the top or the bottom, the rotation of this ball on itself takes place along an imaginary horizontal axis.

how spin works, you'll understand that the way in which balls rebound, especially the cue ball, is not a matter of chance, but the result of a well-calculated spin. Here's a list of the principal types of spin:

topspin: spin forward
backspin: spin backward
right topspin: high and to the right
left topspin: high and to the left
right backspin: low and to the right
left backspin: low and to the left

A review of this list reveals two major spin categories: on the one hand, those that occur relative to the horizontal axis of the cue ball (center, topspin, backspin); on the other hand, those that occur relative to the vertical axis of the cue ball (all the sidespins).

The sidespins, to the right or to the left, are also divided into two categories—natural and reverse—depending on the position of the balls in relation to one another. The natural sidespin intensifies the normal movement of the cue ball following impact and increases its speed. The reverse sidespin tends to push the ball in the direction contrary to its natural direction and slows it down. The result of the natural sidespin is increased, since two distinct forces come together in the same direction; the reverse spin is decreased, for two opposite forces are at work. Review Diagrams 15 and 16 to better understand how this works.

For a given situation, the sidespin (to the right or to the left) completely changes the trajectory of the cue ball after impact. In Diagrams 15 and 16, the natural movement (shown by the dotted line) of the cue ball struck right in the center would be to the right. By adding a right sidespin to the natural movement, the reaction to the right

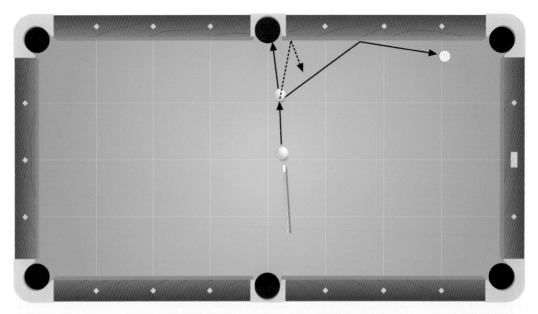

Diagram 15 *Natural sidespin (to the right).*

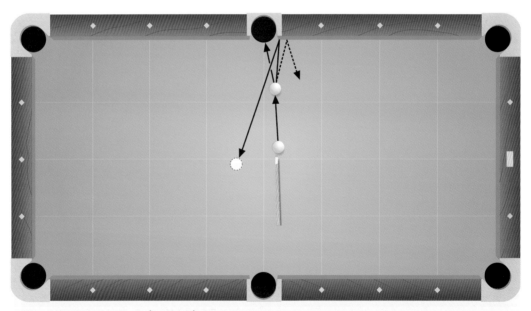

Diagram 16 *Reverse sidespin (to the left).*

Point of contact of the cue on the cue ball (front view) and name of the spin.	Behavior of the cue ball following impact with the cushion (seen from above). The dotted line indicates the approximate location where the cue ball will go after the rebound.
Topspin Center Strike Backspin	
Left Sidespin	
Right Sidespin	
Left Topspin Left Backspin	
Right Topspin Right Backspin	

Diagram 17 *Table showing reflection off the cushion.*

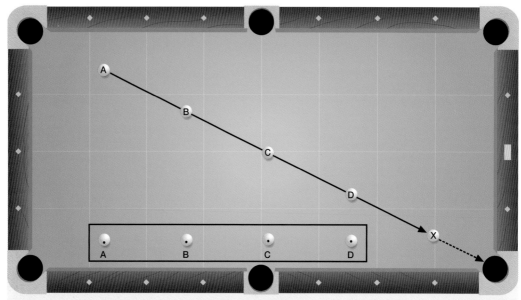

Diagram 18 *The X indicates the ball to be pocketed. The letters A, B, C and D indicate the different positions possible for those within the dotted box, the little black spot indicates the cue's point of contact on the cue ball. To successfully stop the cue ball at the exact place of impact on ball X, the spin and the force of the shot must be increased as the distance increases. In the case of play A, a lot of backspin is needed and the shot has to be hard. In contrast, in play D a moderate shot below center is enough. Plays B and C are in between.*

is doubled and the result, like the speed, is more pronounced. In contrast, the left sidespin, by going against the natural movement of the cue ball, reduces the angle of reflection off the cushion, while also reducing the ball's speed.

For a more complete and detailed description of the different types of spin, refer to Diagram 17.

It's not enough to strike the ball in the spot indicated to be sure of the final outcome. Making the spin work means having a solid mastery of the shot using the cue. You must play your shot while continuing your motion so that the cue follows the cue ball in the same way. In fact, the intensity of the spin depends mainly on the

quality of the cloth, the strength of the shot and the distance separating the cue ball from the object ball. The greater the distance, the less intense the spin will be. In other words, the spin is easy to apply when the two balls are near each other, but it's much more difficult, for example, to make the cue ball return after the impact when the object ball is located at the other end of the table. Note that no spin can be effective if the thrust of the cue is very weak. You always have to strike with a fair bit of force, especially when the cue ball is far away from the object ball. In this case, you have to compensate by playing harder. Diagram 18 shows these principles.

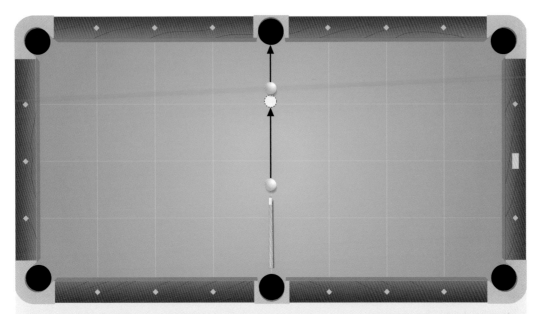

Diagram 19 *If the balls are in a straight line, it's possible to stop the cue ball at the exact spot where contact occurs.*

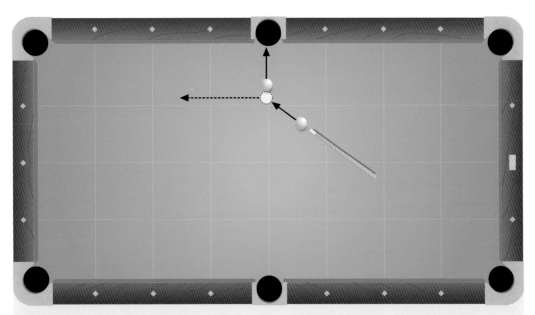

Diagram 20 *When the ball you are trying to strike has to be "cut" at a certain angle, it's impossible to stop the cue ball at the exact spot where contact occurs.*

Moderate backspin.

Often, when you play a ball, you need to leave the cue ball exactly where the impact occurred to prepare the next shot. This is referred to as a "stop shot." This type of shot is only possible when the cue ball, the object ball and the pocket are in a straight line, for if you have to "cut" the ball, i.e. strike it at an angle, that allows the cue ball to rebound off the opposite side.

To do a stop shot, you have to hit hard, slightly below the center of the cue ball.

When used wisely, the spin can transform an apparently hopeless situation into an almost perfect game. In conclusion, as it's practically impossible to describe all situations, here are a few plays where, with the cue ball and the object ball still in the same initial positions, the spin made it possible to prepare the next shot. These illustrations clearly show the need for any serious player to understand the science of the spin.

Moderate backspin.

Right backspin.

Topspin slightly to the right.

Topspin slightly to the left.

Backspin slightly to the right.

Backspin to the left.

A lot of spin to the left, fairly strong.

COMPLEX SITUATIONS

During any game, the ideal way to successfully shoot a ball is to play it directly into the pocket without any interference. Unfortunately, this isn't always possible. The layout of the play on the table can mean that no ball is open in the direction of the pocket or that the cue ball can't directly access a ball at a reasonable angle. In either case, it's impossible to play the shot normally. In such a situation, you have to carefully study the position of the balls in relation to each other in order to determine if it's possible to make what American professionals call a "kick shot," i.e. a combination, ricochet, bricole or carom shot. Indeed, thanks to these shots, you may be able to turn an apparently hopeless situation into an ideal play. The great champion Mike Massey described well the challenge that you must face: "These shots are the product of experience and are played mostly by feel and instinct. To acquire a feel for these shots, you must put in hours of practice to gain any measure of consistency." Be careful. Naturally, everything depends on the stakes of the frame. During a friendly match, you'll seize any opportunity to test your knowledge and take chances. If you miss your goal, you'll benefit from it, for you'll become aware of your mistakes and gain some great experience. However, if it's an important competition, don't risk opening the game to your opponent: if you don't think you can pocket a ball

easily using one shot, play defensively. Missing a risky ball at a critical moment can be the same as offering your opponent the win on a silver platter. However, since nine-ball has replaced 14.1 among the elite of pool, the offensive playing style has essentially replaced the defensive aspect of the game and the approach has now become a lot more aggressive. Therefore, there's been a massive change in the thinking, and the principles of caution that used to guide the pros have given way to dramatic shots: since the frame is very short, participants don't hesitate to resort to the most daring shots to seize victory. It's up to you to assess each time a complicated situation arises whether your chances of winning a risky and uncommon play are good enough to dare to try it. Everything depends on your skill. It's also a question of confidence and your nature.

COMBINATION SHOTS

In pool, a combination shot occurs when the player uses one or several intermediate balls found between the cue ball and the object ball to pocket the object ball. It's always fascinating to play a combination shot, especially if it includes several balls. As soon as the layout of the play seems to favor pocketing a ball, you will likely want to try it. This temptation is very strong among all players and you're probably not the exception to the rule. Nonetheless, you have to resist and not play a combination shot unless there's no other solution, because of the small margin of error of less than 0.04 in. ($^1/_{32}$ mm).

The art to successfully making this kind of shot can't be learned from books, but through experience that can only be gained by repetition. Therefore, it's not a question of des-cribing here all the possible combinations, as there is an almost infinite number of options. You can

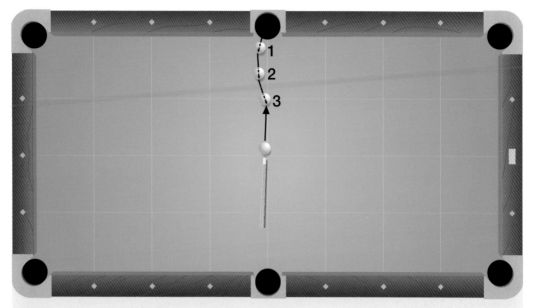

Diagram 21 *The focal point of the cue ball can be found by sighting the pocket and by working back to the last ball.*

play those that you're sure you can make, e.g. when two or several balls are frozen to each other in a straight line with the pocket and close to it. In this instance, all you have to do is aim the cue ball so that it hits the point of contact of the first ball.

Obviously, the farther apart the balls are, the harder it will be to make the combination shot. It's the same if the ball is far away from the pocket, for there's no margin of error. The situation is even more complicated if the combination shot is aimed at two balls. Even if a combination shot sometimes seems easy, always be careful and pay attention. Careful attention can't be emphasized enough.

Always determine your focal point by starting with the object ball, then moving back to the cue ball and not the reverse. Determine the target by first studying the ball closest to the pocket, then the next closest, and so on until you get to the cue ball. Plan these steps meticulously before playing.

When two balls are frozen together, or less than ⅛ in. (3 mm) apart, a curious osmosis phenomenon takes place between them, which causes the second ball to go in slightly the same direction as the first ball. This principle also applies to the cue ball when it's shot at two balls frozen together, or when the cue ball itself is frozen to another ball.

Similarly, even if the two balls appear to be aligned in such a way that they'll miss the pocket, there's sometimes a way to fix the situation by "pushing" the first ball, which will transfer its momentum to the second ball at an angle. A

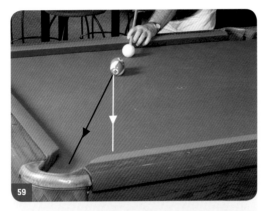

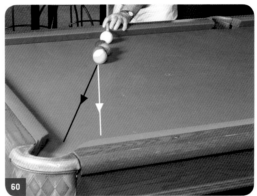

In photos 59, 60 and 61 the white line indicates the point with which the balls are aligned and the black line shows the real trajectory that the ball will travel.

ball that is pushed along the length of a table 9 ft. (2.74 m) in length can deviate up to 1 ft. (30 cm) from its normal trajectory.

When the object ball is frozen to the cue ball, its angular momentum will be emphasized even more if, in addition to pushing on the desired side, you apply the spin on the opposite side. This shot is fairly easy to master and can get you out of a jam at more than one critical moment.

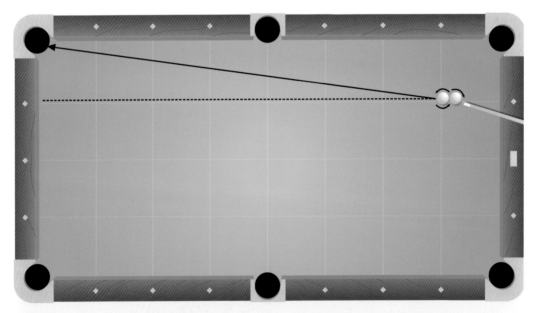

Diagram 22 The dotted line indicates the direction in which the ball is aligned. However, it can be pocketed. Note the angular momentum of the ball attempted, because the cue ball was pushed in the direction of the pocket.

This combination is impossible to do, for it's pushed in the wrong direction.

Note the deflection.

Practice it and learn how to calculate and assess the deflection.

CAROM AND RICOCHET SHOTS

Carom and ricochet (also called "kiss shot") shots have many similarities and are governed by the same principles. As a result, a lot of amateurs confuse them. However, the difference is simple.

In the case of the carom shot (photo 63), the cue ball strikes another ball before touching the object ball, while in the case of the ricochet (photo 64), it doesn't strike an intermediate ball; the object ball itself will strike another ball before being pocketed.

The carom shot isn't used that often in pool or snooker, but it is the basis of European billiards. Even if pool is now very popular in Europe, you can still find a lot of tables with a continuous

A carom shot.

64

A richochet.

cushion known as carom billiards tables. These tables are pocketless and you play with only three balls. The game consists of getting the highest number of consecutive carom shots. To add to the difficulty, certain variations have been introduced, such as three-cushion billiards and balkline billiards (18.1, 18.2, etc.). In three-cushion billiards, the cue ball must hit at least three cushions before striking the last ball. In 18.1 or 18.2 (in France, 47.1 or 47.2), you can only make a limited number of carom shots inside predefined balklines before having to change zones.

The difficulty with this type of shot lies in calculating the exact point off which the cue ball (or the ricochet ball) will rebound after hitting

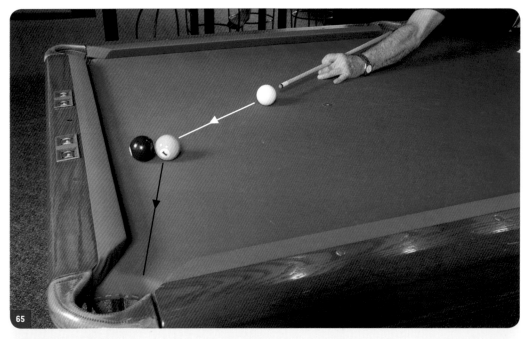

65

Another type of ricochet.

another ball (Diagram 23, A). To determine this, you have to draw an imaginary line perpendicular to the point of contact between the two balls. By following this imaginary line, you'll know where the ball's trajectory will end following the impact.

The challenge is to correctly sense this point of contact. It's a question of scrutiny and of habit. When the balls are stuck, continue as follows: imagine a point that would join the centers of two balls that will ricochet off each other; then, starting at this point, draw a perpendicular line in the direction of the place where the object ball will be directed (Diagram 23, B).

When the balls involved in the ricochet are not frozen together, the principle is the same, except that the point of contact is established with respect to the ball against which the ricochet will take place (Diagram 24). The exact spot is determined by tracing an imaginary perpendicular line (90°) to the center of the ball in question.

You can even do multiple carom shots or ricochet shots under certain circumstances, when the way the balls are arranged on the table lends itself to doing these.

When all the balls are tightly grouped together, review the layout of the play before deciding that no shot will work. Often, a ball is completely aligned with the center of a pocket. Nonetheless, be careful when doing this kind of shot: if you miss your objective, you'll automatically leave the play open to your opponent. If you're not convinced ahead of time that you'll succeed, play defensively.

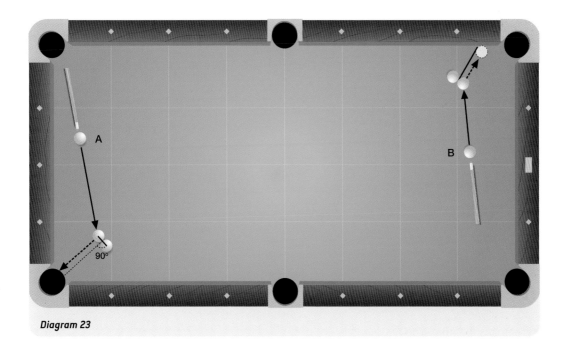

Diagram 23

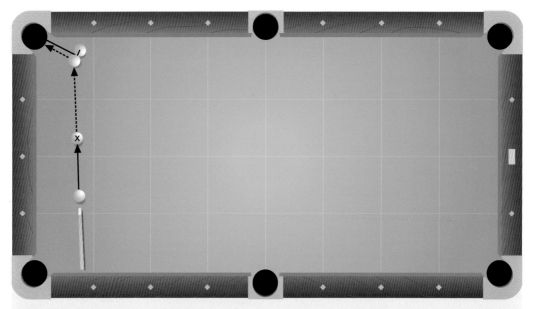

Diagram 24

A double ricochet in a multiple combination shot.

A double ricochet that's difficult to shoot.

A simple bricole.

CROSS AND BRICOLE SHOTS

Cross (formerly referred to as "double"—see the Glossary, page 255) and bricole shots require using the cushion to make a shot with the ball. If the cue ball strikes the cushion before touching the object ball, it's a bricole. If the object ball itself rebounds off the cushion before going into the pocket, it is referred to as a cross.

Cross and bricole shots are always fascinating to watch. But they're considered by professionals as being the most difficult shots to do. To succeed, you have to locate the exact spot on the cushion where the ball will rebound into the center of the pocket. To do this, you know that

An illustration of a shot (the 8-ball in the center off three cushions) that I made a few years ago on a winning ball during a frame of eight-ball played in an organized league.

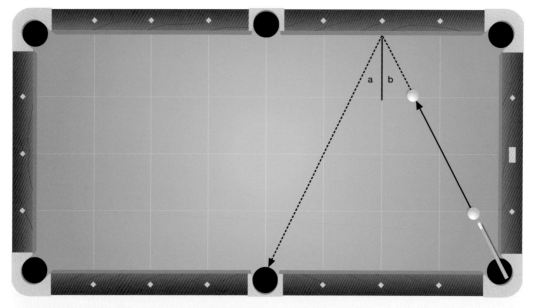

Diagram 25 *In this illustration, angle A is equal to angle B.*

you have to aim at an imaginary point somewhere on the cushion opposite the desired pocket. But how do you determine exactly where the target is? English and American writers teach different, very complex systems on this subject with mindboggling results.

Some amateurs claim that the professionals have a clever technique whereby the diamonds that line the rails serve as points of reference. This popular belief was encouraged by the publication in some books on pool of a series of tables illustrating the rebounds that are possible from different locations. An expert on the topic, Danny McGoorty, who passed away in 1970, explains in his autobiography that all the great pool players instinctively perform cushion shots. McGoorty had the advantage of participating in several major tournaments, including the 1949 World

Championship, and of rubbing shoulders with the greatest masters, including Jake Schaefer, Welker Cochran and the legendary Willie Hoppe, who excelled at pocketless billiards. At the end of Hoppe's book, several tables indicate what the result will be by striking a particular diamond from a particular spot. In his memoirs, McGoorty confirms that Hoppe didn't come up with these designs himself, but rather that John Layton, Bob Cannafax and a few others did. It was the publisher who decided to include them in Hoppe's book. In fact, this diamond system is a nice theory but not terribly practical. Don't believe in the existence of a miracle method that would suddenly enable you to make a cushion shot. Even the professionals are never sure what the result of a cross or a bricole shot will be.

On the other hand, there is, in my opinion, a

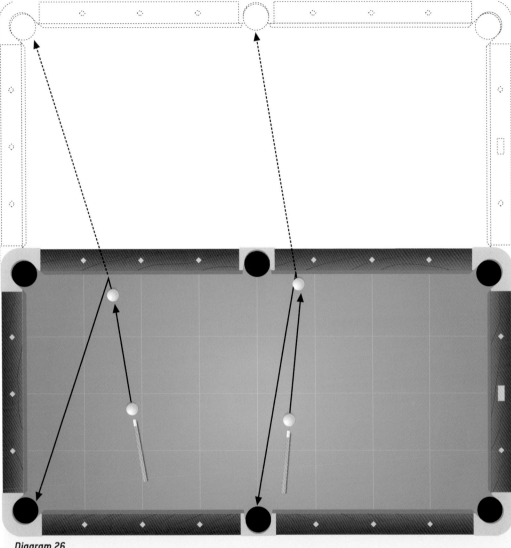

Diagram 26

way of calculating fairly accurately the rebound of the ball off the cushion. I came up with this method and I've been using it for a long time. It's easy to understand, and the results are surprising.

To start, you know that if you play without a spin, the angle at which the ball strikes the cushion is the same as the one at which it will rebound (Diagram 25). To predict more accurately what the ball's reaction will be, all you need to do is imagine that the pocket is located at a distance equal to the width of the table, in the direction of the point to which the ball would be projected if there was no cushion.

Imagine a table identical to the one on which you are playing and aim at the pocket that corresponds to the opposite pocket (Diagram 26). This technique works for all kinds of cross shots, no matter if the object ball is near or far from the cushion or the cue ball. You'll need some time to be able to visualize the exact layout of the table, but you'll note that, in the long-term, this method, even if it isn't perfect, remains the most effective and gets the best results.

It's essential that a ball attempted off the cushion be played with no spin, otherwise its trajectory, once it hits the cushion, may change. In addition, the cross shots must be played moderately hard. If you play too gently, the angle of reflection will be wider. If you play too hard, the angle will tend to be smaller (see Diagram 27).

MASSÉ SHOTS AND JUMP SHOTS

A lot of emphasis was placed early in this book on the importance of holding the cue horizontally and parallel to the bottom (or bed) of the table. The only exception to this rule applies to the performance of massé and jump shots. The goal of the massé shot is to trace an arc, or a curve, using the cue ball. The jump shot forces the cue

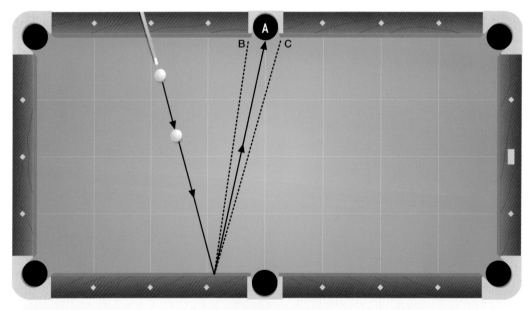

Diagram 27 *If you play a shot moderately hard, the ball will follow the trajectory shown by letter A. If you play gently, the angle will be bigger (letter C, and if you play hard, the angle will be smaller (letter B).*

ball to leave the table bed and rise slightly for a short distance, while following its trajectory. In pool, these two types of shots are rather rare among amateurs, but since the 1990s, the jump shot has been used more and more in high-level competitions, especially in nine-ball. They also help to entertain the spectators during trick shot demonstrations or fancy shots. When you perform a massé, it's almost impossible to know in advance the degree of the curve that the cue ball will follow. Therefore, it isn't a precise shot. This is why the experts rarely use it during an important match.

In European or pocketless billiards, however, the massé is used much more often, given that in most of the frames, all that's required to score a point is to have the cue ball touch the two other balls, regardless of where they are projected. In other words, the room to maneuver is much greater, i.e. the width of the ball, or approximately 2$\frac{1}{4}$ in. (57 mm). In contrast, in regular pool, the margin of error is generally only a fraction of an inch, since the object ball must be sent off toward a specific point.

The massé can be very helpful in snooker. In this game, you have to touch a specific ball belonging to a predefined group (the reds or the colors), otherwise you're penalized at least four points. The player who finds himself at an impasse will sometimes have to resort to the massé to get around the ball in the way.

To perform a massé, hold your cue almost

70

Willie Hoppe, the great American champion in three-cushion billiards a century ago, prepares to perform a massé with raised arm.

Photo: © Billiards Digest

vertically, attack the cue ball on the same side that you want it to go (i.e. left or right) and play hard. "Pinched" between the stick and the baize, the cue ball will start rotating around itself so quickly that its trajectory will be affected, and it will follow a smaller or larger arc depending on the force of the shot and the angle of the cue when attacking. The more the cue is angled, the greater the deflection.

During a frame, whatever the game, the cue ball will often not have access to the desired ball, its trajectory often completely or partially ob-structed by one or several balls. You then have a choice: use one or more cushions to reach the desired ball, or use a massé or a jump shot. It all depends on what is at stake. If you're coming from behind and you want to risk everything, then you can try a jump shot. When not using the massé shot, the pros are resorting more and more to the jump shot to get around any balls in the way. The young and fiery pro Niels Feijen (14.1 world champion in 2008) prefers the jump shot: "For me personally, jumping is easier than kicking. With a kick, you are a little dependant on the rails and choosing between different routes. With jumping, it's more straight forward—get over the blocking ball, then either try to make the object ball or play safe." At this stage, one thing has to be clear: in some games (mainly nine-ball), your shot will be refused if, on its way, the cue ball catches on or taps the ball you're trying to jump over. This detail is fundamental, for it implies that you'll have to execute a higher jump in nine-ball, since you have to be sure that the cue ball will completely clear the obstructing ball. Until the early 1980s, the jump shot was hardly used: at that time, the American pros played pri-marily in 14.1 tournaments, a game that is more defensive than eight-ball or nine-ball. Since each frame is longer, they pre-ferred to play a defen-sive shot rather than risk a chancy jump shot, for which they hadn't developed enough technique. And, if they dared to try a jump shot, they would use their normal cue, since it was always a par-tial jump shot that didn't require a lot of eleva-tion, especially since the shot was allowed even if the cue ball caught on the obstructing ball on its way over. You could only use it to get around the part of the ball that was blocking, which implies that the cue ball generally didn't have to rise more than half the height of this ball, or roughly $1\frac{1}{2}$ in. (40 mm).

In 1983, Earl Strickland, who was 22 at the time, caused quite a stir in the pool community in the United States: this young star was the first to attempt a jump shot during a professional

A partial jump shot, in the sense that the cue ball doesn't have to completely pass over the two obstructing balls that are too close together and preventing the cue ball from moving between them normally, in order to get between them. You can perform this kind of jump shot using an ordinary cue.

championship broadcast on ESPN. This happened during the final match of the Caesars Tahoe tournament against the legendary Steve Mizerak. Strickland won thanks to this spectacular shot! He was the youngest of 119 participants in this nine-ball tournament, and his daring won him his first major title and made him famous. At that time, the jump shot wasn't very well known, but the following year, in 1984, the pro Pat Fleming was the first to use the short cue to execute jump shots in tournaments, thus creating a new fashion that quickly spread among his colleagues. American pros began using and perfecting this technique, which is common today. In the beginning, this new trend was the subject of controversy for a few years among players, but the spectacular nature of the shot caused such a craze among spectators that the pros had to give in and include it in their arsenal. There is now a much shorter and lighter cue specially designed for this shot (see page 36). The jump cue makes it possible to perform a number of plays that are impossible to do using normal cues. It's a lot lighter at approximately 10 oz. (280 g), which allows you to jump over balls that are close to the cue ball. With your normal cue, it's practically impossible to jump over a ball located less than 6 in. (15 cm) from the cue ball. Using a jump cue, some experts are able to pass right over the obstructing ball, which can be as close to the cue ball as 2.5 cm (1 in.), but this is unusual. You should limit the distance to a minimum of 8 cm (3 in.).

Photo: © Cuetec

An illustration of the perfect jump-shot technique: champion Allison Fisher, who was named Female Player of the Decade (2000–2009) in 2010, prepares to execute a jump shot using the short cue specially designed for this purpose.

When you play a shot using the jump cue, you don't have to imitate the filing motion to get ready to shoot. First, you simply need to lean forward as usual and line yourself up to determine the exact spot at which the cue ball should be directed. As soon as you've decided on your target, raise the palm of the hand forming the bridge. Bear in mind that you always play a jump shot with an open bridge, since you have to place the hand forming the support at an extreme angle on your fingertips near the cue ball, for the cue itself will be held at an angle between 30° and 60° relative to the horizontal plane of the table. Aside from using a short cue, two factors will determine the range of the rebound: the angle of the cue and the amount of force used. The higher the angle, the more sudden the jump. And the greater the force, the higher the jump.

Furthermore, there are two ways to hold the cue to play a jump shot: the "pendulum" and the "jab." The pendulum motion is the one normally used in most shots, with the cue balanced in front and at the back like a pendulum balanced under your elbow. You would use this technique (but raising your back hand) if the angle of attack imagined is 45° or less. If the angle is bigger, you'll have to resort to the technique called the jab: hold your cue a little like you would to throw a dart. Strive to align your body and your head in such a way so as not to harm your shot, with the cue held almost vertically in front of you and as close as possible to the side of your head so that you can visualize and understand the angle of attack. You then grasp the cue lightly with your thumb and index finger, your wrist bent back as far as possible and up. Maintain your wrist in this position and use your forearm to give the ultimate thrust that will project the cue toward the cue ball with a quick, lively shot.

From the moment that your bridge is in the final position, it is best if only the back arm moves, while the rest of your body remains motionless. The higher the angle, the higher the cue ball will rise. The most important point to remember is the amount of force needed to make a good shot with enough impact. Since you're striking in the direction of the table bed, the natural tendency is to brake the shot too soon. Avoid making this mistake. Don't grasp your cue too tightly. When it's time to release, go right ahead and apply the force required. Strike quickly and lively like lightning, for the faster the cue leaves the cue ball, the higher the jump. The point of attack is located directly in the center of the cue ball or slightly behind it, for if you attack too high, you risk the ball getting stuck between the tip and the table, which prevents it from rebounding.

When should you resort to the jump shot? Most professionals prefer trying the jump shot rather than choosing a cushion shot. The best opportunity is when the ball that you want to reach is very close to a pocket so that the room to maneuver is greater. Furthermore, the jump shot can't be performed if the obstructing ball is leaning against the cue ball, for you need some distance for the cue ball to get enough speed and rise to pass over the top. Experience will teach you how to assess the distances needed. In the same vein, it's dangerous to attempt a jump shot when the cue ball is perpendicular to the cushion against which the object ball is positioned. It's better if the object ball is not too close to the cushion relative to the striking angle, to give the cue ball enough space to land and remain on the table, thus preventing it from being shot off the table, as shown in Diagram 28. A significant point

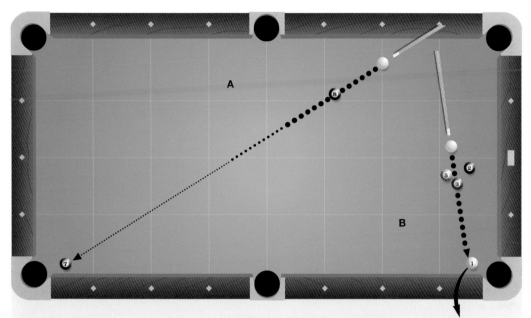

Diagram 28 *The arrangement of the balls in A is ideal for attempting a jump shot because the desired ball (the 7-ball) is near the pocket. In addition, the cue ball has sufficient distance to jump over the 8-ball and land back on the table before hitting the 7-ball. In B, attempting a jump shot over the three blocking balls to try to pocket, or simply to contact, the 1-ball, may run the risk of failing, since it's almost impossible to prevent the cue ball from being shot off the table.*

is to strive to strike the cue ball right in the center, avoiding any spin to the left or the right, otherwise you'll completely miss your shot. To see an example of how to execute a jump shot perfectly, go to YouTube and enter the names Ouschan and Engert. You'll see the best female player in the world execute a perfect jump shot at the ten-ball world championship in the Philippines in 2008.

Before attempting a jump shot, you must first master all the other technical aspects of this play. Most amateurs will never resort to this shot, which is reserved for the experts. Lastly, when using these two types of uncommon shots, be careful not to perform a miscue; you risk tearing the cloth with the tip of your cue.

TRICKS AND FANCY SHOTS

You may have already had a chance to see a player execute tricks on a pool table. In one of his films, for example, Jerry Lewis makes a shot pocketing six balls, one per pocket, at the same time. There's an almost infinite number of possibilities in this area. In 1974, I won a monthly competition organized by the magazine *American Billiard Review* (see the illustration to the right) and in 1982 I published a book called *100 trucs de billard*, which showed how to execute all kinds of tricks and uncommon shots. The comments I received about this book were very positive!

Believe it or not, I even received an email from an amateur in Madagascar who congratulated me and mentioned that the diagrams and explanatory notes were so clear that performing the tricks was "very simple." He was sorry, however, for he couldn't remember to whom he lent his book and asked me where he could get another copy. That book, which was published more than 25 years ago, hasn't been available for some time, and the repeated requests from amateurs convinced me to include those tricks in this book.

The attraction of fancy shots lies in the fact that they seem to be impossible to do at first glance. Some plays, massé and jump, for example, require consummate skill. Yet most are within reach of all players, and the main challenge—the key to success, in fact—is to prepare the play well and to position the balls in the right spot.

Beware of this aspect of the game, however, for performing tricks or fancy shots doesn't improve the caliber of the game. On the contrary, it risks destroying the competitiveness of the player who devotes himself to these plays. Many claim to be the best in the world in this field. Truthfully, in my humble opinion, Mike Massey, an American whom we were able to admire on several occasions at demonstrations held all over Canada, is far better than his competitors in this area. From the time that television began to broadcast the annual trick shots world championship, we've often had occasion to see him at

work, since he has won this competition nine times. His tricks are really spectacular. We sometimes say that the English are difficult to impress or, at least, fairly impassive. You should have seen the reaction of the snooker pros when Massey performed in England in the early 1990s: even the great champions like Davis, Hendry and

TRICK SHOT CORNER! ●

This month, we're privileged to use a shot contributed by our good friend in Canada, M. Pierre W. Morin. He calls it the "5 Banks Shot." As he describes it, it's a "spectacular, but very easy shot. Place the object ball in front of the corner pocket, and the cue ball in front of the next corner, as shown. Hit the cue ball in the center with a hard stroke, striking near the last opposite diamond. The cue ball will hit 5 cushions, before the object ball is pocketed." Try it, fans....but watch those diamonds!

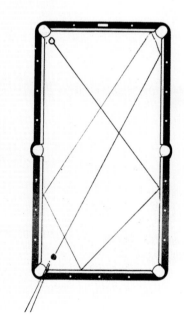

Parrot, among others, were as excited as children unwrapping their Christmas presents. Believe it or not, he performs his most impressive tricks without using a cue, using only his hand to project the cue ball along extraordinary trajectories. He also excels at unimaginable massé shots. One of his main predecessors was Charles C. Peterson, an American who died in 1962 and who was elected to the BCA Hall of Fame not long after. Following him, Willie Mosconi and James Caras also began in this field after retiring from active competition. However, no professional has been both a champion in competitions and an expert in fancy shots. When James Caras came out of retirement in 1967 to participate in the pres-tigious U.S. Open, he had to stop his demonstrations and restrict himself to serious training six hours a day for roughly six months in order to get back into shape. This proves that you can't be the best at regular competitions and trick shot demonstrations. Of course, you also have to have a lot of skill to perform these tricks, but you need even more to excel in important games. First, learn the techniques of pool and master them. The dexterity needed to perform fancy shots will follow.

STRATEGY

Technique isn't everything. You still have to know how to use it, since in the end it's the results that count. You may have the skill to hit the most difficult shots, but if you play without any strategy, you'll remain a mediocre player. You can learn a lot by carefully watching the pros play. But not every-one has a champion at their disposal who can teach them the subtleties of the game. In addition, a good player isn't automatically a good coach. They don't always have the availability, the patience or the talent to communicate the science, nor the good grace to share their secrets. After having the opportunity to see many Canadian and American pros play in competitions, after attending several world championships over three decades, and after having read most of the current literature on the subject, I have enough experience to provide a general outline of the strategies that every serious amateur should know. There are a lot of other elements, but I'll spare you. You'll enjoy discovering them yourself as you progress. Naturally, I left out some dishonest tactics, for I respect pool too much to contribute to tarnishing its reputation.

PLACEMENT

The best pool player is the one who knows how to harmoniously explore all the facets of the game. To excel, you have to be a complete player. Each aspect of technique is a link in the chain, and a chain is only as strong as its weakest link. Even if an amateur is a specialist in cross-table shots, if it's all they know how to do, they'll never become a champion. The good player must excel in all areas and not have any weaknesses. Don't be impressed by pretentious players who use extraordinary spins on every shot: you'll quickly notice that their game has no substance, for they never know in advance where the cue ball will end up for the next shot. No pool player reaches the top without understanding and mastering placement.

Furthermore, it's not enough to place the ball well to be a champion. In a run of 100 consecutive points, in snooker or in pool (14.1), you'll inevitably have a few difficult shots (let's say three or four, if you use placement well). If you're incapable of pocketing any difficult ball, you'll never be able to win these long runs that are the trademark of champions. The best player is the one who, while mastering placement, also has the skill to make difficult shots. If you're competing against a good player and it's your turn, you'll usually find yourself faced with an apparently hopeless play, and the only way to get out of the jam will be to perform a difficult shot. In short, first learn to pocket balls in all situations before thinking about beating the experts.

Your first step: learn the technique so that it becomes instinctive. Before learning playing positioning, you need to learn the basic rules. It's difficult to concentrate on two things at once. In other words, you'll have a lot of trouble preparing and anticipating the next shot if you're focusing on pocketing the object ball. All professionals, over the course of their careers, have missed a fairly easy ball because they were only concentrating on placing the next ball. This will happen to you at the start. Continue, nonetheless, for mistakes are inevitable.

GLOBAL APPROACH

In what order should you pocket the balls on the table? Naturally, there's no precise answer to this question: everything depends on their arrangement, on your way of seeing the situation, on your skills and on your weaknesses.

You've already noticed during friendly games that your opponent doesn't always choose the ball that you would have attempted. This is because everyone has their own idea of the play. It would be unrealistic to define all the rules that can guide you in this area. The essential principle is to always choose the simplest solution. Faced with several situations, play the easiest one. For example, if you have a choice between a ball that's close and directly in line, on the one hand, and a distant combination shot on the other, choose the first one. Naturally, this major rule will sometimes have to be revised if you want to save a position for the next ball or break a group of balls that are in the way. However, in general, avoid complicating the play unnecessarily. Ease and simplicity are the ideal approach.

SCATTERING THE BALLS

In all games of pool and snooker, a good part of the placement must be devoted to breaking up compact groups of balls here and there on the table. When it's your turn, your main concern, before even starting to play, will be to pick out the solitary balls positioned strategically and to roll the cue ball where you'll be able to make it ricochet towards the groups that need to be broken up (Diagram 29).

Indeed, after striking the ball to be pocketed, the cue ball must rebound toward the groups in the way. Sometimes you'll have to prepare the break well in advance in order to get the cue ball into a favorable position (Diagram 30).

Contrary to what you might think, you don't have to play with a lot of force to scatter the balls. Excessive force risks sending one or several balls off the table and, in particular, pocketing the cue ball. Most of the time, moderate force is enough to scatter the balls. Many experts break up the groups gently, which allows them to anticipate where the balls will go when they scatter.

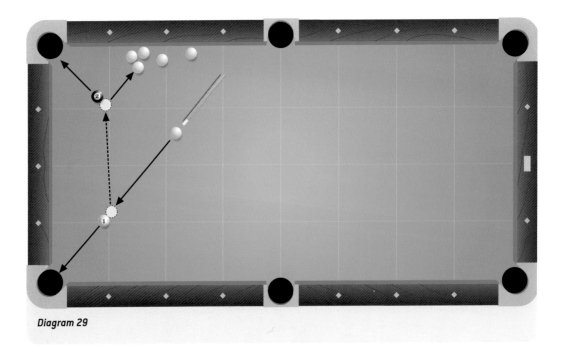

Diagram 29

Never wait to pocket all the solitary balls before breaking up compact groups: you risk finding yourself at an impasse if the balls in motion come to a stop in a difficult location. Therefore, it's better to have a few options. Organize your play to keep one or two balls "in reserve" near the other pockets as shown in Diagram 30.

In addition, avoid moving the balls that have direct access to a pocket. Even if several balls are very close to one another, it's much better to leave them undisturbed if it's possible to pocket them. By disturbing them, you risk placing them in a situation that is even more difficult.

Once all the balls have scattered, determine a plan aimed at ensuring that the cue ball is always in a favorable position to pocket other balls. For games of 14.1 or line-up pool especially, watch that it's placed in the best location possible at the end to start again when the balls are returned to the table.

Avoid rolling the cue ball from one end of the table to the other with each shot. A long shot is always dangerous. Not only do you run the risk of pocketing it, but you won't be able to figure out where it will stop. Proceed in steps. Pocket all the balls located at one end of the table, then pocket those located at the other end. It's better to free the top of the table first, then play the balls at the bottom end. Make every effort to observe these few rules and your skills will improve.

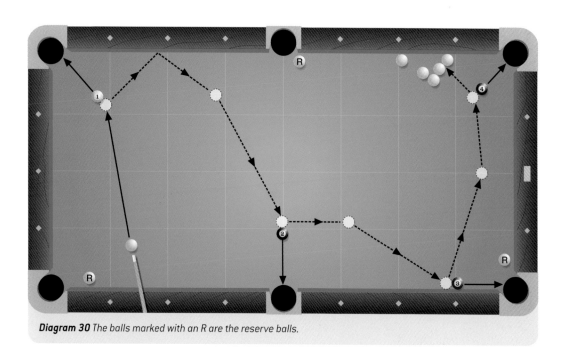

Diagram 30 The balls marked with an R are the reserve balls.

CONCENTRATION

Cliff Thorburn, who in 1980 was the only Canadian to become a snooker world champion, explained that during Georges Chénier's demonstrations (several times Canadian champion in the 1950s and 1960s), some non-pool-playing spectators found the show boring because all the shots appeared too easy. Those in the know were literally hypnotized by Chénier's extraordinary mastery and sensitivity. His concentration was intense and unshakeable. In fact, to appreciate the way professionals play, you have to have some knowledge of pool.

Furthermore, you'll notice that the champions always have easy shots to perform. In fact, of 100 successful shots made by a professional, you would, without a doubt, be able to do 99 of them. Why is it then that you can't beat them and you can't match them? It's a question of concentration and positioning. While you strive to concentrate on one ball out of 10, the professional concentrates intensely on each shot. It's just like school: some students only need 10 minutes to learn a theory, while others might need two hours. It's concentration and the way of working that change everything. Even if you were to read one lesson for hours and hours, if your mind is elsewhere, you won't retain anything. It's the same thing in pool, where, to excel, you have to "read" the game by giving it everything you have. Avoid playing randomly or blindly. It's just as easy to play well as it is to play poorly. In fact, when played seriously, pool requires an intellectual effort as constant and intense as bridge or chess. Often, it's concentration that separates the expert from the mediocre player. Former Quebec champion Claude Bernatchez won, among other things, a major tournament in Chicago in June 1996. After his win, a journalist asked him if the cheers of the spectators, who were applauding the Bulls NBA win on the big screen next door and not the pool players, had bothered him. Bernatchez answered that he didn't notice anything and added, "When the concentration is there, you can play guitars, or Christmas music, that does not bother me."

TRAINING

Billiards is 5% skill and 95% training.

JOE BALSIS

Joe Balsis learned to play pool at a young age, but he started his professional career only at the age of 40. His rise was meteoric. In the space of 28 months, he participated in 10 tournaments and won five, including the most prestigious. He was world champion in 1965. Therefore, he knows what he's talking about when he says that:

"To become a proficent player, the same formula applies: 5% is to master fundamentals—and practice is the other 95%."

You'll sometimes despair that your game is uneven: today, everything's going badly, while yesterday you were playing like a champion. Don't get too upset: all amateurs experience difficult periods during which bad luck seems unrelenting. Remember that the professionals play five to eight hours a day on average, 365 days a year. If you play once or twice a week, it's perfectly normal that your game is sometimes inconsistent or disjointed. You miss easy shots? You probably haven't practiced enough. Your level of skill will be directly proportional to the number of hours you'll have spent on the game. Normally, it takes many years of experience and perseverence to train a champion. If you have great ambitions, know that the best—in fact, the only—way to achieve them is to practice regularly, at least one hour a day and, if possible, to measure yourself against a better player. To beat them, you'll have to be better than them. John Pulman, who was a professional snooker world champion for 10 years, explains that after he became amateur champion in 1946, he had to practice nonstop for eight to 10 hours a day for five years to be able to join the professional ranks. There's no magic formula: the key to success is to practice every day.

COMPETITION

Rivalries and winning are the very essence of sports. A lack of serious competition is probably the main handicap and the worst hindrance for good players. To advance, you must at all costs measure yourself against players who are stronger than you are. When an amateur reaches a certain level, it becomes difficult for them to put their knowledge to the test because they lack a serious opponent. Of course, this problem is not specific to any region, it is the same everywhere. Today, people have the opportunity to see professionals on television or to attend games of great skill and to expand their knowledge. It wasn't always like that. In 1966, when Georges Chénier was forced to go into semi-retirement due to health issues, he moved to Toronto. At that time, Ontario was the only province in Canada that could guarantee a professional a reasonable living. Fortunately, this is no longer the case. Today, you can register and participate in competitions that are organized on a regular basis in most pool halls in most regions. It's a good opportunity to meet and face very strong players from whom you'll gain immeasurable experience. In fact, this is one of the best ways to learn!

In all sports, it's healthy and normal to have a certain degree of emulation among competitors.

The passionate will to win is fundamental to winning. On the other hand, your pride shouldn't cause you to refuse to play a game when you aren't sure of winning. You won't learn anything playing against inferior players, and "to win without risk is to win without glory." If your opponent seems stronger, this should motivate you to challenge them, for you'll benefit greatly, regardless of the outcome of the match. Unfortunately, a lot of amateurs don't see it this way and refuse to play unless there's no risk of losing. Such a negative attitude could backfire on them, for the caliber of their game, far from improving, would plateau and perhaps even decline. At the beginning of my career, I participated in three professional tournaments in the United States. Even if my chances of winning were zero, and despite the costs incurred, I believe the experience was immeasurable. The caliber of my game improved more than twofold. This example should help you to understand the need to always find real competition.

DEFENSE

A veteran of pool in Ontario, Gus Ness, explains that he had occasion to receive valuable advice from Georges Chénier in the 1960s. "Once I was about to pot a ball which would have led to me winning the frame but passed it up. It was difficult and I was afraid that if I had missed, it would cost me the game. George got quite angry with me. 'If during the course of the game you are presented with an opportunity to win the game and you pass it up, you don't deserve to win. Winners find ways to win and losers find ways to lose.'" In addition to being a visionary, Chénier belonged to the class of winners and he knew how to seize all opportunities. This is exactly the attitude that prevails today. With the huge popularity of nine-ball, the offensive aspect of the game has basically taken over. The technique has advanced, and the way to contemplate strategy has been transformed: we play all out because the game is very short and we can't pass up the chance to win. Over the last 20 years, the caliber of the game has risen surprisingly, and amateurs have an opportunity to see the pros at work on television and borrow their techniques. In the past, when continuous and straight pool were in style, the rhythm of the game was much slower and more deliberate.

In most sports, defense plays an important role and can turn a foreseeable loss into a victory. For example, it would be unthinkable for a hockey instructor to only use the forwards during a game. Each time an opportunity presents itself, and no other reasonable option exists, you have to resort to a defensive shot to save the situation. Remember this: even if the win seems guaranteed, never take any undue risks and don't give your opponent any chances, especially during an important game. Unfortunately, amateurs have a tendency to brake their game when they are ahead. This attitude is very bad. As the great star baseball player, Yogi Berra, said: "It ain't over till it's over."

Of course, in pool as in other sports, the best defense is still a good offense, especially in nineball. No one has ever won by only playing defensively, and sometimes you have to take some calculated risks to come out the winner. The whole problem lies in maintaining a happy medium and in playing it safe wisely and at the right time. During an important game, don't hesitate to resort to a defensive shot if the arrangement of the balls on the table doesn't reasonably allow for a ball to be pocketed. The safe shot is the one where the goal is not to pocket the ball, but to leave your opponent, when it's their turn, with a play that is so difficult that they won't be able to make a good shot.

The best players in the world sometimes play several defensive shots in a row. The duration of a professional championship game often reveals the style, offensive or defensive, of the opponents. A frame of 150 points generally runs about 90 mintues. In the 1973 world championship, the champion, Lou Butera (the fastest player in history) won the frame in 21 minutes, during which he played a run of 150 balls. In 2009, at the 14.1 world championship, the famous American pro Johnny Archer was defeated by the player who would go on to win the tournament, the Frenchman Stephan Cohen, during

a rather dull game that lasted four hours. The duration indicates that the two players exchanged a considerable number of defensive shots, which doesn't mean they aren't excellent players. But each one respected his opponent and didn't want to make a mistake that would have allowed the other one to advance to a win.

Lastly, only experience will teach you how and when to play defensively. Develop it.

NERVOUSNESS

To quote Quebec hockey coach Pierre Creamer: "Certainly, there's a lot of pressure on the players during a final ... but this is a normal situation. Pressure is a part of hockey. The players have stage fright before the game, but when the first minutes are over, everything is better. Anyways, it's a good thing, for, just like with actors, when an actor has stage fright, he usually gives his best performance. Nervousness is good when you can overcome it."

These observations don't apply only to hockey, but to all sports, including pool. Often, there doesn't have to be much at stake to cause tension among the competitors. In a tournament, you'll sometimes have the impression of being more nervous than the others. This is a false impression. In fact, all players feel a certain degree of tension, but the difference is in controlling yourself. You'll have to learn how to live and play despite the stress. Some players don't want to admit that they're nervous. Others are so proud that they refuse to participate in major competitions so they don't have to show just how nervous they become. Don't make this mistake. In the long run, you'll get used to playing despite the tension, and you'll even benefit from it. Some pros are very nervous, and I've even seen their whole body shake. However, this doesn't prevent them from having a fantastic run.

Here's another story. Mike Sigel has won the highest number of tournaments in professional pool in the United States: 101 titles. He was the first American pro to break the barrier of $100,000 in tournament winnings during the 1986–87 season. After dominating the 1980s so spectacularly, and justly earning the title of Player of the Year in 1986, this great champion suddenly disappeared from the scene at the end of 1994. He wasn't seen again in any tournaments for several years. Where did Sigel go? The answer was surprising. Before disappearing, he had won two major titles: his 100th in March 1994 in Philadelphia, Pennsylvania, and his 101st a month later in Worcester, Maine, during competitions that brought together the 34 best players in the world. Watching him, everyone thought he had nerves of steel, that he was the most solid star and the most talented in the American pool community! Here are the surprising revelations of columnist Mike Geffner (Sigel's greatest fan), published in the magazine

Billiards Digest: "The last time I saw Sigel, he indeed appeared on the verge of a nervous collapse. It was at the Valley Forge event, as he took a break outside the playing area during a late-tournament match: with his hands shaking, he dragged on his cigarette what seemed like a thousand times in the space of two minutes, while muttering something about what an idiot he was for putting himself through so much pain and suffering for such little money. I remember feeling so sorry for him. Yet, typically, when it was over, Sigel had once again captured first place." Five months later, after ranking fifth in the nine-ball world championship in Las Vegas, Mike Sigel retired from competition after a brilliant career lasting more than 20 years. He came back to the game a few years later, but the best years were behind him.

You can learn the following lesson from this story: if playing in a tournament is stressful, you can feel better knowing that even after 100 competitive wins, one of the best players in history felt even more nervous. All in all, don't get hung up about it. On the contrary, rest assured that, in the long run, you'll get rid of this handicap and you'll be able to play very well despite the tension.

In addition, respect who you are and don't try to imitate the behavior of others if it doesn't suit your nature. You tend to be calm? All the better. But if you're excitable, for goodness' sake, be yourself. In England, the pros that attract the crowds are those that are out of the ordinary, like

Jimmy White and Ronnie O'Sullivan. The same phenomen exists in the United States with Earl Strickland. Since pool isn't the most spectacular sport, long live the colorful participants. However, a word of caution: don't overdo it. In 1984, in Bude, England, Christopher Gifford, aged 21, who had just won, was so thrilled that he swallowed a ball. He almost choked to death, owing his life to one of his teammates, David Gilbert, who performed mouth-to-mouth resuscitation. "It wasn't the thing to do," says Gilbert. "He started waving his arms, running back and forth without being able to breathe, and shaking like a madman. His cheeks were purple and his lips, blue." Later, at the hospital in Stratton, the doctors were able to remove the ball from Gifford's throat, but they kept the young man under observation. He said: "I am seriously thinking of giving up billiards." Reports have mentioned several similar incidents elsewhere. In Tredegar, England, several back teeth had to be removed from a young man to get a ball out of his mouth. Others, less fortunate, died from asphyxiation. In New York in the 1960s, it had become trendy among some teenagers to place pool balls in their mouths to show off to their friends. It's much more difficult to remove them. One medical specialist invented a device used to remove pool balls from the mouth.

CONFIDENCE

One of the lessons I've learned from competition is that you've got to believe you can win, but you've also got to want to win. Belief and desire can truly move mountains...

MIKE MASSEY

During any competition, a lack of confidence is just as harmful as overconfidence. The first makes you play timidly while ignoring your opponent and the second prevents you from using all your resources.

Never underestimate your opponent: this kind of attitude often leads to defeat. Irving Crane, seven-time world champion, stressed that at the start of his career, he had the fault of giving his rival a chance, when he was ahead at the start of the frame. All amateurs have, more or less, this habit that seems inscribed in human nature. You must fight this weakness. Willie Mosconi believes that, to become pool champion, you have to have a "killer instinct." He even insists that: "When the knife is inside, twist it."

Respecting your opponent doesn't mean fearing them to the point where you are completely powerless. As Mika Immonen says: "Respect everyone, but fear no one ... Before going to war, remember this: your ablity to get rid of your own doubts and limits is the way to success." To win, you have to have great confidence in yourself and the certainty that you're capable of coming out the winner. If you feel beaten in advance, your chances of winning are pratically zero. Forget about the stakes, your opponent's reputation and the spectators, and concentrate on the game. Don't be negative; if you stop looking for all the things working against you, your confidence will blossom. Remember that the ability to win can be found inside yourself. It's a matter of patience, effort and will.

OVERCONFIDENCE ...

In 1925, the old *Billiards Magazine*, eager to teach pool players a billiards-related moral, offered a recap of a legendary game between champions Erwin Rudolph and Charles (Chick) Seeback in Sayre, Pennsylvania. During the contest, a cat (remember, it was almost a century ago) crept near the table carrying a recently captured mouse in its grasp. Leading 120-17 in the 125-point game, Rudolph, upon seeing the cat, remarked to his opponent, "See, you have got as much chance to win as that mouse." After the mouse escaped and left the attention of the players and spectators, Seeback promptly ran the next 108 balls and won.

CAROM BILLIARDS

In North America, we use the expression "European billiards" to describe pocketless billiards. This is misleading, for the sport is played not only in Europe, but also around the world: in Asia, Central America, South America, Africa, Russia and Japan. The correct term is "carom billiards." In fact, this variation is a very old form of pool that replaced the others around the 18th century. While North America and the Anglo-Saxon countries adopted some varieties of pool in the 1800s, most of the other countries hung onto billiards in its initial form, at least until quite recently. Today, pool is constantly gaining in popularity, even in countries where pocketless billiards dominates. During the same period, pocketless billiards has become more popular in the United States among older players, but it's almost certain that it won't ever beat pool in popularity among Americans. In Quebec, as in the rest of Canada, pocketless tables disappeared a long time ago from public halls, but a table was designed a while ago allowing for sections of the cushions to be adjusted and moved, enabling a pool table to be transformed in no time into a pocketless billiard table for those who would like to try this game.

In most of the European billiard games, three balls are used: two white ones, one of which is marked by two colored dots, and a red one. These balls are slightly bigger than regular pool balls, with a diameter of $2^3/_8$ in. (60.5 mm), compared to 57 mm ($2^1/_4$ in.), i.e. $^1/_8$ in. (3.5 mm) bigger. At first, such a small difference may seem negligeable, but those in the know will tell you the opposite is true: it's huge.

In an open game, the game consists of ensuring the cue ball touches the two other balls in the same shot (carom) and with no restrictions. It was for this game that the Dion brothers of Montreal conceived a method to achieve an almost uninterrupted series of carom shots. For some obscure reason, in France their discovery was baptized "the American," but "the Canadian" would have been more appropriate, given the nationality of the inventors. The open game is the easiest game to play in pocketless billiards, and many amateurs have played runs of 100 or even 1,000 consecutive points. In 1935, Charles C. Peterson scored 20,000 points in 1 hour, 41 minutes and 8 seconds during a demonstration in Chicago.

Other variations were invented to make the game more difficult. Thus, in the cushion game, the cue ball has to hit at least one cushion before touching the first ball in the carom. In the red game, the cue ball must always hit the red ball first.

Balkline billiards was also introduced. In this game, four lines are drawn on the cloth, parallel to and a set distance from each cushion. In 14.1 or 14.2, this distance is 14 in. (35.6 cm). In 18.1 and 18.2 (in France, 47.1 and 47.2), it's 18 in.

(45.7 cm). These lines divide the table into nine zones: the central zone is a free zone in the sense that you can play an unlimited number of consecutive carom shots. In the eight remaining balks the player can only play a limited number of carom shots and must then try to make the balls switch balks. In 14.1 or 18.1 (47.1), the player can play only one carom in the eight lateral zones and must go elsewhere in another zone. In 14.2 or 18.2 (47.2), the player can play a maximum of two consecutive carom shots in each balk. The best player in the history of 18.2 (47.2) was probably the American Jake Schaefer Jr., who ran a few runs of 400 consecutive points in the 1920s.

Currently, the most popular game played on pocketless tables is without a doubt three-cushion. This is the game of champions, of world competitions. The player must try to make the cue ball hit at least three cushions before completing the carom shot. As a result, the shot is successful in the following four instances: a) the cue ball hits one ball, then touches three cushions before hitting the second ball; b) the cue ball touches three cushions or more before hitting the two balls; c) the cue ball touches one cushion, then the first ball, then two cushions or more, and finally the second ball; or d) the cue ball hits two cushions or more, then the first ball, then a cushion, and finally the second ball.

Hitting the same cushion three times (shot with a spin) before completing the carom is considered a succesful shot.

This is probably the variation where the diamonds are the most popular, although the most famous experts all play instinctively. To give you an idea of how hard the game is, note that a run of 10 consecutive carom shots in three-cushion billiards is an excellent run. The best players in the world sometimes achieve a run of 20 points in their career. The great Turkish champion Semih Sayginer ties the incredible world record for the highest run: 31 consecutive points (the same as the Colombian-American Hugo Patino). The world champions in this game since 2000 are as follows:

2000	Dick Jaspers, Netherlands
2001	Raymond Ceulemans, Belgium
2002	Marco Zanetti, Italy
2003	Semih Sayginer, Turkey
2004	Dick Jaspers, Netherlands
2005	Daniel Sanchez, Mexico
2006	Eddy Merckx, Belgium
2007	Ryuuji Umeda, Japan
2008	Marco Zanetti, Italy
2009	Filipos Kasidokostas, Greece
2010	Daniel Sanchez, Mexico

Which type of billiards is the most interesting and the most difficult? Is it carom, snooker or pool? Accurately answering this question would be like trying to solve the square of a circle. These varieties of billiards are so different from each other that it's impossible to come up with any valid comparisons. In fact, all the ways of playing billiards are fascinating for those who know even a little about it. If you have the opportunity to play carom billiards, do it and you'll see for yourself that it's difficult to rank this type of game—not to mention snooker or pool—with any certainty.

THE RULES OF POOL

Even if each organization promoting pool tournaments in the United States adopted rules that were a little different from those of the Billiard Congress of America (BCA), these rules would still be similar. The BCA generally governs pool. This governing body compiles statistics, sanctions tournaments, notes records and, especially, issues the official rules for the different games of pool played in the United States. The British have a similar organization for snooker, the World Professional Billiards and Snooker Association. The Europeans have the Union Mondiale de Billard for carom games. Over the last few years, globalization has also affected pool, and there is now an international organization that covers 89 countries. The World Pool-Billiards Association (WPA), whose principal merit is that it obtained a consensus on the rules of the different games (mainly the games of eight-ball and nine-ball) was established, and "standardized" rules were (finally) announced with the significant achievement of being unanimous. Curiously, since Quebeckers played the same type of billiards as Americans, i.e. pool, you would have expected them to immediately adopt the American rules, but the language barrier and less extensive communications several decades ago meant that uncertainty reigned. Until 1979, Canada didn't have an organization overseeing pool. Over the long term, the lack of an ultimate authority caused a certain kind of anarchy to take hold in the Canadian world of pool, in the sense that the rules changed from one region to another, often even from one city to another. In 1978, the Fédération de Billard du Québec was founded, which is now the Fédération Québécoise des Sports de Billard, and it has been able to impose uniform regulations identical to those used elsewhere. These are called standardized rules. And, for many years now, we have a strong national organization—the Canadian Billiards & Snooker Association (CBSA).

Rules are essentials. All that's needed is for the followers of pool to consult them and apply them. The international rules were designed by the best players in the world and their goal is twofold: to make the game easier to play and to eliminate any argument. On the contrary, the regionalisms, made up of confusing, illogical and absurd rules, which were prevalent in Quebec (and probably elsewhere in the francophone world where pool is popular) complicated the game and encouraged misunderstanding. It's much simpler if everyone understands of the rules, makes them known and sticks to them. These objectives have largely been achieved.

Therefore, you'll find here the latest regulations in effect today almost everywhere in North America. They are almost identical, except for a few details, to those that are in effect on the professional circuit worldwide.

RULES COMMON TO ALL GAMES

All games of pool share some rules. Rather than repeat these generalities for each individual game, here's a summary of the rules that apply to all the variations.

THE CUE BALL IS THE WHITE BALL

In other words, the cue is used to strike the cue ball directly, which is projected toward the other balls with the goal of pocketing them. Only the tip of the cue may come in contact with the cue ball. Otherwise, i.e. if a player touches the cue ball with something other than the tip of their cue, it's an illegal shot leading to a foul and the loss of a turn. Aside from professional championships observed by competent referees, in most pool competitions in North America, the principle of the foul against the white only is applied, which means that a participant is not penalized if they accidentally move a ball other than the white one. All games described later on are played with 15 numbered balls, except for seven-ball, which is played using the first seven balls, nine-ball, which is played using the first nine balls, and 10-ball, which is played using the first ten balls. To start the game, the balls are racked in the shape of a pyramid using a triangle (or in the shape of a diamond for nine-ball, or a hexagon for seven-ball), on the foot spot (the main spot).

To start, the player places the cue ball any-where within the break box. This zone is located in the upper quarter of the table and is bounded by an imaginary line drawn between the two side diamonds to create a line parallel to the upper rail (Diagram 31).

CUSHION SHOT

In Quebec, we used to use a random draw to decide the order of the players at the start of a frame. Since roughly 1980, most amateurs have adopted the very simple method used in pro-fessional competition: lagging (or back and forth). The two participants (or a representative from each team) stand side by side at the head of the table, and each plays one ball at the same time, aimed at the foot cushion to make it rebound (photo 73). The player whose ball stops closest to the head cushion may choose the order of the players. This method should be adopted and followed by all amateurs.

CUE BALL IN HAND IN THE BREAK BOX

During a game, each time the regulation

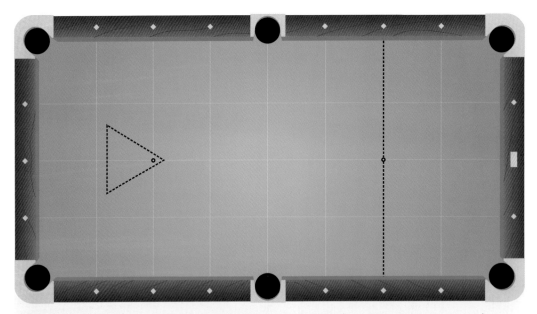

Diagram 31 *The break box is located in the quarter at the head of the table (bounded here by the dotted line), opposite the end where the balls are placed at the start of the game.*

This is how to decide the order of the players at the start of a game in professional competitions.

stipulates that the cue ball must be played from the break box, the player has to place it in this box to make their shot. Therefore, they can place it near the imaginary boundary line without touching it. While playing, they must ensure that the cue ball completely leaves the break box before hitting a numbered ball. He must then either play directly against a ball located outside the box, or by making the cue ball leave the box and return using one or more cushions to make a legal shot on a ball located inside the box.

BREAKING THE EQUIPMENT

A player is not penalized when they use a rake and the head of the rake breaks or falls on the table and touches one or several balls. In this case, the balls are simply returned, as closely as possible, to their original positions, and the player continues. The same thing applies if the game is disturbed by something outside the game; the balls are then returned to their original positions and the player continues.

EIGHT-BALL

In eight-ball, any human being can beat you during any game.

Minnesota Fats

Many amateurs think that Minnesota Fats (Rudolph Wanderome) was a world champion. His detractors state that, on the contrary, his only merit is to have contributed a lot to promoting pool without ever having been champion. It's true that Fats never won a major tournament. He was elected to the BCA Hall of Fame in 1984, not for his performance in tournaments, but as the most famous personality in pool (he died on January 18, 1996). One thing is certain. Minnesota Fats expressed a great truth when he said the words quoted in the epigraph. Indeed, the popularity of eight-ball is due, in large part, to the fact that in this game, the chances of winning are almost the same for everyone. With a little luck, even a beginner can beat a champion. In fact, eight-ball is 45% luck and 55% skill. Whether you win or lose, there's no need to get hung up about it.

EIGHT-BALL STRATEGY

In the game of eight-ball (as in nine-ball), more than in all the others, the best defense is a good offense. The priority is to scatter your own balls while avoiding doing the same to those of your opponent. Indeed, if your two last balls are frozen in a position with no way out, this can cause you to lose the game. Many make the mistake of pocketing from the start all (or almost all) their balls without pocketing the main one, the 8-ball. Avoid this at all costs, for your opponent then has free access to all their balls. If they are even slightly skilled, they can easily end the game with their first shot. This is why, if some of your balls are trapped in a group, you should scatter them first, then pocket the separated and easy balls. Here's a good tip: if, at the start of the game, the 8-ball is

near a pocket and you don't think you can end the frame, set yourself up to place one of your balls between the 8-ball and the intended pocket. This way, your opponent won't be able to end the game either, and you'll be almost sure to have at least one more opportunity to come back to the table. And remember that a game of eight-ball is never over until the 8-ball is pocketed.

THE RULES OF EIGHT-BALL

Warning: in eight-ball, every region, or even every pool hall, has its own rules. To achieve one ideal and common rule, two goals were set. First, to make the game as easy and as simple to play as possible, and second, to clear up any confusion in order to eliminate any disagreement among participants. The more complex the rules, the more frequent the conflicts. Therefore, the regulations that we are proposing have been thought out based on these factors. They're the fruit of long experience and deserve to be learned and followed by all players.

The rules common to all games (mentioned above) apply here in terms of the equipment and the way the game is played, except when they conflict with the following regulations.

1. How to Play the Game

This game is played using a white ball and 15 balls numbered from 1 to 15. One of the players (or a team) must pocket the group of lower-numbered balls (1 to 7) and their opponent (or the opposing team) must pocket the higher-

Don't place the cue ball right in the center of the break box to open a frame of eight-ball.

Instead, place the cue ball to the left or the right, and your chances of randomly pocketing one or several balls will increase. Personally, I prefer striking the second ball with a right backspin, as shown in this photo.

numbered balls (9 to 15). To win, the 8-ball must be legally pocketed, i.e. after all the balls in a player's group have been pocketed.

2. Designating the Balls

There are two ways to play eight-ball.

The first way to play is called eight-ball call shot. The player must indicate before each shot which ball they intend to try to strike and in which pocket they intend to pocket it. The player is not obliged to say what his intentions are if the shot is obvious, only when there are several options. If the referee or the opposing player is unsure as to the intentions of the player, they must ask him what will be attempted before the player leans forward to take the shot. If the player wants to play a combination or a cushion shot, they must say so in advance, but do not have to specify the number of cushions or the number of hits or ricochets: the ball is good even if there are two or three ricochets. If any balls are pocketed accidentally or illegally, they remain pocketed. There's one exception: the opening shot (also called the break), where the player doesn't have to announce their intentions, as the aspect of luck is accepted and the opening player continues to play if they legally pocket a ball with the shot.

The second way to play is called free eight-ball. In this instance, no shot has to be announced in advance. The player's only obligation is to pocket any ball in their group in any pocket, except the 8-ball. The player must announce the pocket into which they intend to send the 8-ball. The players must agree before the start of the game if they're playing call shot or not. The same principle applies to tournaments, where the organizers must indicate before the start of the tournament which version—call shot or not—will be in effect.

3. Placing the Balls

At the start of a frame, the balls are placed at the foot of the table, tightly packed in the shape of a pyramid using a triangle. The first ball at the apex of the triangle must be on the foot spot. The balls are distributed randomly except for the 8-ball, which is placed in the center, while a low-numbered ball and a high-numbered ball are placed in the two lower points of the triangle.

4. Determining Player Order

The order of the players is decided by lagging. In the following games, the winner of the previous frame performs the break, with one exception: in a tournament or any other form of competition, the break may alternate, provided the organizers have announced this in advance.

5. Performing Jump Shots and Massé Shots

Jump shots and massé shots are allowed, provided they are correctly performed, i.e. the player doesn't accidentally disturb the ball with their hand or their cue. Although the rule "cue ball fouls only" is in effect during a match with no official referee, there is, nonetheless, a foul when the player, while attempting to get around a ball blocking the object ball by using a jump shot, a deflection shot or a massé shot, moves the ball (whether it's moved by the player's hand, cue or bridge).

6. Performing a Legal Break

To perform a legal break, the opening player must place the cue ball behind the head string (break box) and must either a) pocket one ball, or b) project at least four balls at the cushion.

If the opening player doesn't perform a legal break, there's no foul, but their opponent may either a) accept the position of the balls to be played as is, or b) replace the balls in the triangle with the choice of performing the break themselves or of forcing the other player to retake the break.

7. Pocketing the Cue Ball on a Legal Break

If the opening player pockets the cue ball during a legal break, a) all the pocketed balls remain pocketed (except the 8-ball, see rule no. 9), b) there's a foul, and c) the table remains open.

The opponent has the cue ball in hand in the break box and must meet the requirements mentioned in the section Cue Ball in Hand in the Break Box (see page 109), as per the rules common to all the games.

8. Projecting Balls off the Table on the Break

When a player projects a numbered ball off the table on the break, there is a foul and the opponent has the choice of either a) accepting the position of the balls as is, or b) taking the cue ball in hand in the starting zone and playing it.

9. Pocketing the 8-Ball on the Break

When the 8-ball is pocketed during the break, the opening player has the choice of either a) retaking the break, or b) replacing the 8-ball on the spot and continuing their turn. If the opening player pockets the cue ball and the 8-ball during the break, their opponent has the choice of either a) retaking the break themselves, or b) replacing the 8-ball on the spot and starting their turn with the cue ball in hand in the break box.

10. Open Table

The table is said to be open as long as the choice of the groups (high balls or low balls) hasn't been decided. As long as the table is open, a high ball, a low ball or the 8-ball can be struck first to pocket the selected ball. However, when the table is open and the 8-ball is struck first, the pocketed ball doesn't count but remains pocketed and the player loses their turn. Their opponent continues the frame with the table open.

In the case of a foul on an open table, any ball pocketed illegally is not returned to the table.

11. Assigning a Group of Balls

A group of balls (high or low) is assigned to each player in the following manner. The choice of high-numbered or low-numbered balls is not decided by the balls pocketed during the opening shot. Whether the opening player pockets one or several balls on the break or not, the table remains open immediately after the break. The only consequence for the opening player who pockets a ball on the break is that they continue to play. The choice of groups will be decided after the break when one of the players succeeds in legally pocketing the designated ball.

After a group has been decided, if one player mistakenly pockets a ball from the opposing group, the opponent must declare the foul as soon as it occurs and before the next shot. Otherwise, the groups are reversed, i.e. the player who made the mistake keeps the group of balls on which they played the shot.

12. Performing a Legal Shot
As each shot (defensive or not) is played, except during the break or when the table is open, the player must strike the ball in their group first and either a) pocket a numbered ball, or b) ensure that the cue ball or a numbered ball strikes the cushion.

Note: A player can send the cue ball to the cushion before it strikes the ball in their group, however, after making contact, they must either a) pocket the designated ball, or b) ensure that the cue ball or a ball in their group strikes the cushion. Otherwise, there's a foul.

13. Performing a Defensive Shot
A defensive play is allowed and doesn't have to be announced, with the one exception that, for strategic reasons, a player can choose to pocket a ball in their group and interrupt their turn at the table by announcing in advance that their shot is defensive. This kind of defensive pocketing is legal. The player must notify their opponent in advance; if not, they'll have to continue playing. Any ball pocketed during a defensive shot remains pocketed.

14. Continuing the Game
A player continues to play until they miss legally pocketing a ball in their group. When a player legally pockets all the balls in their group, they attempt to pocket the 8-ball.

15. Committing Fouls
When there is a foul, the opponent gets the cue ball in hand, i.e. they can play the cue ball anywhere on the table (the break box only exists for an open table). The goal of this rule is to prevent intentional fouls that can place the opponent at a disadvantage. A player with the cue ball in hand can place it either with their hand or any part of their cue (including the tip). When positioning the cue ball, any forward stroke motion of the cue that touches the cue ball is considered a foul, unless the shot is legal.

16. Performing Combination Shots
Combination shots are allowed. However, the 8-ball can't be used as the first ball of a combination except if the table is open.

17. Illegally Pocketing Balls
A numbered ball is illegally pocketed when a)

it's pocketed at the same time a foul has been committed, b) the designated ball is not pocketed in the designated pocket, or c) the player announces in advance that their shot will be a defensive one. The balls pocketed illegally remained pocketed.

18. Projecting Numbered Balls off the Table
When any numbered ball is projected off the table, there's a foul (except with the 8-ball, where the frame is always lost). Any ball projected is not returned to it's spot, which means that it's left in the pocket or in the return bin for the balls.

19. Shooting the 8-Ball
When a player attempts to pocket the 8-ball, pocketing the cue ball or committing a foul doesn't mean the frame is lost, if the 8-ball isn't pocketed or projected off the table. The opponent then gets the cue ball in hand.

Note: The 8-ball can never be pocketed using a combination shot.

20. Losing the Game
A player loses the frame for the following reasons:
a) Commits a foul while pocketing the 8-ball (exception: see rule no. 9: Pocketing the 8-Ball on the Break).
b) Pockets the 8-ball while playing the last ball of the player's group.
c) Projects the 8-ball off the table at any time during the frame.

d) Pockets the 8-ball in any pocket other than the one designated.
e) Pockets the 8-ball when it's not the object ball.

Note: Any foul must be declared before the next shot, otherwise it won't be counted against the player that fouled.

21. Tie Game
If, after three consecutive turns at the table by each of the players (six turns in all), only the 8-ball and two numbered balls remain on the table, and the players agree that attempting to pocket or to move a numbered ball would result in the loss of the game, the game is cancelled and restarted, and the break is awarded to the first player.

Note: Three consecutive fouls don't lead to the loss of a game of eight-ball.

THE GAME OF NINE-BALL

*In **nine-ball**, the break is certainly important, but the most important thing is the next shot. If you pocket a ball with the next shot, you win. Otherwise, most of the time, you lose.*

STEVE MIZERAK

Even if the game of nine-ball is relatively new compared with eight-ball or continuous pool (14.1), it has quick-ly become entrenched and has carved out a prominent place for itself in North America since the 1980s, to the detriment

ANSWERS TO A FEW FREQUENT QUESTIONS REGARDING THE RULES OF EIGHT-BALL

1. On an open table, after the opening player has performed the break without pocketing a ball, when it is my turn, I call a high ball, but I miss it and, in addition, the cue ball strikes a low ball. Is there a foul? Does my opponent get the cue ball in hand in the break box? (Question submitted by François Sogny of France.) **ANSWER:** Since the table is still open, you can even use the other group of balls to play your own and you don't have to call it (rule no. 10). Your only obligation is to call which ball you're playing and into which pocket you're playing it. Therefore, you'll simply lose your turn and you aren't penalized.

2. What are a player's obligations when they play defensively? Do you have to ensure that the cue ball touches one or several cushions after hitting a numbered ball, or is there no obligation other than to move the cue ball where you want? (also submitted by François Sogny.) **ANSWER:** See rule no. 12, page 114 regarding the conditions that have to be met for a shot to be legal ("defensive or not").

3. After the break, when the opening player has failed to pocket one ball, if the next player calls a high ball and misses it, does the table remain open or is the opponent obliged to continue with the low balls? **ANSWER:** The table remains "open" (which means that the next player still has a choice) as long as one of the participants hasn't legally pocketed a ball.

4. What happens if, on the break, I pocket two low balls? Or if I pocket two low balls and a high ball? Do I then have to continue with the low balls? **ANSWER:** The only consequence when you pocket one or several balls on the break is that you remain at the table for the next shot, but you still have the choice, and the table is still open until one of the participants legally pockets a numbered ball after the break.

5. After pocketing all the balls in my group, I realize that the 8-ball is near the corner pocket, but that one of my opponent's balls is blocking the path, since it's on the edge of the intended pocket. I call that I will attempt to pocket the 8-ball in the same pocket, I play, I shoot the 8-ball at the blocking ball, which falls in the pocket, followed by the 8-ball. My opponent insists that I lost, for they claim that I can't pocket an opponent's ball when playing the 8-ball, especially if the other ball falls in before the 8-ball. **ANSWER:** You won. If you have no other balls remaining except the 8-ball, your only obligation is to call where you'll pocket it. Of course, the cue ball must touch the 8-ball first, but it isn't important that you pocketed one or more of the other balls using the same shot, whether it happens before or after you pocket the 8-ball. Obviously, you would have lost if you had also pocketed the cue ball.

of all the other varieties of billiards, even snooker. In an era of speed and drama, this game truly matches the mentality at the turn of the millenium. It revolutionized the world of billiards. Veterans strongly criticized how much it leaves to chance and the quickness of the execution. But its young fans have demonstrated that the game of nine-ball calls on all of a player's resources and that you can't excel at it without consummate skill, as dramatic and uncommon shots are often unavoidable in order to win. In particular, nine-ball does away with the great caution that snooker or continuous pool (14.1) demand. The game is so short that you can never allow yourself to give up the slightest opportunity. As soon as a shot is possible, you have to attempt it, other-wise there's a huge risk that your opponent will end the game without allowing you to make a single shot. Therefore, this is the ultimate offensive and the most exciting game.

THE STRATEGY OF NINE-BALL

It can't be said often enough, but the secret lies in the break: it's the opening shot that often decides the outcome of a match. As Mike Massey underlines: "If you are not breaking well in 9-ball, it doesn't matter how well you are running balls because you're not going to win against an opponent who is breaking well. He will simply run more racks than you." The pros spend a lot of their training practicing breaks. Most of them place the cue ball near the head string—not right in the middle, but approximately 4 in. (10 cm)

from the cushion, to the right side of the table for right-handers, to the left side of the table for left-handers—and rest their cue on the rail to play. The strike required to perform the break isn't a regular shot. A lot of force needs to be applied, i.e. all the power you're capable of. To be able to apply all this energy, you need to change your usual stance: stand closer to the table, lean forward a little less and distribute your weight differently on your legs with your upper body leaning slightly back. In addition, you have to exaggerate the preparatory motion and, to do this, press the hand forming the bridge less firmly on the table. Hold the cue more loosely than usual. As you strike, your waist and upper body will be projected forward at the same time as your arm. Avoid jumping while playing, for this will cause you to lose some of your energy, which you need to channel completely to propel you forward and not upward.

The goal of the break is not only to scatter the balls and to pocket at least one, but also to get into position to be able to continue. It's not just about applying a lot of power; you also need to be accurate. The point isn't to have the cue ball to contact the 1-ball just anywhere, for you greatly risk finding yourself at an impasse with the next shot. In other words, not only do you have to think about scattering the balls well and pocketing at least one of them, you also have to think about positioning the cue ball so that you'll be able to continue. When you watch the great champions play against each other on television, you must have noticed their intense concentration and the vast number of preparatory motions they make before performing the break. These movements aren't irrelevant; they're designed to ensure the greatest accu-racy possible. According to the experts, even the greatest world champions miss pocketing a ball at the break 60% of the time and they pocket the cue ball 10% of the time!

The first pitfall to avoid is pocketing the cue ball, which is often equal to presenting the win to your opponent on a silver platter. But then, you ask, where do you aim on the 1-ball? You can never anticipate exactly where the 1-ball will stop after the break. Therefore, you have to ensure that the cue ball goes to a spot where it will be possible to strike the 1-ball, wherever it is. Where is this ideal place? Right in the center of the table, or the spot closest to the center. At the break, the 1-ball is somewhat compressed against the compact pack of the other balls and it receives a push in the opposite direction. This is why it often ends up at the other end of the table. It's understandable that it will be a lot easier to play it on the next shot if the cue ball is in the center of the table. What should you do then when performing the break to ensure the cue ball stops as close as possible to the center of the table? This is what preoccupies most champions. Even if you can never be absolutely sure of getting it to stop in the center of the table, the following method is the one recommended and used by all the pros: aim as directly as possible at the center of the 1-ball in a completely straight

This is how the balls are placed (in the shape of a diamond) at the start of a game of nine-ball.

line with the cue ball. In addition, it's essential that the cue contact the cue ball right in the center, or slightly below center, and that no sidespin be applied. If you play correctly, the cue ball, after striking the pack, will go backwards and hopefully stop near the center of the table. Good luck with the remaining balls.

THE RULES OF NINE-BALL
The rules common to all the games (mentioned above) apply here with respect to the equipment and the playing of the game, except when they conflict with the following regulations.

1. Object of the Game
The goal of this game is to pocket the 9-ball. You win when you pocket the 9-ball on the break or with any other legal shot.

HOW FAST CAN A POOL BALL MOVE?

In 1996, at the annual pool exhibition of the BCA in Minneapolis, an engineer specializing in the design and development of measuring and control devices, Dr. George Onoda of the IBM Research Center, used a micro-computer equipped with two laser beams to calculate the maximum speed at which the pros could play the cue ball on the break. The margin of error of his device was less than 1%, and he determined that, between the break shot and the moment the ball struck the diamond (the balls are placed as in a game of nine-ball), it lost on average $1/2$–1 mph (0.8–1.6 kmh) in speed.

The pros—23 men and 15 women—who participated in the competition were each allowed three attempts. The best was Sammy Jones (the husband of Loree Jan Jones), who achieved 31.1 mph (50 kmh) pocketing five of nine balls on the break. It was surprising to realize that the size and the weight of the player were not necessarily determining factors. Thus, Buddy Hall, who has a fairly imposing physique, was ranked 22nd (second last) with a speed of 21.3 mph (34.3 kmh). In addition, the best players on the circuit don't necessarily beat the speed records, proven as Strickland was ranked fifth, and Archer, seventh. Among the women, Jeanette Lee, at 28.3 mph (38.3 kmh), is the fastest while champion Allison Fisher achieved a modest 18.6 mph (29.9 kmh), which hasn't prevented her from completely dominating the world pool circuit among the female pros for many years.

2. How to Play the Game

The balls numbered 1 to 9, as well as the cue ball, are used. With each shot, the cue ball must contact the ball whose number is the lowest on the table, but the balls don't have to be pocketed in numerical order. Any ball is legally pocketed provided the cue ball strikes the lowest-numbered ball on the table first. You never have to announce in advance which ball you're attempting nor which pocket you're aiming at. When a player pockets a ball using a shot considered legal, they remain at the table and continue to play until they miss, commit a foul, or win the frame by pocketing the 9-ball. When a player misses their shot, their opponent must continue the game by assuming the position left by the previous player. However, after a foul, the next player has the privilege of placing the cue ball anywhere on the table. A match is over when one player has won the requisite number of frames.

3. Placing the Balls

At the start of the game, the balls are racked in the shape of a diamond, with the 1-ball placed at the apex of the diamond and opposite the head spot, the 9-ball in the middle, and the other balls at random. The opening player places the cue ball anywhere in the break box to perform the break.

4. Determining Player Order

The order of the players is decided by lagging. For the following games, the winner of the first game performs the break. Exception: in a tournament or any other form of competition, the break can be done by alternating (with no regard given to whichever player may have won the previous frame), provided the organizers have announced this in advance.

5. Performing a Legal Break

The requirements for the break are the same as those for the other shots, with the following exceptions.

a) The opening player must ensure that the cue ball touches the 1-ball first, and they must either 1) pocket a ball, or 2) shoot at least four balls at the cushion.

b) If the cue ball is pocketed or projected off the table, or if the preceding conditions (see (a)) are not met, there's a foul and the opponent has the cue ball in hand anywhere on the table.

c) If, on the break, the opening player projects one or several numbered balls off the table, there's a foul and the opponent has the cue ball in hand. The ball is not returned to the table (except if it's the 9-ball, in which case it will be returned to the spot or, if other balls are on its spot, as close as possible at the foot of the table).

6. Playing the Game

Immediately after the break, the player can play a push-out shot (see the following rule). If the opening player pockets one or several balls on a legal break, they can either a) play the push-out shot, or b) continue to play until they miss, commit a foul, or win the frame.

When the player misses the ball or commits a foul, their opponent returns to the table and continues playing until they miss or commit a foul during their turn, and so on. The frame ends when the 9-ball is pocketed on a legal shot, or if the referee ends the frame (default) following a major infraction of the rules.

7. Performing a Push-Out Shot

Immediately after the break, the opening player (or their opponent if the opening player hasn't pocketed a ball) can play a push-out shot, which involves sending the cue ball anywhere on the table without having to project it off a cushion or hit a numbered ball; all the other rules apply. The player must announce their intention of playing a push-out shot before performing it, otherwise the shot will be considered a normal shot.

The balls pocketed on the push-out shot remain pocketed, except the 9-ball, which is returned to the head spot. Following a push-out shot, the opponent has the choice of either a) playing the cue ball from this position, or b) skipping their turn, i.e. allowing the player who made the push-out shot to continue. There's no foul during a push-out shot if all the rules (except rules 9 and 10) are followed.

8. Penalizing Fouls

When a foul is committed by a player, they lose their turn at the table and their opponent plays; no pocketed ball is returned to the table (exception: if the 9-ball is pocketed illegally, it's returned to the head spot). In addition, the opposing player has the cue ball in hand anywhere on the table. Several fouls committed on the same shot equal one foul.

9. Performing an Irregular Shot

It is considered a foul if the cue ball doesn't contact the lowest-numbered ball on the table.

10. Performing a Cushion Shot

It's a foul if the player makes the mistake of not sending a ball to the cushion or the cue ball to the cushion after it's struck the lowest-numbered ball without pocketing a ball.

11. Playing Cue Ball in Hand

After a player has committed a foul, their opponent has the cue ball in hand and can place it anywhere on the table with one restriction: the cue ball must not be placed in such a way that it touches another ball. The player can adjust the position of the cue ball as long as they haven't played the shot.

12. Projecting Balls off the Table

A ball is considered to have been projected off the table when it stops somewhere other than on the playing surface. This is a foul and the ball is not returned to the table (exception: when the 9-ball is projected off the table, it's returned to the head spot). The opponent then plays with the cue ball in hand.

13. Performing Jump Shots and Massé Shots

Jump shots and massé shots are allowed, provided they are correctly performed, i.e. the player doesn't accidentally disturb the ball with their hand or their cue. Although the rule "cue ball fouls only" is in effect during a match with no official referee, there is, nonetheless, a foul when the player, while attempting to get around a ball blocking the object ball using a jump shot, a deflection shot or a massé shot, moves the ball (whether it's moved by the player's hand, cue or bridge).

14. Committing Three Consecutive Fouls

If, during the same game, a player commits three consecutive fouls in three turns at the table, they lose the frame. A warning must be given to the player at fault between the moment they commit the second foul and the third foul, otherwise they remain at two fouls even if they commit a third.

15. End of the Game
The frame begins at the break, when the cue ball leaves the break box, and it ends when the 9-ball is legally pocketed, or when a player commits a foul leading to loss of the game.

16. Tie Game
If the referee feels that neither player is really trying to win because of the positioning of the balls, he or she must announce this decision, and each participant is then allotted three turns at the table. Then, if the referee still feels that no progress has been made to win the game, they must declare that the game is at a stalemate and cancel it. The player who started the frame is once again asked to perform the break.

THE GAME OF SEVEN-BALL

The game of seven-ball is, in fact, a shorter version of nine-ball, and it's practically identical except for a few differences. It is played with only seven balls (from 1 to 7) instead of nine. At the beginning of the frame, the balls are placed in the shape of a perfect hexagon, with the 7-ball in the center, surrounded by the six other balls, with the 1-ball in front facing the usual spot where the point of the triangle is set at the start of the frame for most types of pool. The main

This is how the balls are racked (hexagonally) to start a frame of seven-ball.

difference lies in the fact that, immediately after the opening player has performed a legal break, their opponent has to choose the side of the table (i.e. any of the three pockets on one side) on which they will pocket the 7-ball. The opening player will have to pocket the 7-ball in one of the three opposing pockets. In the end, failure to pocket the 7-ball in one of the three pockets assigned at the start will mean losing the frame. The frames are ultra-quick, lasting on average only three minutes each! In addition, you can balance the strengths when the opponents are at different skill levels. Thus, the strongest player can be forced to pocket the 7-ball in only one of the pockets designated at the start of the game, immediately after the legal break. Or, inversely, the weakest player can be given the right to pocket the 7-ball in any of the six pockets.

THE GAME OF TEN-BALL

Another game that closely resembles nine-ball,

with the difference that 10 balls are used, i.e. the balls numbered from 1 to 10. Just a few years ago, this game was hardly played, but ten-ball has since become one of the games preferred by champions because of the difficulty of pocketing the 10-ball on the break. This reduces the element of luck. Adding a ball may seem harmless, but in reality, this slightly complicates the game and, in particular, makes it much more difficult to pocket the 10-ball on the break compared with pocketing the 9-ball in nine-ball. At the start of the frame, the balls are placed in the shape of a triangle, with the difference being that the last row of five balls is completely eliminated. The 1-ball must be placed at the apex of the triangle and the 10-ball in the center of the third row. A

This is how the balls are racked (in the shape of a triangle but using only 10 balls) with the 10-ball in the center, at the start of a game of ten-ball.

major difference between the rules of 9 ball and the rules of 10 ball is that you must call the ball and pocket in 10 ball (similar to 8 ball) while you do not have to call the shot in 9 ball.

CONTINUOUS POOL (14.1) AND LINE-UP POOL

The idea of this game is to get the balls in the pocket and to get position for the next shot.
GEORGES CHÉNIER (1970)

Georges Chénier, who died in 1970, was one of the best pool players in Canadian history. He was also the only player in the world to excel at snooker and at pool. He set the record in the snooker world tournament in 1950 in England (a run of 144), and another in the pool world tournament in 1963 in New York (a run of 150). He can rightly be considered the highest authority on the subject. In an interview given to a journalist in Toronto a few months before his death, Chénier said: "Snooker is 25 percent luck, but straight pool is only five percent luck."

Indeed, continuous pool (14.1) is considered the most scientific game in pool. It calls on all of a player's resources: position, spin, accuracy, determination, concentration, etc. And, in particular, in continuous pool, skill represents the greater part: 95%. If you're good at continuous pool (14.1) you'll automatically excel in all the other types.

Until the early 1980s, continuous pool (14.1) was the game of champions, the one played at all the important competitions. In the early 1990s, it was more or less abandoned, but it has become fashionable again over the last few years, such that a world championship was reinstated in 2006. It's the ultimate scientific game, requiring consummate skill. If you have great ambitions, practice this game in particular.

THE STRATEGY OF CONTINUOUS POOL (14.1)

In essence, the strategy of the game of continuous pool is to ensure that the last ball is placed in a position that allows the cue ball to rebound off the pyramid formed by the 14 other balls when they are repositioned in the triangle. All of a player's shots must be played with this goal in mind if they want to play a consistent run. Once the play is scattered, identify the break ball, i.e. the one that will remain the last one on the table. The key ball is also very important: you'll play against it to ensure the cue ball remains where it is not only possible to pocket the break ball, but also to project the cue ball against the pack of 14 balls that remain, placed in the shape of a pyramid. Photos 79 to 84 show the different ways of opening the frame at the start of each turn.

In continuous pool, there are some defensive shots that occur often and you have to know

79

84

them to be able to respond to your opponent. These different defensive plays are often used by professionals to prevent their opponent from scoring. Remember that at least one ball (or the cue ball) must always be projected against the cushion when making these shots, otherwise it may cost you up to 18 penalty points for three consecutive fouls.

THE RULES OF CONTINUOUS POOL (14.1)
The general rules common to all the games apply here, especially those relating to equipment, cushion shots, ball placement and the start of the game. Specific rules are listed below.

1. Performing the Break
The starting player has the cue ball in hand to perform the break, and has to place it inside the break box. They can play directly against the rack or off one or several cushions, provided at least two balls are projected towards the cushion in addition to the cue ball. They can also call the ball, which will be counted if it's pocketed. If the player doesn't meet these requirements, they'll be penalized two points, and their opponent will have the choice of accepting the position or of requesting a new break. The player that commits a foul loses two points for each missed break, and their opponent can request that they start again as long as they're not satisfied with the conditions. If the player pockets the cue ball or projects it off the table while performing the break, they lose one point, and this foul is taken into account in the penalty for three consecutive fouls.

2. Duration of the Frame
The score required is decided by the participants or the organizers of the meet. In major tournaments, each frame consists of 200 points.

3. Designating the Balls
Only the desired ball and the object pocket have

All pool professionals, without exception, perform the defensive shot shown here to open the game. If you play gently, with a right sidespin on the cue ball, it will return to the other end and the rack will remain practically intact.

Here's another defensive shot showing what follows the preceding shot.

Another frequent defensive shot in 14.1. Played gently, the cue ball stops right at the apex of the triangle, and a ball hits the cushion so that the shot will be legal.

This photo and the following one show similar situations. By playing gently between the second and the third balls, the cue ball stops very close to the rack, leaving your opponent to play with no way out.

to be announced in this game, unless the shot is an obvious one. In this case, the referee must name the ball and, if they make a mistake, the player must correct the call before performing their shot. Combination, ricochet, carom, cross-table and bricole shots are allowed and don't have to be called. Similarly, when the player attempts to strike a ball off a cushion (kick shot or bricole), they don't have to announce the number of cushions the cue ball will touch before striking the object ball. If the position of the balls appears to favor pocketing one of them, there's no need to call the shot, but simply to designate the ball and the pocket. When the designated ball receives a double hit (double ricochet) from the cue ball or from another ball before being pocketed, it's valid. Lastly, a ball is valid provided it's pocketed in the object pocket, whether it touches one or several balls or whether it travels around the entire table before being pocketed.

4. Repositioning the Balls

In continuous pool (14.1), the balls are returned to the table only when 14 of them have been pocketed, the 15th remaining where it stopped on the table. The 14 balls in question are repositioned using the triangle, and the space for the missing ball is left open at the apex of the triangle next to the head spot. When the triangle is removed, the 14 balls are racked in the shape of a pyramid and the player continues to play, generally using the 15th ball to open the game. The player can, nonetheless, play directly against the rack if they prefer, provided they satisfy the rules of shooting the ball off a cushion or the cue ball off a cushion after hitting a ball.

5. Interference by the Balls During Replacement

If, by coincidence or otherwise, the player pockets the 14th and 15th balls on the same shot, they are credited for both, and all 15 balls are racked again. The player must continue to play from the spot where the cue ball stopped.

If the 15th ball prevents the 14 other balls from being placed inside the triangle, it's positioned on the head spot.

If the cue ball and the last ball both prevent the 14 other balls from being racked, the 15th ball is returned to the triangle with the 14 others, and the player, with the cue ball in hand, must continue to play from the break box.

If the cue ball prevents the balls from being racked inside the triangle, the following rules apply:

a) The player has the cue ball in hand as long as the last remaining ball isn't in the break box.

b) If the break ball (the 15th ball) is inside the break box, the cue ball is placed on the head spot.

c) If the 15th ball is already on the head spot, the cue ball is then placed on the center spot.

In all instances, the player has the choice of playing the cue ball directly against the 15th ball or the rack, provided they obey the rule of playing the ball off the cushion.

6. Playing with the Cue Ball in Hand

The player has the cue ball in hand at the start of the frame, if the cue ball was pocketed or projected off the table, or if there was interference during the replacement of the 14 balls inside the triangle. The cue ball is not considered played as long as it isn't projected outside the break box in the direction of the playing area.

If, when they have cue ball in hand, the player places it outside the break box and is warned of this by the referee or by the opposing player,

they lose they're turn; they're penalized one point if they still play it from this position. In addition, the next player has the choice of accepting the position or of requesting that the play be returned to how it was before the error was discovered. However, if the cue ball is outside the break box, and the player plays before the mistake is noticed, the shot is valid if they succeed in pocketing a ball.

When the player has the cue ball in hand during a frame, they can play it directly off any ball outside the break box. If the ball is located directly on the line bounding the break box, the player who has the cue ball in hand can play off this ball provided it's located mostly outside the break box. In other words, even if the ball touches the line, it's allowed provided the bottom is outside the line.

7. Foot on the Floor

The player must have at least one foot on the floor during play, otherwise it's a foul, leading to the loss of one point.

8. Balls in Motion

When a ball, whether it's the cue ball or another ball, is in motion or is spinning on its own axis, it can't be played as long as it's still moving. Failure to follow this rule is a foul penalized by one point.

9. Ball Rebounding out of the Pocket

If, when it's pocketed, the ball rebounds onto the table, it isn't considered pocketed. And if it's the ball designated by the player, they lose their turn. The ball in question is left on the spot where it stops on the table. This rule applies even if the rebound of the ball on the table is due to the fact that a pocket is full. The player at the table is responsible for emptying the pockets to avoid the overflow from affecting the successful pocketing of the remaining balls.

10. Jump Shot

A jump shot is allowed if it's purely accidental, or if the player raises the butt of the cue and strikes the cue ball in the center or on top. The jump shot is illegal if the player uses the cue to push it under the cue ball, like a shovel.

11. Push Shot

The push shot is legal provided it's done in one initial motion and the cue contacts the cue ball only once.

12. Projected Balls

If the cue ball is projected off the table, it's a foul equal to pocketing the cue ball. Therefore, the player loses their turn, loses a point, and a foul is recorded against them. If the designated ball is projected off the table, it's a simple mistake which doesn't lead to a penalty, but the player loses their turn and the ball is returned to the line. If, at the same time the designated ball is pocketed, another ball is projected off the table, this does not constitute an error and the ball is simply returned to the string. The ball pocketed

on the shot is valid. The lighting system, when it's installed above the table, is considered part of the equipment. If a ball hits the light and falls back onto the table, it stays where it fell. A ball that stops on top of the cushion is considered out. If a ball leaves the table, rolls along the cushion and falls back onto the table unassisted, there's no foul. It remains where it stops. If someone prevents a ball from falling off the table or comes in contact with a ball rolling along a cushion, it's considered projected off the table.

13. Cue Ball Error

If a player, whether inadvertently or due to distraction, uses another ball instead of the white one as the cue ball, it's a foul that leads to the loss of one point. The next player must accept the balls in the position in which they are found after this shot.

14. Penalties

Penalties are deducted from the score of each player. A player who has not yet scored a point and is penalized, is then in a deficit, and the penalties will have to be deducted from any subsequent valid points.

15. Ball Frozen Against a Cushion

When a ball is frozen against a cushion or located at a distance less than the diameter of the ball, a valid defensive shot can't be played by placing the cue ball immediately opposite this ball or by touching it. The player must either a) pocket this ball, b) send it to the other cushion after striking the ball frozen to the cushion, or c) ensure that the cue ball touches another cushion after striking this ball. The number of defensive shots is limited to two consecutive shots for each player. The third shot becomes a foul that leads to the penalty of three consecutive fouls.

16. Defensive Shot

The defensive play is legal. The player is not obliged to reveal their intentions but can do so. By performing a defensive shot, the player must send at least one numbered ball off the cushion or ensure that the cue ball strikes a numbered ball, then a cushion. Otherwise, it's a foul, and the player loses one point and their turn.

17. Ball off the Cushion

If the player misses the ball called, there's an error; they lose their turn but they are not penalized if they obey the following rule.

In all instances, and for all shots, whether defensive or not, the player must ensure that the cue ball touch at least one ball, that one ball is projected off the cushion, or that the cue ball is projected off the cushion after touching another ball. Otherwise, the player loses their turn and a point, and a foul is recorded against them. The same rule applies when, missing a shot, a player fails to touch any ball with the cue ball, they lose their turn and one point, and a foul is recorded against them.

18. Penalty for Three Consecutive Fouls

Each time a foul is committed, it's recorded against the player that made the foul. To erase this foul, the player must perform a legal shot during his next turn. If a player commits three consecutive fouls, they lose a point for each foul and are debited an additional penalty of 15 points on the third foul (total penalty: 18 points). In addition, they must reopen the frame as at the start by following the rule on breaks; for the player that commits a foul, performing a break erases their three consecutive fouls and play continues.

THE GAME OF LINE-UP POOL

The game of line-up pool has been the equivalent in Quebec of American continuous pool (14.1) among older players.

THE STRATEGY OF ALIGNMENT

Your main concern in line-up pool is to ensure that the cue ball stops as close as possible to the foot cushion once the 15th ball is pocketed so that you can strike the next ball. Indeed, all the balls are repositioned in a straight line starting at the head spot, and the 11th ball should be located approximately 1 in. (20–22 mm) from the foot cushion, as shown in photo 90. If you place the cue ball very close to the cushion, it then becomes possible to successfully pocket up to seven consecutive balls in the two foot pockets. You can make the cue ball either back

90

In line-up pool, this is how the 15 balls are repositioned when you have successfully pocketed all of them. You continue your series by playing the first four or five balls in the row beginning at the foot cushion, while controlling the movement of the cue ball in order to be in a better position for the next ball.

91

After pocketing four or five of the first balls of the row, set up the play so you can get an angle on the cue ball to break the line of balls that are left so that you can continue your run.

up after each shot, or move forward according to the situation and your personal skill.

In practice, however, don't wait until the eighth ball to break the line, for you run the risk of failing. Once you reach the fourth or the fifth ball, set up the play so that the cue ball, while pocketing the next one, is projected into the line of balls and opens the play so you can continue your run (see photo 91).

At this stage of the game, a lot of players make the mistake of using excessive force to scatter the balls. By playing too hard, you run the risk of also pocketing the cue ball. In addition, it's possible that the attempted ball may rebound out of

the pocket and onto the table because of the force of the shot. This shot doesn't require a lot of force. A shot made with moderate force will be enough to scatter all the remaining balls and to allow the cue ball to end up near the center of the table, the spot that offers the best options for playing the next ball.

Quebeckers hold the worldwide high scores for straight pool. The world record in competition belongs to Alain Martel, who successfully played a run of 451 in front of witnesses on the evening of January 19, 1988, during a league match held in a pool hall located north of Montreal. Gaston Leblanc holds the record in a provincial championship with a score of 351, earned in a tournament in 1991 in Saint-Georges de Beauce. Moreover, Leblanc also shot four runs of more than 300 points during his career.

THE RULES OF STRAIGHT POOL

All the rules are the same as for line-up pool (14.1), except for the replacement of the balls after each round.

REPLACEMENT OF THE BALLS

After each round or run, i.e. when a player misses, all the pocketed balls are returned to the table and lined up between the head spot and the middle of the foot cushion (photo 90). There's space for 11 balls along this line; the four others, if necessary, are lined up in the direction of the center of the table. If a player plays a run of 15 balls, they're all repositioned on the line, and the player continues to play, performing the next shot from the spot where the cue ball came to a stop after the previous shot. If the cue ball stops on the line, the other balls must not be frozen to it, but placed nearby.

THE GAME OF SNOOKER

Even if we omitted the integral rule, many will certainly find it useful to know some of the technical data for indicating on the cloth the positions where the various markers are located to help place the balls on the table in snooker. Snooker is popular in most countries with a British background. It's best played on tables that are 6 x 12 ft. (1.8 x 3.6 m) or 5 x 10 ft. (1.5 x 3 m) in size. Twenty-one balls are used, as well as the cue ball.

15 red (1 point each)
1 yellow (2 points)
1 green (3 points)
1 brown (4 points)
1 blue (5 points)
1 pink (6 points)
1 black (7 points)

POSITIONING THE BALLS

The position of the balls on the table is indicated by the black spots glued onto the baize at the locations indicated in Diagram 32. A semicircle in the shape of a D is drawn on the line marking the break box. The radius of this circle is 11½ in. (29.2 cm) for a table 6 x 12 ft. (1.8 x 3.6 m) in size. Each time the player has the cue ball in hand during the frame, it must be placed inside this semicircle. The player can then play in all directions and attempt a ball, even if it's inside the D.

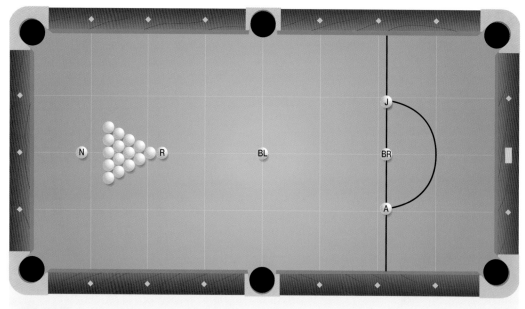

Diagram 32

PART II

THE TRICKS

INTRODUCTION

Since 2000, trick and fancy shot competitions or championships have been shown regularly on television sports networks. Did you know that you can play most of the tricks you see, provided you have the basic technique and you know how to prepare and perform the shot? Nonetheless, one clarification: we have to distinguish between the tricks performed on a pool table and those that are practiced in carom billiards, i.e. on a pocketless table, more commonly found in Europe. What we call fancy shots are played on 10 ft. (3.1 m) tables, and each participant must successfully perform the required figures imposed in three attempts. The quality of the execution of each figure is recorded, and the referees assign a number of points based on a coefficient that takes into account the degree of difficulty (from 5 to 10 points). We won't discuss this type of billiards, only the trick shots played on pool tables. Clearly, if you have the opportunity one day, don't miss watching a demonstration of carom billiards by Turkish champion Semih Sayginer, a virtuoso who performs with disconcerting ease incredible shots involving fantastic massés that cause the cue ball to follow erratic trajectories! It follows along exaggerated curves, stops to return along its path and strikes two or three cushions before completing its carom against the second ball. These extreme massés, where the cue is held vertically, are not within the grasp of many players, and, moreover, there are many fantasy plays for which only he knows the secret. To see the skill of this champion, go to YouTube and search by entering his name. You won't believe your eyes!

I'm proud to say that I was the first to publish a book in French on the topic in 1982, a book entitled *100 trucs de billard*, which was a bookstore success. A few years later, I received a letter from one of the great American masters, Larry Grindinger, whose feats were featured twice in publications such as Ripley's *Believe It or Not!* In 1994, Ripley's published a diagram illustrating an incredible play during which Grindinger performed an 11-cushion shot. To give you an idea of what this is like, you'll find later in this book, among all the tricks, a diagram of a nine-cushion shot, which is exceptional. Grindinger wanted to create an association of pool trick players (Trick Shot Shooters Association) and invited me to become a member. What flattered me the most was that he paid me a great honor by describing one of my brilliant tricks in these words: "To Pierre, I love your five-ball pyramid shot. It is one of the greatest trick shots of all time. Regards, Larry Grindinger." I had already surprised several people with this trick, in particular in 1986, in the 14.1 world championship practice room in Philadelphia. Even the famous champion, Danny Diliberto, rushed over to congratulate me after watching me perform the trick, adding that he would include it immediately in his own routine of demonstration tricks.

With respect to the trick shot championships

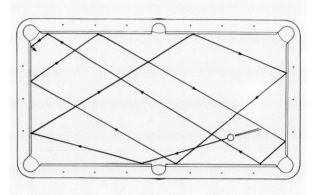

In 1994, Larry Grindinger became the first pool player in history to execute an 11-rail bank shot.

that have often been shown on television over the last few years, as impressive as these shots are, remember that most of them are nothing more than variations on or adaptations of tricks that are explained later in this book. Indeed, you'll find here the basic elements to perform and (we hope) achieve most of the feats that the pros do during these competitions. Certainly, these artists have the honor of demonstrating their skills before thousands of spectators, and with the pressure of a televised competition, which isn't easy. But if you persevere and carefully follow my instructions, you'll nonetheless have the satisfaction of being able to do them from time to time!

During my career, I realized that the tricks and fancy shots are the part of pool that inspires the greatest interest among most amateurs. How many times has someone asked me to explain, perform or replay such and such a trick? Everyone wants to learn a few tricks to impress friends when they come to visit. We're always pleased to see the reactions of surprise and the astounded faces of the spectators. Whether you are an expert or a simple amateur, performing a pool trick or fancy shot has probably always fascinated you. Movies and television, within the framework of sports broadcasts or advertising, come up with some trick shots on occasion. The player makes the ball jump, forces the cue ball to follow a whimsical trajectory, pockets a ball using several cushions, or even pockets several balls in one shot.

All the tricks have at least one thing in common: they all present some degree of real or apparent difficulty. In most instances, the amateur will have the impression that the trick is almost impossible to do, or at least very difficult. As impressive as these plays are, did you know that most of them are within your grasp? With training, you can perform most of the tricks executed by the champions. Naturally, it's possible that your success rate might not be as high as theirs, but you'll still have the satisfaction of succeeding occasionally.

It's harder to learn a trick from a book than from a qualified teacher. Indeed an expert beside you can see your mistakes and point them out to you immediately. When you use a book, you have to discover your errors yourself. I know something about this, since I learned a large part of my tricks from books or magazines and, as the Chinese proverb says, "It is easier to know how to do something than to do it." You need a lot of patience and perseverance to achieve most of the shots shown.

A friend invited me one day to try his new pool table in his basement. After a few frames, he asked me to show him some tricks. I explained to him in detail how to prepare and perform at least 20 different tricks, and he was able to do almost all of them after me. A few weeks later, I met him by chance and I asked him if he was doing well with what he had learned. He confessed that he remembered only one of the tricks. This anecdote shows that you can't become an expert in one day. The danger that awaits you in reading this book? Jumping too quickly into one trick or another without stopping to absorb any of them in particular. If you give in to this temptation, you'll risk forgetting everything.

Before moving from one trick to another, master the first. Even if you've tried it without success several times, don't give up. Continue and you'll end up discovering the mistake you overlooked, and remember that all the experts had to go through this stage. Indeed, the best way to learn consistency in the way you perform and reproduce a trick successfully is to spend several hours trying it over and over again until you've mastered it perfectly. If you're striving to become a master in this field, be prepared to spend up to a whole day repeating the same trick. Don't be content to succeed once every 10 times; redo it until you can perform it correctly 10 times in a row! As I often say about tricks, the hardest part is having the patience to learn them. And remember that it's harder to do a trick in front of an audience than on your own.

When you perform tricks in front of an audience, you have to remain calm. I know excellent players who were incapable of doing tricks in public, for they would fly into a terrible rage each time they had the bad luck to miss their shot. If you're incapable of accepting the fact that you may miss a shot from time to time, stop right now. When you fail, you need to laugh and ask the spectators to give you a chance by letting you try it again. However, don't be stubborn and insist on trying a trick more than three times. I've already seen a supposed champion try the same trick 12 times in a row without success. In the end, the spectators made fun of him, some even offered to teach him! His stubbornness made him look ridiculous in the eyes of the spectators instead of making him look better. If you miss a trick three times in a row, make a joke of it, such as, "This trick is absolutely impossible," or, "Sometimes, this doesn't work," or simply: "I'll try it later."

Don't be presumptuous. Don't pretend to be a better player than the others. You'll have to go through a laborious learning process, just like everyone else, and redo each trick several times before mastering it. This warning isn't to discourage you; on the contrary, it's to make you aware that no one has the innate science in this field and that success is only possible through hard work. You tried 10 times and couldn't do it? It's normal. Persevere. You'll get results.

When I wrote this part, I wanted to show that the magic of pool is accessible. Therefore, I tried to demystify this aspect of the game and show that there are no miracles, rather, that for each trick there's a recipe that anyone can learn with a lot of training and patience.

Another important warning: you learned a few tricks on your table that you master fairly well. You're proud of yourself and rightly so. You're going to play elsewhere, at a neighbor's or a relative's or a friend's and you really want to show off. But what a disappointment! You can't do any of your shots; you constantly miss. What's happening? In fact, there's nothing to worry about. You've simply discovered something new: that each table is different and has its own personality. The quality of the baize, the lig hting, whether the table is balanced and, in particular, the rebound of the cushions represent a lot of unknown factors. Some tricks that require three, four or five cushions to perform are almost impossible to do on some tables, especially commerical or residential tables. The next time you attend a trick shot demonstration by a specialist, pay particular attention to the first tricks they do. You'll notice that the player is testing the cushions at the start of their show. This is essential to allow them to make the necessary adjustments.

Where do the tricks explained in this book come from? What's their source? Who's the inventor of each one of them? These are some of the questions it's impossible to answer with certainty. Approximately 60% of my tricks are inspired by other works, books or magazines. However, it's impossible to discover the real creator of each one. Furthermore, there are probably as many inventors as there are tricks, for a pool player, as brilliant as they may be, can hardly hope to create a trick that is truly original in their career. Rare are the books that mention the source of each trick, an impossibility because of the lack of documentation on this topic. The only ones who have taken the trouble to do any in-depth research on this topic are historian Mike Shamos, curator of the Billiards Archives, and writer Robert Byrne of California. Shamos devoted many articles to this topic for 20 years in his interesting column (appropriately titled "Chronicles") in the magazine *Billiards Digest*, in Chicago. As for Byrne (who was elected to the prestigious BCA Hall of Fame), he spent eight months retracing the origins of tricks and fancy shots. The result of his discoveries can be found in the book entitled *Byrne's Treasury of Trick Shots in Pool and Billiards*, published in 1982.

Don't believe that the tricks explained later in this book are a recent invention. Most of them were conceived 100 years ago or even earlier! In a book published in London in 1807, White tells stories of some tricks practiced as far back as 1789, or many years before the invention of the leather tip. The first true book on pool tricks is probably that of Fred Hermann, published in New York in 1902 and entitled *Tricks and Games on the Pool Table*. His book was republished in 1967 and is the source of a few tricks shown in this book. One of the best, *Trick and Fancy Pool Shots Exposed*, was published in 1908 in Boston by Joe Hood. Then, in 1948, the champion Jimmy Caras published *Trick Shots Made Easy*. Simple in design, this little book is actually excellent and, furthermore, was the inspiration for almost all amateurs. There's also a guide by Mosconi, *Winning Pocket Billiards*, published in 1965, which contains a section on 18 spectacular tricks. In 1978, another American, Willie Jopling, published a booklet with loose-leaf sheets containing approximately 25 tricks, some of which were previously unpublished. Some of my difficult shots were inspired by another book by Robert Byrne, *Standard Book of Pool and Billiards*, published in 1978. The most recent one is *Massey's World of Trick Shots*, published by Mike Massey in 2003. Finally, tricks published in various magazines also helped me. Over the last few years, a number of experts in this field have shown many in the magazine *Billiards Digest*. Currently, Mike Massey is considered the great-est tricks and fancy shots specialist. He puts on roughly 240 demonstrations a year, and his shows are highly appreciated. He has won almost every trick title and championship, and you can see his achievements regularly on television sports channels. He's in high demand not only in the United States, but throughout the world, and he claims to have traveled nearly 5 million km in his career to put on demonstrations: spectators in 35 countries have had the opportunity to see him at work. He's charismatic and very dramatic, and he has a great sense of humor.

This book has the benefit of giving order and logic to the presentation of pool tricks. In addition, I strived to simplify the diagrams by making them clearer and more accurate. This can't be said of many books of this type, for most works on the topic lack clarity and accuracy.

The usual rules don't apply to tricks and fancy shots. Indeed, in most of the tricks, the rules have to be broken, for example, to play a push shot, strike the ball while in motion, touch the ball with the hand, place the ball on top of the cushion or a chalk cube, or use pieces of equipment in performing a trick. Remember to warn spectators that pocketing the cue ball has no bearing on the success of the trick. The trick is good even if the cue ball is also pocketed.

Naturally, the diagrams will guide you as to how to place the balls when you try the tricks illustrated in this book. You'll realize perhaps that some plays are difficult to do on your table: if this happens, you'll have to make some adjustments to succeed. You may have to move the balls slightly in one direction or another, or change your spin or the force of the strike. If you persevere, you'll probably learn what can be called the "trick instinct." By playing them, you'll find it easier to understand or discover the trick behind each one.

As I already explained in the first part on techniques, sometimes a spin has to be applied to make some shots. A ball is played without a spin when the cue strikes the cue ball right in the center. A spin is applied when the tip of the cue contacts the cue ball somewhere other than in the center. There are a lot of spin options: high (topspin), low (backspin), right, left, top left, top right, bottom left and bottom right. Each of these spins causes the cue ball to follow a different trajectory after colliding with another ball or with the cushion. However, it becomes laborious to always repeat, for example, "apply the spin to the top, slightly to the right," or any other similar expression. Rather than express it this way, I prefer to adopt a clock system, one that's already used by many writers. This method is simple and accurate. For example, the spin on the top, slightly to the left would translate into an "11 o'clock spin." Accord-ing to this system, the cue must strike at the spot that corresponds to that time. If you say to play a 6 o'clock spin, this means that you have to strike the bottom of the cue ball. Below is a diagram showing these different spins with the corresponding descriptions.

- The shot directly in the center is neutral, in the sense that no spin will be applied so that the cue ball follows a normal trajectory.
- The 12 o'clock spin corresponds to a topspin and moves the cue ball forward.
- The 6 o'clock spin corresponds to a backspin and makes the cue ball move backward.
- The 3 o'clock spin corresponds to a sidespin to the right and increases the cue ball's projection towards the right.
- The 9 o'clock spin corresponds to a sidespin to the left and increases the cue ball's projection toward the left.
- The spins at 1:30, 4:30, 7:30 and 10:30 are intermediate, and produce the corresponding trajectories.

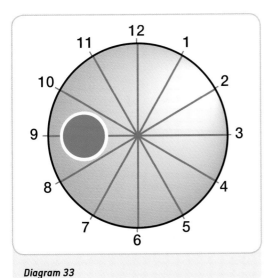

Diagram 33

This system also helps to teach pool. If you teach someone to play and you want them to strike the cue ball in a specific spot, you don't need to explain the desired spot (e.g. low and slightly to the right); all you need to do is tell them to strike at 5 o'clock. This reminds me of something that happened a few years ago when a group of friends was playing pool in a local hall. One of the players complained that he couldn't make what was a rather easy shot: "I don't understand," he said, "I strike the ball at 2:08, but this doesn't work." Another player at the next table replied: "You're behind and you're two hours late. Strike at 4:08 instead and you'll get it!" This funny anecdote shows the need to always know the correct time, or in other words to know how to apply the correct spin.

Often, instructions specify that you must "freeze" two balls, one against the other, or to a cushion. This means that they have to stick to each other, but if the quality of the cloth on the table isn't the best, which is often the case, it will be difficult for you to make them stick together. If this happens, here's how to freeze the balls against each other. Place them in the required position and hold them there with one hand. Take another ball and use it to gently strike the balls you want to freeze. Not only will the balls stay put, but you'll also be able to return them to the same spot in days or weeks to come. Indeed, this maneuver leaves marks on the cloth that are imperceptible to the eye, but it allows the balls to return to the same positions.

In conclusion, I would like to remind you of this quotation by the great Raymond Ceulemans, three-cushion world champion: "A mediocre player says that he knows how to score a point when he makes a good shot one time out of 10. A champion says that he doesn't know how to do it when he misses one time out of 10."

EXPLANATION OF PICTOGRAMS

Under the trick name and diagram, you'll find three symbols that show the following:

Degree of Difficulty

 I assessed the degrees of difficulty with 1 being very easy and 5, very difficult. In some cases, positioning the balls is complicated, and sometimes the trick requires a lot of skill. Obviously, this assessment is very subjective and you may find the trick easier (or more difficult) than indicated.

Force Required

 A thermometer, measuring from 1 to 10, indicates the force needed to play the trick, with 1 being very gentle and 10 being the maximum force you're able to produce.

Strike Location

 A dial similar to a clock with a shaded dot indicating the approximate point where the cue should attack the cue ball. Each table is different, so you'll sometimes have to modify the point of attack to perform the trick.

1. THE CROSS-TABLE SHOT

Place all the balls in a straight line starting in the center, as shown in the illustration. The goal of this exercise is to perform 10 consecutive cross-table shots into the center pocket. However, note that you grab the cue ball with your hand after each shot and you place it yourself for the next cross-table shot. Strive to turn your cue with each shot to avoid a miscue. In the beginning, you'll find this play difficult, but if you practice regularly, you'll improve very quickly. When you become more skilled, you'll be able to go faster and strike more quickly. It's possible to shoot up to 15 balls this way, provided you leave enough space between each of the last five balls.

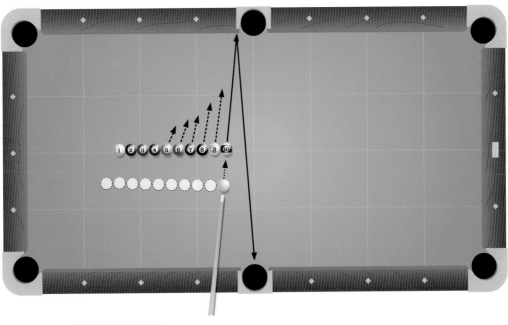

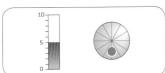

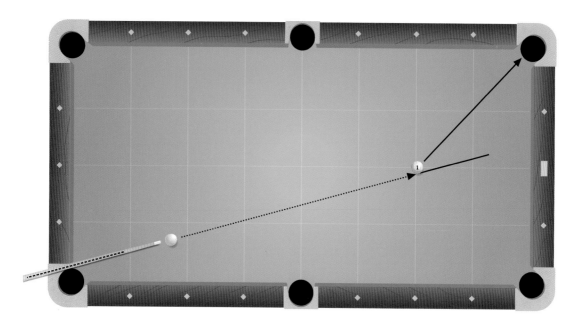

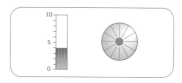

2. A USEFUL TRICK

Here's a situation that arises frequently in pool games. This is what we call a spot shot, meaning that after a ball is pocketed, you have no other choice but to play the ball placed on the head spot. Even if this type of ball is relatively easy to pocket, it does happen that, because of the tension or the stakes of the game, the person performing the trick feels some hesitation and sometimes even misses the shot. There's a trick that many pool professionals advocate to make it

easier to perform. Place the cue ball on the table and line it up between the object ball and the inside corner of the opposite pocket, as shown in the diagram. Simply aim at the far right side of the ball. By playing this way, the impact will occur at exactly the right spot, and the ball should be sent directly into the pocket. It's a technique that I use and that is surprisingly effective. Practice this shot, for it will be very useful during major games when nervousness reduces your skill.

3. HOW TO AVOID THE CORNER
OF THE CENTER POCKET

Here's another situation that sometimes arises during pool games. The cue ball and the object ball are both frozen against the same cushion but separated by the center pocket. Those who know a little about pool know that, with this kind of shot, there's a high risk that the cue ball will catch on the corner of the center pocket in passing, such that its trajectory will be completely changed, as you can see in the diagram below. This possibility is even greater when you take into account that, on some tables, the cushion is not exactly straight, but bent slightly inward.

To overcome this danger, raise the butt of your cue a little and play the shot with moderate force by applying a 7:30 spin, as shown in the diagram. The cue ball will trace an arc, pass approximately $1/4$ in. (8 mm) from the cushion opposite the center pocket and come back along the cushion to hit the ball at the right spot. This trick requires consummate skill, for not only is it difficult to do, but there's also the risk that the cue ball will be pocketed. Repeat several times.

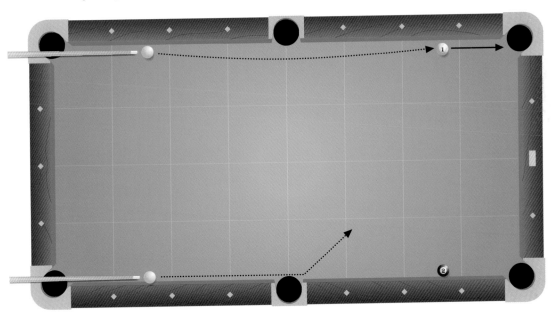

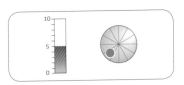

4. DESPERATE CROSS-TABLE SHOT

Place the 1-ball and the 2-ball one behind the other on the head spot and hold the cue ball in hand. This kind of play sometimes occurs in competition. At first glance the situation seems to be hopeless. However, it is possible to hit the 2-ball with a cross-table shot, as shown in the illustration. Simply play the cue ball on the left side of the 1-ball with moderate force. A slight deflection will be transmitted to the second ball, and after a few attempts, you'll probably be able to make this cross-table shot into pocket A.

Obviously, as with any other uncommon shot, it's better to have had the chance to try it several times on the table you'll be using to perform it.

Note: Since the way balls rebound differs from one table to another, you may not be able to do this shot as shown on some tables. In this case, the 2-ball may be pocketed in pocket B, not with a cross-table shot, but with a double cross-table shot. You'll have to try it a few times to know if you'll be able to make this shot.

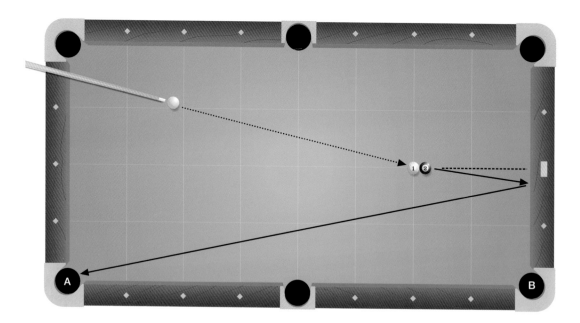

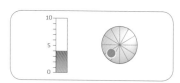

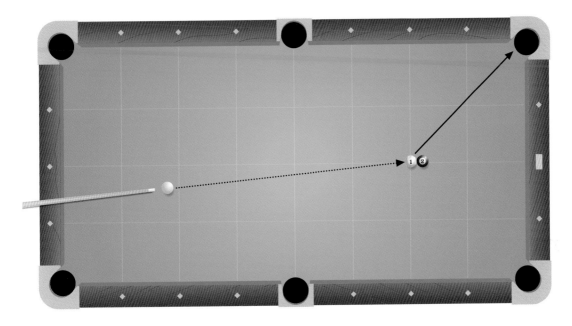

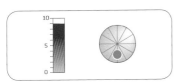

5. A SLEIGHT OF HAND

Place the balls as shown in the illustration and line up the 1-ball and 2-ball starting at the head spot. Is it possible to pocket the 1-ball in the left corner? Certainly not each time, but you should be able to do it once every five times.

Note the position of the cue ball: it's not in the center, but approximately 5–6 in. (12–15 cm) from the center, and this detail is essential for performing this shot.

Apply a lot of backspin, play hard and strike the 1-ball right in the center, i.e. right in the middle relative to the cue ball. It's difficult to explain what happens. In fact, it seems that the 1-ball is caught between the cue ball and the 2-ball, which causes the cue ball to double kiss, impossible to see with the naked eye because of the speed at which it happens. Because of the strike angle, the 1-ball is projected toward the pocket. Even if you can't do this trick every time, your satisfaction will be all the greater when you do it successfully.

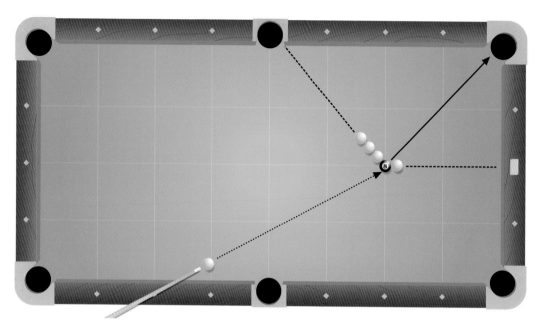

6. WHITHER THE 8-BALL?

Here's a trick that is as simple to place as it is to do. In addition, similar situations will arise during some games and it will be an advantage for you to have faced them already. Place the 8-ball on the head spot and place the other balls as shown in the illustration, lining up the row of four balls with the corner of the center pocket. Before placing the cue ball on the table, ask the spectators if it's possible to pocket the 8-ball in the designated pocket. Lastly, place the cue ball at the approximate spot as shown in the diagram and strike hard at 4 o'clock, aiming at the right side of the 8-ball. The other balls will move away and the 8-ball will be sent directly into the intended pocket.

7. FROG JUMP

This trick is as old as the hills ... or rather, pool. It was illustrated in one of the first books on pool, published in 1827 by a Frenchman named Mingaud (see "The Chalk," page 32). Surround the cue ball with several balls so that there's no direct access to the 8-ball placed on the edge of the opposite corner pocket. Announce that you'll be attempting to pocket the 8-ball without playing a combination shot, which appears impossible at first. The secret: don't strike in the direction of the 8-ball. On the contrary, play fairly hard, slightly raising the butt of your cue, in the direction of the closest cushion, at an angle perpendicular to this cushion. Apply an 11:30 spin. As soon as it hits the cushion, the cue ball will jump over the blocking balls and hit the 8-ball. This is a perfectly legal shot and can be useful in a game of eight- or nine-ball.

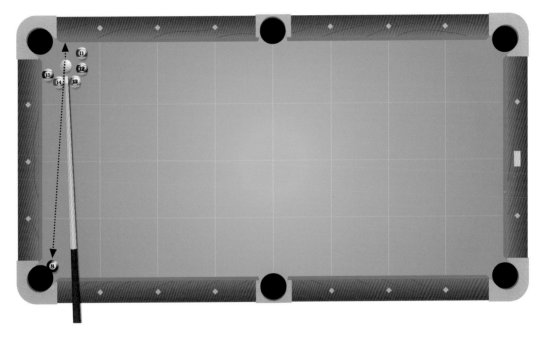

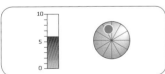

8. A CONVENIENT PASS

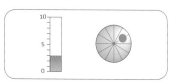

At first glance, it's impossible to pocket the 2-ball in the corner, given its position. However, there's a way to do it. Aiming at 2 o'clock, press the tip of your cue against the cue ball. Next, push, following through with the cue. Being jammed between the cue ball and the cushion, the 2-ball will be projected along the cushion into the corner pocket. It's important not to do any preparatory back-and-forth motions with the cue, for you have to use the push shot. Usually, this type of shot is illegal during a game, but since this is a trick, the rules don't apply.

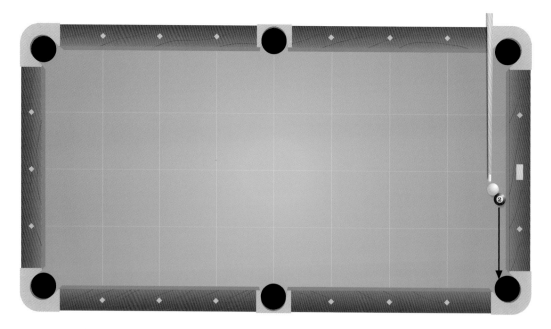

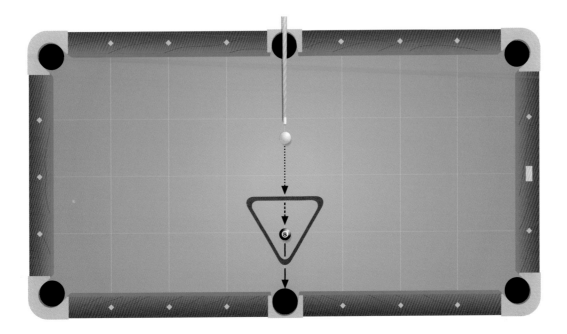

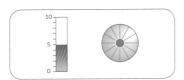

9. SIMPLE

Place the cue ball and the 8-ball in a straight line between the two center pockets, then place the triangle on the table, ensuring that the apex is in front of the opposite center pocket and that the side of the triangle closest to you is parallel to the cushion. The 8-ball is inside the triangle approximately 2 in. (5 cm) from the side, and the apex of the triangle should be approximately 4 in. (10 cm) from the center pocket. Then announce to your audience that there is a way to pocket the 8-ball in the center without removing the triangle. Some people will probably suggest a jump shot.

After waiting few minutes, perform the trick. Simply play a fairly hard shot in the direction of the 8-ball. Naturally, the cue ball will hit the side of the triangle. Therefore, the whole triangle will move toward the center pocket. The side of the triangle will hit the 8-ball, which in turn will also move toward the pocket. At the same time, the apex of the triangle will move to the inside of the pocket, leaving enough space for the 8-ball to fall into the opening. This trick is so simple that it will leave the spectators stunned, disbelieving and surprised not to have figured it out sooner.

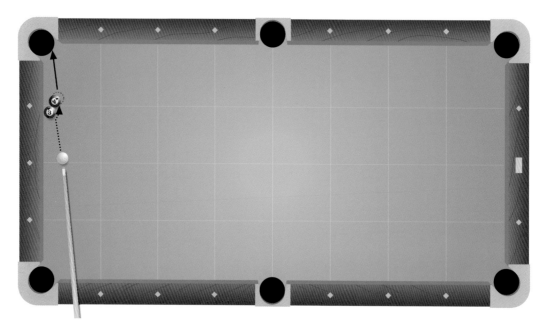

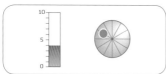

10. UNEXPECTED BYPASS

The 3- and 4-balls are frozen against each other at such an angle that it seems impossible to pocket the 4-ball in the corner. If a player tries to play the 4-ball without touching the 3-ball, they'll never succeed. The secret is to brush against the 3-ball by applying a lot of 10 o'clock spin. The 3-ball will push the 4-ball toward the outside, while the cue ball will continue along its course. In fact, the cue ball will ricochet off the 3-ball, and continue along to hit the 4-ball while it's moving. This trick is perfectly legal and can be useful during a game, for it comes up fairly often.

11. A USEFUL DOUBLE KISS

Sometimes, in some games, especially seven-, nine- or ten-ball, you have to ensure that the cue ball touches a specific ball first, but you actually want to pocket a different ball. This is what you see in the diagram, where the player must first strike the 1-ball, although they want to pocket the 9-ball. It's impossible to play a cross-table shot with the 1-ball, for there would be a double kiss. The easiest way to hit the 9-ball is to play the 1-ball directly, in a straight line, and apply a 4:30 spin. The 1-ball will act like a buffer, caught between the cushion and the cue ball. There will be a double kiss, and the cue ball will come back to strike and pocket the 9-ball. Practice this shot and master it, for it will come up from time to time during matches.

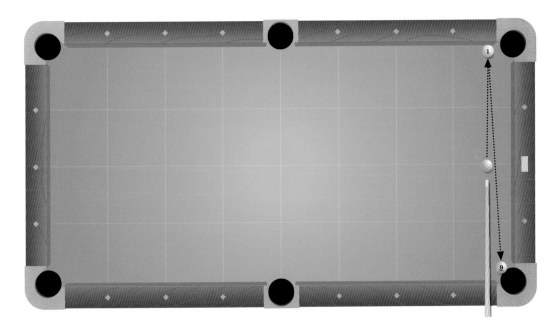

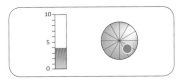

12. A THIN SLICE

In the same situation as in trick no. 11, there's another way to pocket the 9-ball. Apply a lot of sidespin to the left (9 o'clock) to graze the 1-ball but not touch it. Immediately after the cushion is struck, the left sidespin will ensure that the cue ball pushes the 1-ball into the pocket and rebounds to hit the 9-ball. This trick is more diffi-cult than the previous trick, for the angle of the cut is slightly more than 90°. Therefore, it's recommended that, in addition to applying a lot of spin, you raise the butt of your cue more than usual (approximately 15°), which adds more spin.

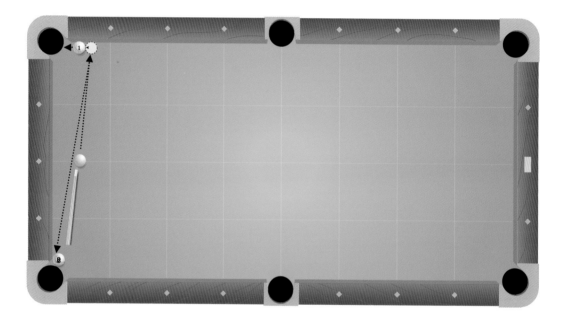

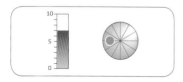

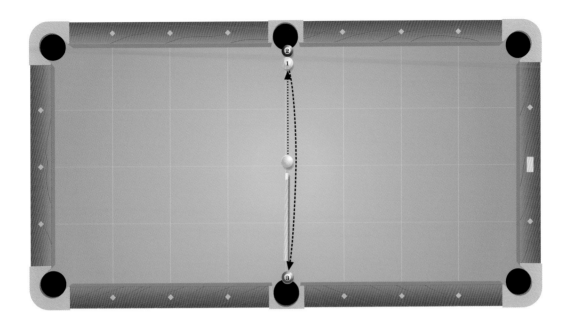

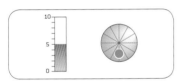

13. A DEVASTATING BACKSPIN

Look at the diagram. In general, in a combination shot using the 1- and the 2-ball, the 1-ball will stay put or it will move to one side or the other. However, there's a way to pocket not only the 1- and the 2-ball, but also the 3-ball, in a single shot. To do this, the four balls must be placed in a perfectly straight line, with the cue ball positioned almost in the center of the table between the two center pockets. Carefully aim at the center of the 1-ball and strike hard with a lot of backspin. The reverse rotation of the cue ball will change into a forward rotation toward the 1-ball, which will follow the 2-ball into the center pocket. At the same time, the backspin will ensure the cue ball moves back to pocket the 3-ball.

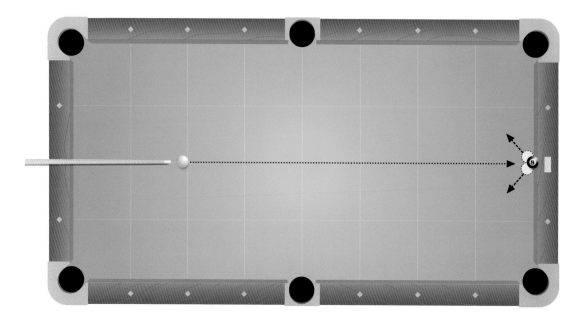

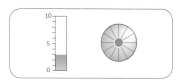

14. SURPRISE !

Do you think that tricks are a recent invention? Think again, as this trick was illustrated in one of the first books on pool devoted to tricks, published in 1902 by Fred Hermann! This trick is probably the best known and the easiest of all the tricks contained in this book. Freeze the two balls against the cushion as shown in the illustration. Next, place the 8-ball on top of the cushion, pressing equally against the two other balls. Announce to the spectators that you're going to play in such a way that you'll touch the 8-ball first. How can such a sensational feat be

done? The answer is simple. After making the spectators wait for a few minutes, gently play in the direction of the 8-ball. As soon as you take the shot and the cue ball is in motion, strike down hard on the cushion near you with your fist, or hit the table with your hip. The vibration will instantly transfer to the entire table, and the weight of the 8-ball will move the 1-ball and 2-ball apart. Before the cue ball reaches the other end, the 8-ball will have fallen onto the table and the collision will happen as announced.

15. THREE IN THREE

Place three balls as shown in the diagram. It's better to align the three numbered balls slightly along the outside corner of the pockets, for the shot will cause a deflection, such that the two balls will head off at an angle to the inside.

Although only three balls are involved, this trick is more difficult to do than other plays that appear much more dramatic. As a result, practice placing the balls carefully to increase your chances of succeeding as much as possible.

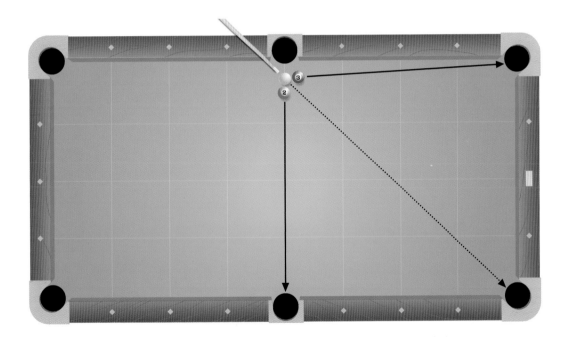

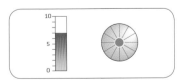

16. ELEMENTARY, MY DEAR WATSON!

This trick is a practical application of the elementary principle of physics: any action causes an opposite, equal reaction. Create a row of nine or 10 balls frozen against each other along the foot cushion, starting near the left corner pocket. Ask a spectator to tell you the number of balls that they would like you to pocket in the corner pocket in one shot. The number chosen can be one, two or three balls at most. To pocket the desired number, take an equal number of balls and place them at the other end of the cushion, frozen one against the other. Then, play your shot by pushing these balls in the direction of the row. You'll notice that if you used only one ball, only one ball in the row would be pocketed. If you use three balls, as shown in the diagram, the last three balls in the row (marked with an X) will be pocketed. The secret to doing this trick? As mentioned, you must "push" with your cue instead of performing a normal shot. Some might find this trick simple, but for those who don't know it, this play is, in some ways, of "scientific" interest.

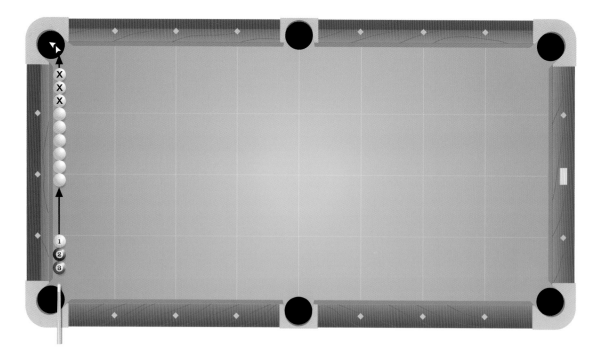

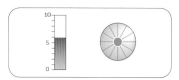

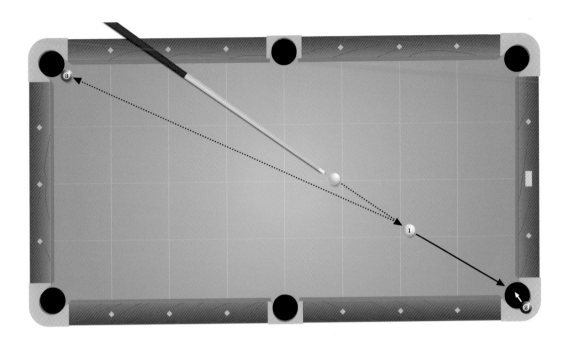

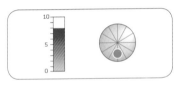

17. THREE AT A DIAGONALE

Here's a trick that will allow you to check if you have mastered the backspin. The 2-ball is perched on a cube of chalk, which is balanced behind and over the corner pocket. Ensure that the chalk and the 2-ball are leaning slightly toward the inside of the pocket. You'll pocket the 1-ball in the same corner and ensure that the cue ball moves back-ward to pocket the 3-ball. Strike hard with a 6 o'clock spin. When the 1-ball lands in the bottom of the pocket, the vibration will move the 2-ball into the same pocket. If you prefer, to start, you can place all the balls, i.e. the cue ball and the three other balls, in a perfectly straight line, making this trick easier to perform.

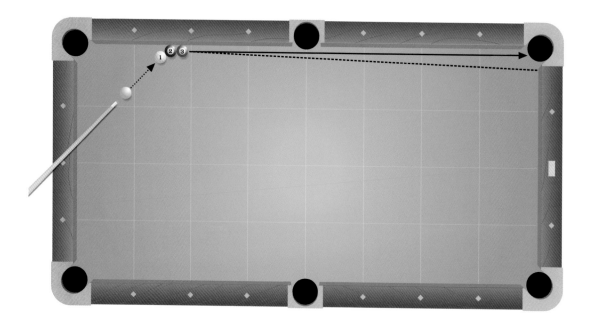

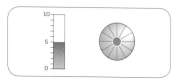

18. TAKE ME FOR A RIDE

This trick is one of the funniest in this book, and it's almost impossible to guess its secret. It's almost magic. Place three balls and the cue ball as shown in the illustration and ask a spectator (preferably a good player) to strike the 1-ball in order to pocket the 3-ball at the other end. In fact, on a normal table, the 3-ball is impossible to pocket this way, as shown by the dotted line. However, there's a way to do it! Ask another spectator (preferably a player that isn't so good) to come and perform the shot. They'll be able to pocket the 3-ball, provided you discreetly moisten the point of contact between balls 2 and 3. Put saliva on your finger and moisten the point of contact while placing the balls. To fool the spectators, it's better if you put saliva on your finger while the first player tries the trick, as their attention will be focused on that player. If possible, always choose a woman to do this trick, for men don't like to be beaten by a woman, even in pool!

19. THE 8-BALL IN THE CORNER

Here's a trick that is both spectacular and easy to perform. Use the diagram to guide you in placing the balls, watching that all the balls are frozen one against the other and also that all the balls are touching the cushion except for the last one, which is placed at an angle. At first glance, it appears to be impossible to pocket the 8-ball in the corner pocket because of the obstacle posed by the five balls. However, doing it is child's play if you place the balls correctly. Play fairly hard by pushing in the direction of the 8-ball. All the balls will begin to move, the two last ones moving apart to allow the 8-ball free access.

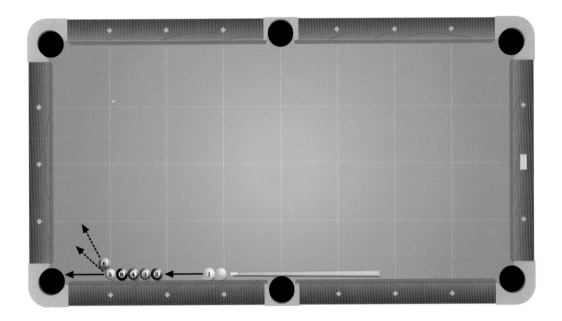

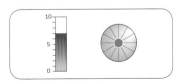

20. THE INSURMOUNTABLE BARRIER

This game is divided into three steps. First, place the balls as shown in illustration A to create an insurmountable barrier in the middle of the table. Next, place the cue ball on the head spot on the side opposite the 8-ball, announce that you're going to pocket the 8-ball without using a combination shot and without making the cue ball jump. After giving the spectators a few seconds to try to find a solution, perform your shot. For this second step, play a shot with no spin and with moderate force in the direction indicated in illustration B. Final step: as soon as you make the shot, quickly lay down your cue on the table along the cushion closest to you, the butt pointed to your right (illustration C). The cue ball will quickly arrive and hit your cue, but since the cue is not elastic like the cushion, the cue ball won't rebound but will continue on its course along your cue to end up at the 8-ball.

Important note: When you place your cue on the table, don't place it right against the cushion but close to it without touching.

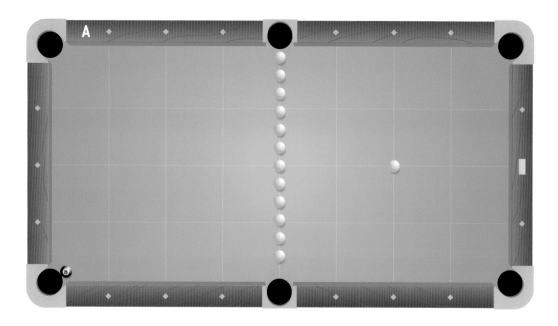

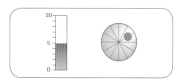

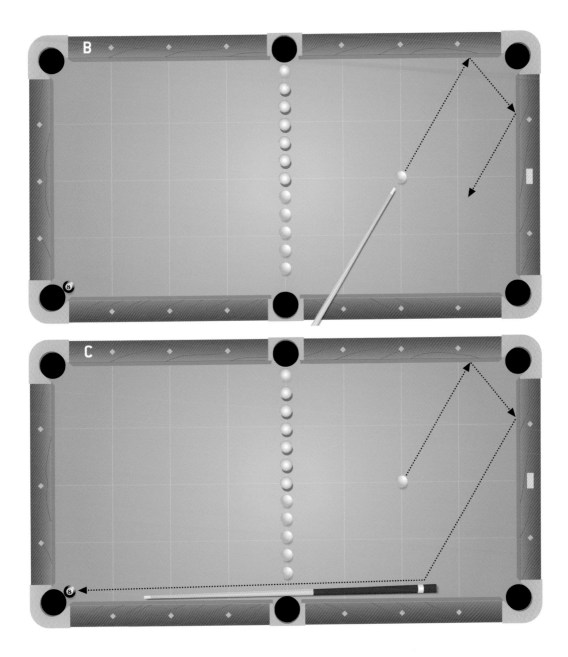

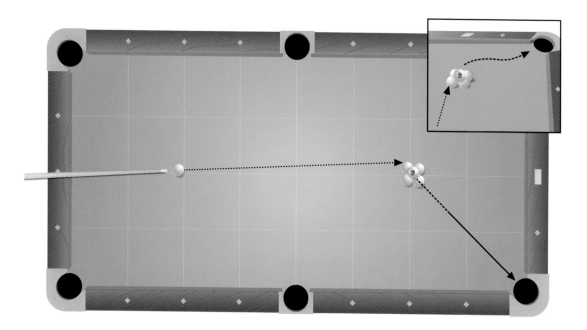

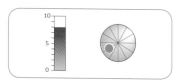

21. THE PYRAMID

This is a spectacular and easy trick to perform. Spectators really like situations that are out of the ordinary and, thanks to this trick, they'll be satisfied. Tell them that recently, during a game of nine-ball, you found yourself faced with an unusual situation. Not only did you solve the impasse, but you also won the game. You have to form a pyramid using five balls, with the 9-ball placed at the apex and the 1-ball in the bottom left corner. The hardest part about this play is to hold in place the four balls that form the base. This will be especially difficult on a new, good-quality cloth. The chosen spot faces the head spot, with the four balls placed parallel to the

cushions. Once you've created a pyramid that will stay put, quickly stand at the other end. Avoid touching the table, for the slightest vibration will make the weight of the 9-ball cause this unusual structure to collapse. Place the cue ball in the center of the break box and announce that you'll pocket the 9-ball in the right corner. To do this, you just need to play the left ball (the 1-ball) hard and the thrust will lift the 9-ball, which will then jump over the other ball and land in the right corner pocket. Finish by saying as naturally as possible, "If one day you find yourself faced with this situation, you'll know how to get out of it ..."

22. THREE BALLS IN THREE POCKETS

For this trick, you'll need three balls: the cue ball, the 2-ball and the 3-ball. Unscrew a cue to form two pieces and place the two pieces as shown in the diagram, ensuring that all the points of contact touch. These four points of contact are as follows: the tip of the cue has to press against the butt, the butt has to press against the cushion, and the two balls have to be frozen to each corresponding section of the cue. Announce to the audience that you're going to pocket "three balls in three pockets," i.e. the cue ball, the 2-ball and the 3-ball, without explaining any further with another cue, play fairly hard

and without any spin in the direction of the opposite cushion. As soon as you perform the shot, hurry to lay your cue on the table. Lean slightly forward and open the pocket of your jacket opposite the place where the cue ball will return. The impact of it against the shaft of the cue will cause the two numbered balls to be pocketed in the two corner pockets. Moreover, by hitting the shaft, the cue ball will be projected into the air and fall down into your jacket pocket: "three balls in three pockets." Lastly, the secret of this trick is to wear a jacket!

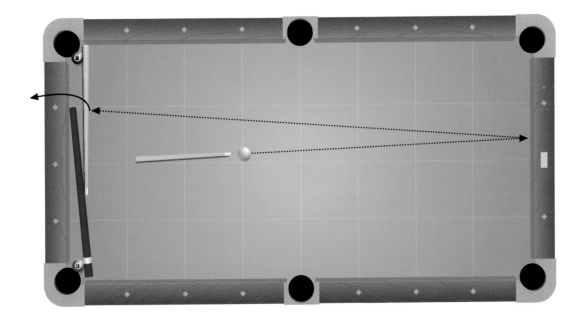

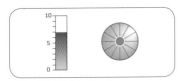

23. A HAPPY ENDING

First, place the cue ball and the 8-ball approximately as indicated in the diagram. Then, before performing the trick, tell the spectators the following story: "The other day, I played several frames of eight-ball at the pub and, at the end, they had me play the best player in the place. As I was about to beat him and end the game, he suddenly threw his cue on the table between the cue ball and the 8-ball, saying that I wouldn't be able to pocket the 8-ball. (At the same time, place a cue in this position.) I made fun of him, saying that I would be able to pocket the 8-ball, even if he put another cue on the table between the 8-ball and the pocket, which he promptly did."

At this point, stop for a few moments to lay the second cue flat on the table as shown in the illustration, so that there is a distance of roughly 1 ft. (30 cm) separating the two cues. Then, announce to the spectators that you will now attempt to repeat this feat. Raise the butt of your cue approximately 20°–30° relative to the horizontal plane and play fairly hard, applying a 6 o'clock spin. The cue ball will bounce over the first cue and hit the 8-ball, which will bounce, in turn, over the second cue, and the trick will be played.

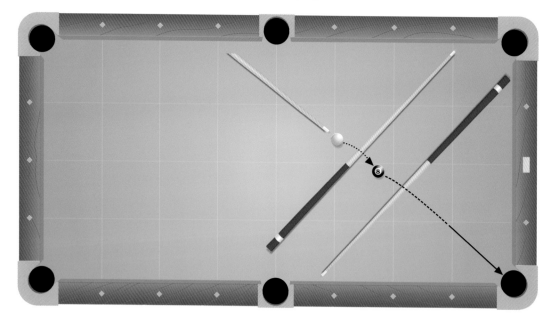

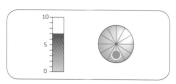

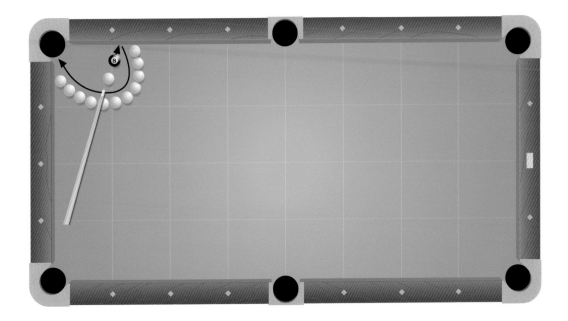

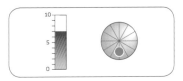

24. A WALL OF BALLS

Form a semicircle with the balls that runs from one cushion to another, approximately 5 in. (12 cm) from the corner pocket. Next, place the cue ball and the 8-ball inside this wall and announce that you are going to attempt to pocket the 8-ball in the corner. Aim at the center of the 8-ball and apply a backspin on the cue ball. The 8-ball will strike the cushion, return to rebound off each of the other balls and finally drop (hopefully) into the pocket.

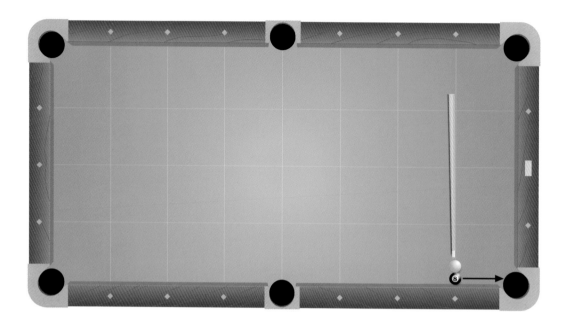

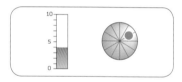

25. THE PUSH SHOT

The performance of this trick requires an illegal shot commonly called the push shot. How do you pocket the 8-ball in the corresponding corner pocket? Slowly press your cue against the cue ball, without performing any back-and-forth motion. It's essential that you don't strike the cue ball as usual, but simply push it. Aim and apply a 2 o'clock spin. As soon as your cue touches the cue ball, push the cue ball straight forward. The secret to doing this trick is to always hold the cue glued to the cue ball without making any preparatory motions.

26. THE CIGARETTE PACK TRICK

Here's a dramatic and yet disconcertingly easy trick. By performing it, you'll never fail to astound your audience. Don't ignore the preparations, otherwise you're certain to fail. Borrow a package of cigarettes from a spectator and remove the contents, keeping only the cardboard packaging. Then, place it upright on the table, near the spot indicated on the diagram. Next, carefully place the 5-ball on top of the pack. To place the other balls, refer to the diagram. The key to success is to place the five balls, the point of the triangle and the cigarette pack in a perfect line. In addition, ensure that the side of the triangle is absolutely parallel to the cushion. Play the shot moderately hard by striking right in the center of the cue ball. The cigarette pack will be projected into the air and the 5-ball will fall on the table. The cue ball will immediately rebound off the triangle and pocket the 5-ball in the center, while the four other balls drop into the other center pocket.

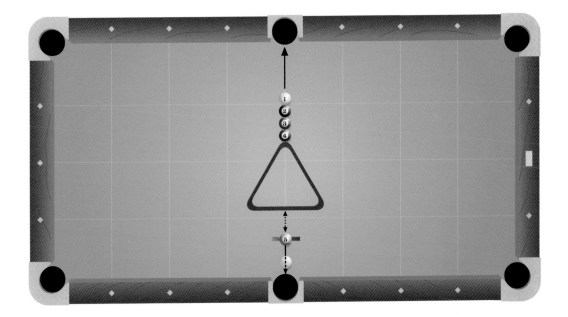

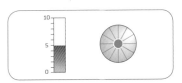

27. REVERSE PUSH SHOT

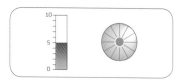

How do you pocket the 8-ball in the opposite corner pocket? Play toward the cushion at an angle similar to the one indicated in the diagram by aiming at the center of the cue ball. Hurry to remove your cue, so that the cue ball can rebound toward the 8-ball, which will be projected into the opposite pocket. You may need to attempt this a few times to be able to do this trick, as the rebound off the cushions, which varies from one table to another, and may require you to modify the strike angle.

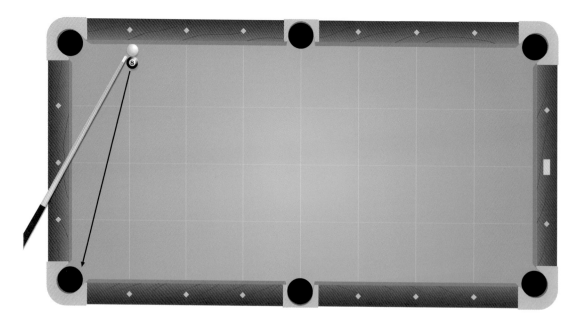

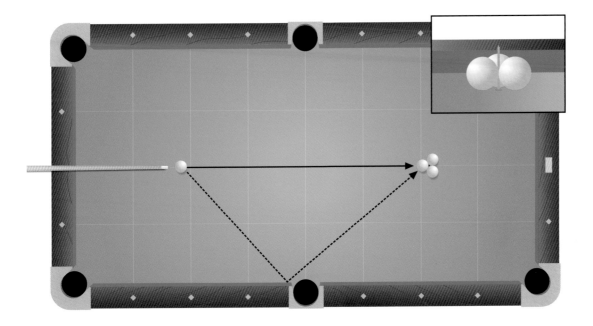

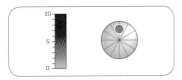

28. THE HIGHLIGHT OF THE EVENING

Freeze three balls on the head spot and place a wooden match upright in the middle, between the balls, as shown in the inset. You can also use a nail or a very thin cigarette. Dare the spectators to make the match fall by playing from the break box. You'll be surprised to see how difficult this trick is. Some people will think that it's possible by playing a shot off the cushion, as shown by the dotted line, but this isn't the solution. The best way to do it is to aim at the center of the first ball of the triangle, play hard and apply a lot of 12 o'clock spin. The three balls will scatter. Carried away by its own momentum and by the topspin, the cue ball will hesitate a fraction of a second, then rebound toward the match. It's essential to strike the first ball right in the center, otherwise the cue ball will roll to the side of it. Therefore, make every effort with this trick and take the time you need to aim at the right spot, remembering to apply a lot of topspin.

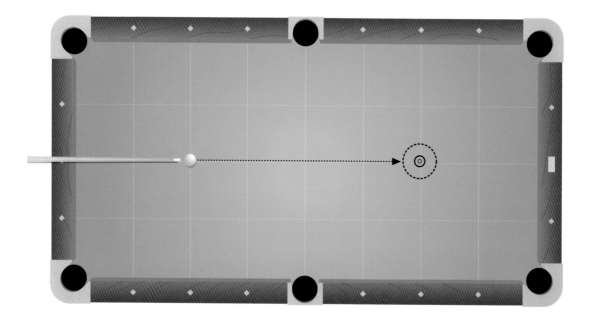

29. REMOVE THE COIN FROM THE CIRCLE

This is an old trick that you may have had occasion to see at a fair. Using the chalk, draw a circle approximately 6 in. (15 cm) in diameter around the head spot. Next, place a ball on the spot, then balance a coin on the top. The point is to play from the break box and make the coin fall outside the circle. As simple as this trick might seem, it's difficult to do. In fact, there are two ways of doing this trick. First, you can play very, very, very gently, so that the cue ball comes to a stop against the ball. The coin will not be projected into the air, but it will follow the motion of the ball and fall outside the circle. Alternatively, you can play very hard with a lot of 12 o'clock spin (as in trick no. 28), but strike the ball right in the center. Carried along by its own spin, the cue ball will continue on its course and strike the coin before it falls on the cloth, thus projecting it outside the circle.

30. A FULL GLASS

Place a glass on the edge of the cushion, near the rubber. Next, place a quarter on the rubber, approximately ¼ in. (8 mm) from the edge of the glass, as shown in the illustration. Then, place the cue ball perpendicular to the glass and the coin. Play a moderately hard shot toward the coin. Under the force of the impact, the rubber will be compressed and cause the coin to rebound directly into the glass. It's an easy trick and very dramatic. Practice, and amaze your friends. One word of warning: since the elasticity of the cushions is not the same from one table to the next, you should without a doubt try this trick once or twice on a new table before performing it.

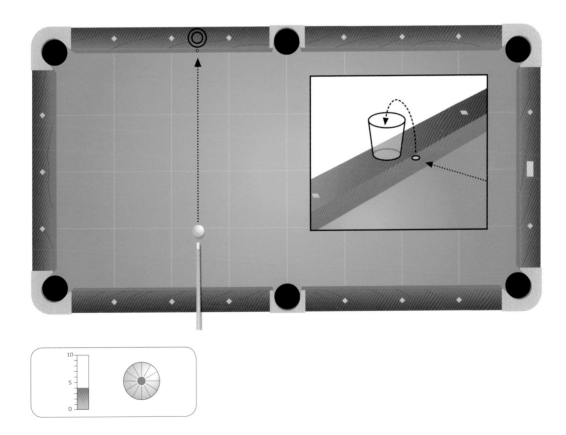

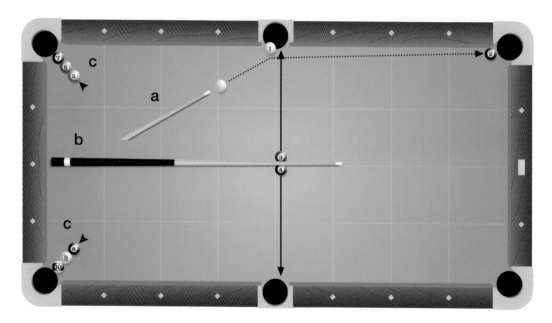

31. 10 BALLS WITH ONE SHOT

Place 10 balls as shown in the illustration, taking care to freeze the 3-ball and the 4-ball in the middle of the table. With pool cue in hand, tell your audience that you are going to pocket the 10 balls that are on the table in one shot. Everyone will think that you're going to shoot hard. The performance of this trick is divided into two steps. First, play fairly gently toward the 1-ball, so that the cue ball also pockets the 2-ball at the other end. As soon as the shot is made, quickly go on to the next step. Firmly lower your cue between the 3-ball and the 4-ball, which will both head off toward their corresponding center pocket. As soon as your cue is lying on the table, release it and use your hands to push the six remaining balls into the corner pockets on either side of you. This trick is easy to do and spectacular. The faster the execution, the more the spectators will be surprised.

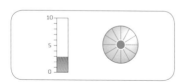

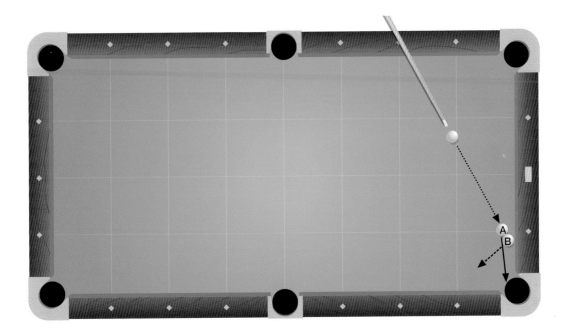

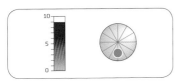

32. ELIMINATION I

The three balls are lined up as follows: balls A and B are frozen against the cushion near the corner pocket, while the cue ball is placed farther away, in a straight line. Is it possible to pocket ball A in the corner? Definitely. Play hard with a lot of backspin, right in the center. Ball B will move away and ball A should head toward the corner pocket.

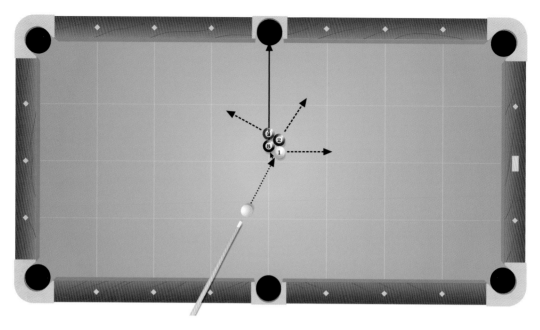

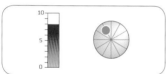

33. ELIMINATION II

On this diagram, the trajectory of the 8-ball toward the center is blocked by the 3-ball. Therefore, one would logically expect you to indicate that you will pocket the 3-ball in the center. However, it's possible to pocket the 8-ball in the center pocket. To do this trick, it's essential that the four balls be absolutely frozen against one another. Place the cue ball at the approximate spot indicated on the illustration and play fairly hard,

applying an 11 o'clock spin, taking care to aim first at the 1-ball on its left. The 1-ball will push the 2-ball, which will also push the 3-ball, thus opening a path to the 8-ball toward the center pocket. After colliding with the 1-ball, the cue ball will continue and ricochet off the 8-ball, which is then set in motion. The trick is to strike the 1-ball first. The rest will happen automatically.

34. ELIMINATION III

The cue ball, 1-ball and 3-ball are placed in a straight line. The 1-ball and the 2-ball pose an obstacle preventing the cue ball from accessing the 3-ball. Is it still possible to pocket the 3-ball without making the cue ball jump and without using the cushion? The simplicity of the answer will surprise you: play fairly hard in a straight line, applying a 12 o'clock spin. The 1-ball and the 2-ball will move away in the direction shown by the two dotted arrows. At the same time, the topspin will ensure the cue ball continues on its course to pocket the 3-ball.

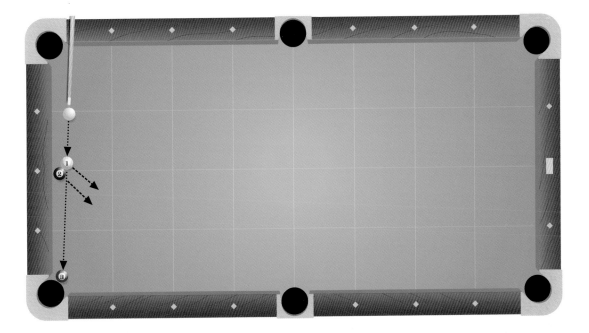

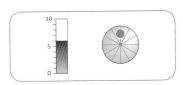

35. *THE HUSTLER* TRICK

During a sports broadcast shown on American television one Saturday afternoon in 1979, the talkative Minnesota Fats positioned the balls and announced to the crowd that he had done this trick a million times during his career. He missed two times in a row! Right away, Willie Mosconi repositioned the balls and did the trick. In fact, this trick is very difficult. In the film *The Hustler*, which came out in 1961, the player portrayed by Paul Newman has his thumbs broken because he wins a bet with one of the gangsters by doing this trick. Hold your cue parallel to the cushion by raising your hand to form a bridge and by raising the butt very slightly. Strike the cue ball from above by using a topspin at

1 o'clock or 1:30, which will ensure that, immediately after the impact, the cue ball will reverse a little and follow a strange curve by moving to the right to allow the 8-ball to pass. In addition, because of the 1:30 spin, a slight deflection to the left will be transferred to the 8-ball so that it should rebound, not in a straight line, but toward the opposite pocket. The most complicated part is to quickly remove the cue as you make the shot to avoid preventing the 8-ball from passing by. At the start, you'll think this is impossible, but try it 100 times if necessary and eventually you'll discover how to make the shot correctly.

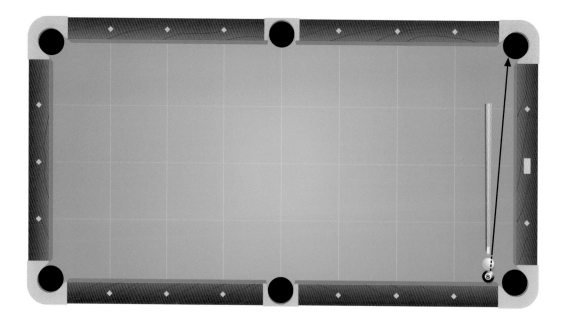

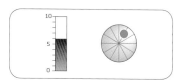

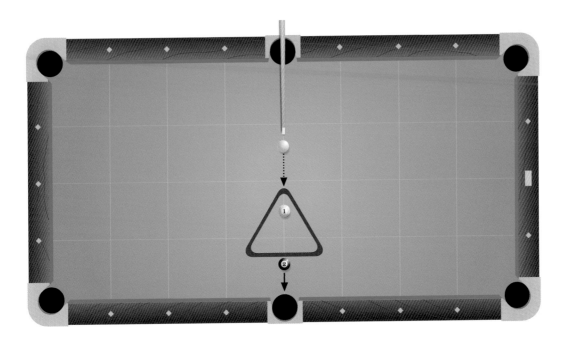

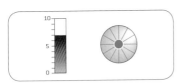

36. WHO WOULD HAVE THOUGHT!

This trick is divided into two steps. Note that the triangle isn't on the table during the first step. First, line up the three balls approximately 1 ft. (30 cm) from each other, opposite the two center pockets, as shown in the illustration. Then, ask the spectators if it's possible to pocket the 2-ball in the opposite center pocket, telling them you aren't going to use the 1-ball, move it, or make the cue ball jump. At this point,

the triangle is still not there. After a few moments, announce that you are now going to do the trick, and move on to the second step. Take the triangle and place it as shown in the illustration, the point aimed in your direction. Play the cue ball off the end of the triangle, which will push the 2-ball into the opposite pocket. You had to think of it!

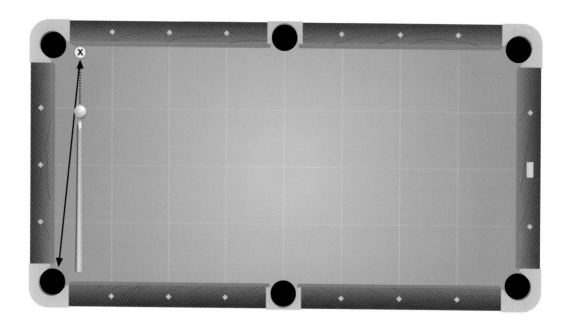

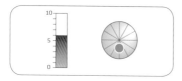

37. ELEVATOR

Is it possible to pocket ball X with a cross-table shot? Most players would reply no, because of the double kiss of the cue ball, which won't have the time to move away to open the path for ball X. However, there's one way of playing this cross-table shot. Allen Hopkins, 1977 world champion, seems to be the inventor of the method used here. Raise the butt of your cue to an angle of approximately 30° and play fairly hard, with a spin slightly below center. In fact, this is an application of the jump shot. The cue ball will bounce toward ball X, using it as a trampoline to rise into

the air. At the same time, ball X will rebound against the cushion and pass *underneath* the cue ball. For the reasons explained in Diagram 28 (see page 89), in the "Massé Shots and the Jump Shots" section, the hardest part of this trick is to avoid projecting the cue ball off the table. Once you've found the right force and the appropriate strike angle (30°–35°), the cue ball will simply bounce almost straight up 12–18 in. (30–45 cm) and fall back onto the table. This is the most difficult part, but persevere.

38. AN UNUSUAL SPRINGBOARD

Take the chalk cube and place it face up on the second diamond on the right rail, then carefully place the cue ball on this unusual springboard. The trick involves pocketing the 1-ball placed on the head spot, so that the cue ball then hits the second ball on the edge of the pocket in the other corner. To do this, you'll have to apply a 5 o'clock spin.

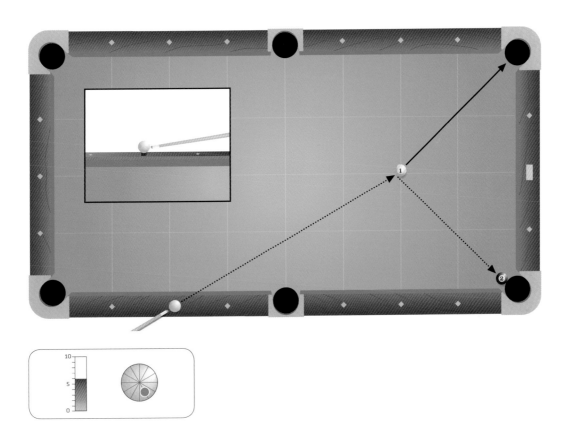

39. WHICH ONE WILL FALL FIRST?

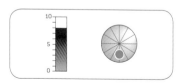

You must use the cue ball to align the two balls with each corner pocket. Position it on the head spot and place one ball beside the other in the direction of the pockets, leaving a space of approximately $1/8$ in. (3.5 mm) between the cue ball and each of the two balls. When the two are carefully lined up, gently remove the cue ball, taking care not to move the two other balls. Then, place the cue ball at the other end, in the center of the table, opposite the imaginary line marking the break box. Now, aim right in the middle, between the two balls, so that the cue ball hits them at the same time. Child's play you say! Careful. This trick is a lot more difficult than it appears. Before deciding that it's simple, try it several times and you'll realize that it deserves a lot more thought.

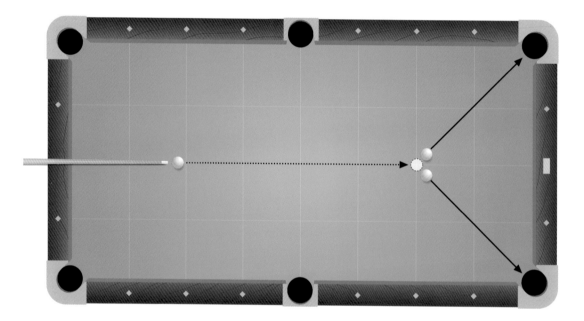

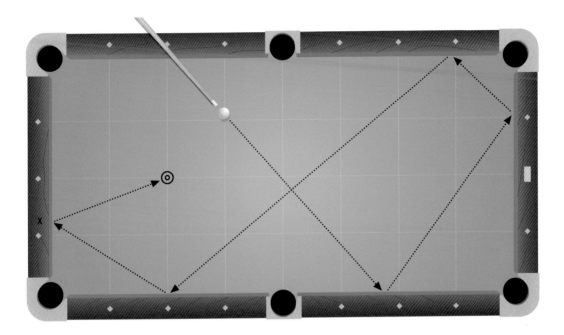

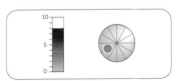

40. MAKE THE COIN DROP

After placing one ball on the head spot, balance a coin on top of it. Next, give the cue ball to a spectator and dare them to make the coin drop, specifying that they must to ensure that the cue ball hits five cushions before touching the ball on which the coin is sitting. The player can place the cue ball anywhere on the table. Even for those who know this trick, a few trial shots will be needed to find the right spot to initially position the cue ball. Place it near the spot indicated in the diagram and you should be able to do it after a few attempts. Note that at the final rebound by the cue ball off the cushion (at the spot marked with an X), the last angle is much smaller than the others. You'll realize that each table really does react differently. This trick was shown on American television in 1979 during a skills competition between six professionals, and Peter Margo did it on his first attempt.

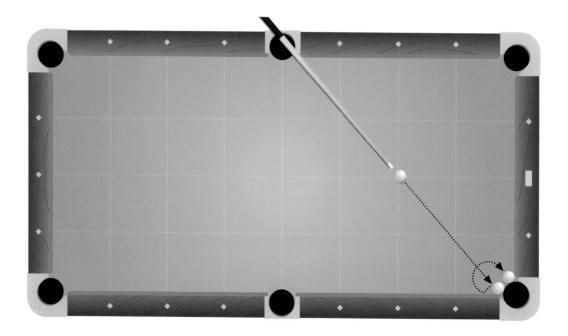

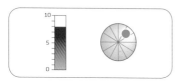

41. THE REVERSE EFFECT

This is probably the shot for which I received the most comments in my career as a pool player, after people saw me perform it during a television commercial for a Canadian brewery. This commercial was broadcast during hockey games at the time when the Quebec Nordiques entered the National Hockey League. I pretended to play a frame of eight-ball and my supposed opponent was flabbergasted to see me play. The unusual behavior of the cue ball always surprises spectators, who find it difficult to believe that a player can apply this kind of reverse motion to it. Strike hard and high at approximately 1:30 and don't aim the ball on the right directly at the center, but slightly to its right. You can do this trick using moderate force, but the harder you shoot, the greater the reverse motion and the more spectacular the trick. This shot is easier to do on a newer, 100% wool cloth. You run the risk of not being able to do it on a worn or low-quality cloth.

42. MACHINE GUN NOISE

Create a row of nine or 10 balls located approximately 2¼ in. (6 cm) from the cushion. To place them the right distance from the cushion, use another ball as a way of measuring the distance. Next, place the 1-ball, 2-ball and 3-ball as shown in the diagram. Aim at the 1-ball by cutting it a little on the side of the 2-ball. Play moderately hard with a lot of spin to the top and the right (2 o'clock). The cue ball will strike the 1-ball, rebound off the 2-ball, then the spin will ensure that it's propelled toward the 8-ball by pushing away, one by one, each of the balls in the row, which will produce a curious noise, like that of a toy machine gun.

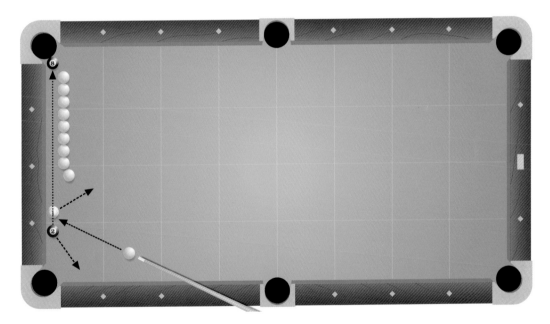

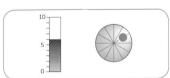

43. FOUR BALLS IN THREE POCKETS

Group four balls in pairs near the space located around the head spot. Align the balls at each end with the corner of the pockets, as shown by the dotted line in the diagram. The two center balls must not be frozen against each other. Play fairly hard and apply a 3:30 spin. This was one of the favorite shots of the legendary Irving Crane, seven-time world champion.

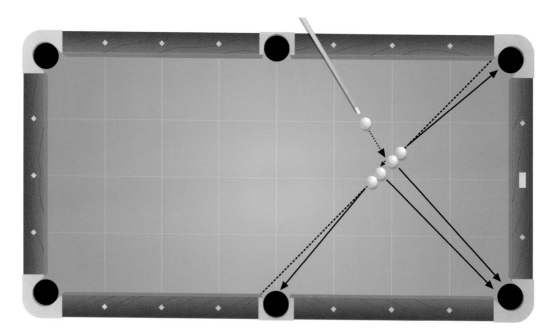

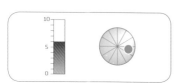

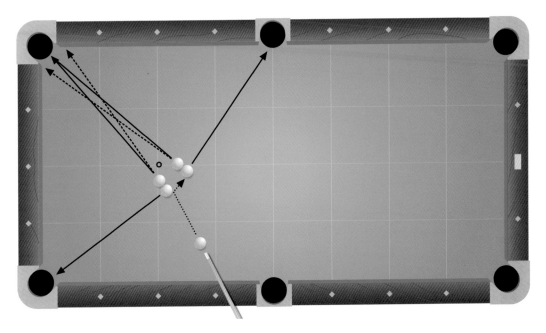

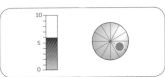

44. DOUBLE COMBINATION I

Place four numbered balls near the head spot, as shown in the illustraton. The two first balls should be 2 in. (5 cm) apart. Take care to line up the last ball in each combination with the opposite corner of the pocket, as shown by the dotted line. Play fairly hard, applying a spin at 4 o'clock and aiming at the first ball on your right. The cue ball, after striking the first combination, will immediately rebound off the other, so that the four balls should each sink into the desired pocket.

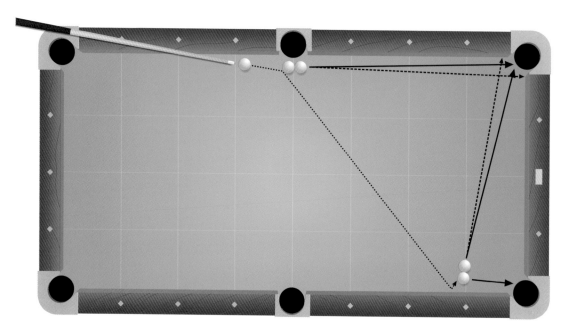

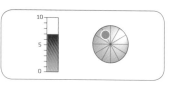

45. DOUBLE COMBINATION II

This shot is more difficult than it appears. It consists of four balls in a double combination. Once again, make every effort to line up the last ball of each combination as shown by the dotted line, for this detail is essential to doing this trick. You should first begin by practicing each combination individually. When you have understood and mastered the principle of each one, it will be easier to do both with one shot. Play fairly hard with an 11 o'clock spin by aiming at the right side of the first ball. The cue ball will continue on its course to hit the second combination after hitting the opposite cushion.

46. TRAY TRICK I

Pool amateurs like to see tricks in which you use tools like the triangle, the rake, the cues, the chalk or any other pool accessory. Here, you'll use the tray. Note that you have to use a tray with a rounded edge, not a sharp edge, as you can see in the inset. All the balls remain in the tray except for the 8-ball and the cue ball. Place the tray perpendicular to the cushions, taking care that box X is opposite the head spot. Place the cue ball as indicated in the diagram and aim at a point near the second-last diamond on the opposite rail, applying a 4 o'clock spin. The cue ball will strike three cushions, rebound off the tray and end its path at the 8-ball, opposite the center. Note the curve followed by the cue ball after rebounding off the tray. This is a really spectacular and easy trick to do.

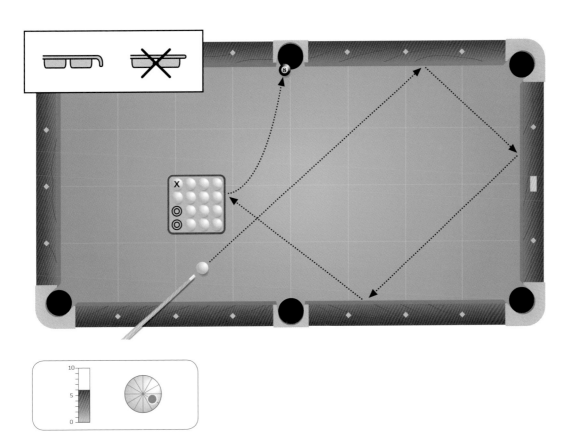

47. TRAY TRICK II

This is a trick similar to the previous one where you use a tray. Once again, all the balls must be left in the tray except for the 8-ball and the cue ball. This time, however, the tray is not quite in the same spot, since box X, opposite the head spot, is placed in exactly the reverse of box X in the previous trick. Once again, play hard and aim at a point near the second-last diamond on the opposite cushion, applying a 4 o'clock spin. The cue ball will hit three cushions, rebound off the tray, strike the opposite cushion near the center and finally hit the 8-ball, which will fall into the pocket. It's another spectacular and relatively easy trick to do.

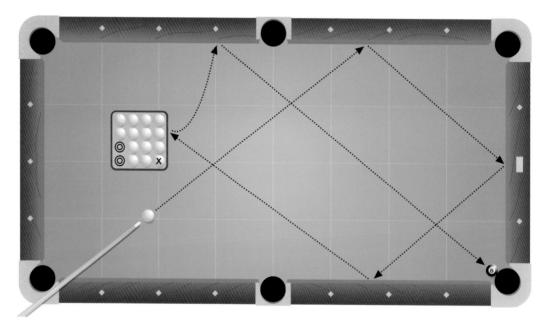

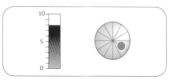

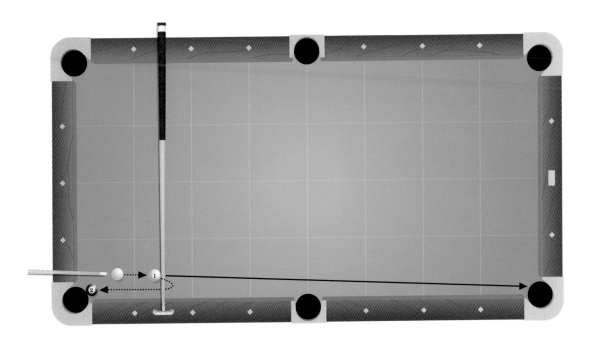

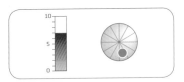

48. OVER THE RAKE

Place the rake on the table so that the head is resting on top of the cushion, near the last diamond. Next, place the 1-ball on the table, near the rake, as shown in the illustration. The cue ball must be placed near the 1-ball, which is lined up directly with the pocket at the other end. Raise the butt of your cue and apply a 5:30 spin. Play fairly hard. The 1-ball will be pocketed at the other end. At the same time, when the cue ball hits the 1-ball, it will jump over the rake and fall back onto the table, while the backspin will ensure that the cue ball reverses to pocket the 2-ball. This trick is very difficult to do. In addition, you risk damaging the tip of your cue, as I've done in the past. You'll

also notice a little white spot on the cloth near the location where the cue ball was sitting when it was struck: this means the cloth has thinned in this spot.

During a show he gave in the moments before the final frame of the world pool tournament (14.1) in New York in 1981, the professional Lou Butera did this spectacular trick on his second attempt. Moreover, in 1974, the Canadian Sports Hall of Fame published an impressive book entitled *Great Canadian Athletes*, and one whole page was devoted to Georges Chénier, who is photographed doing this trick.

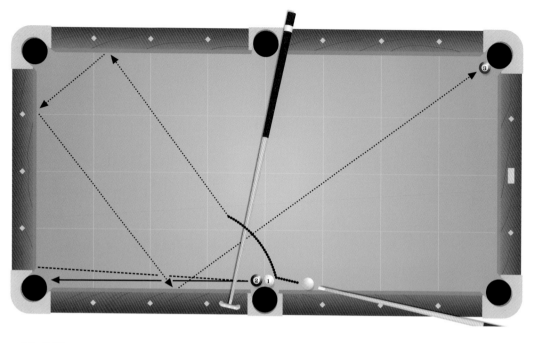

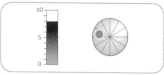

49. OBSTACLE COURSE

This trick is somewhat similar to trick no. 48, in the sense that the cue ball jumps over the rake to pocket the 3-ball after hitting three cushions. First, ensure that the 1-ball and the 2-ball are frozen against each other near the center pocket. The head of the rake rests on top of the cushion, almost between the center pocket and the closest diamond, so that there's enough space underneath to allow the 2-ball to pass. The 2-ball is not directly lined up with the pocket, but rather with the corner, as shown by the dotted line. Since the 1-ball will be struck on the right side, the 2-ball will deflect slightly toward the corner pocket.

To make the cue ball jump over the rake, just raise the butt of the cue when you make your shot. Aim at the right-side of the 1-ball, applying a left sidespin to the cue ball and playing fairly hard. The 1-ball will be the first one pocketed in the center; the 2-ball will travel along the cushion to end up in the corner. When the cue ball contacts the 1-ball, it will bounce over the rake and follow the trajectory indicated in the diagram. Be patient and note the spot where the cue ball is placed at the start. It's worth it to learn this trick to impress your friends.

50. COMPLICATED ROUTE

Take care to place the balls exactly as shown in the diagram. Aim so that the cue ball strikes the 1-ball right in the center and play hard with a lot of 11 o'clock spin. The 1-ball will move away, while the cue ball, propelled by the topspin, will strike the 2-ball. While this is happening, the 1-ball will travel a complicated route during which it will strike three cushions before ending up in the same pocket as the 2-ball. This trick is difficult to do, for you have to test the cushions multiple times, particularly as the elasticity of the cushions isn't the same from table to table. In addition, there's the risk that the cue ball will block the path of the 1-ball. Before attempting this trick, you should ask the spectators to allow you several attempts so that you can succeed.

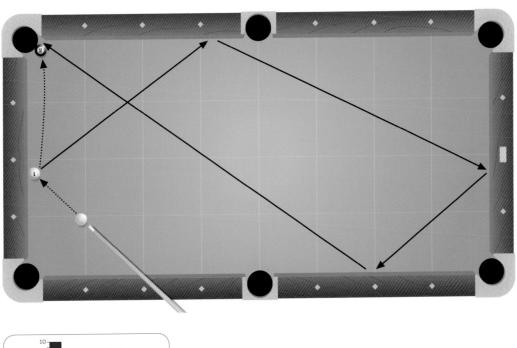

51. SPECTACULAR DOUBLE KISS

After organizing the balls in the shape of a pyramid, move the three top balls and position them as shown in the diagram, so that the 8-ball is in the middle of the three. Announce to the spectators that you're going to pocket the 8-ball in the corner at the other end. All you have to do is play hard against the first ball. The 8-ball, after a double kiss against the pack and the opposite ball, will come to rest in the pocket located diagonally opposite, at the other end.

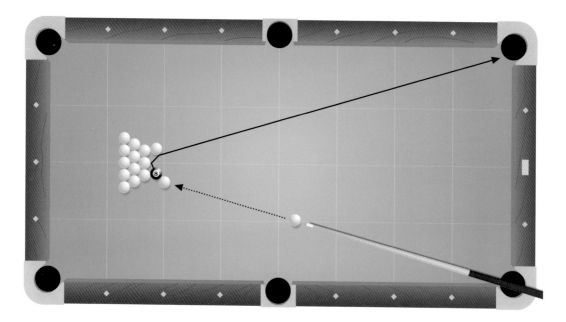

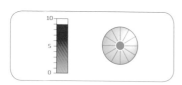

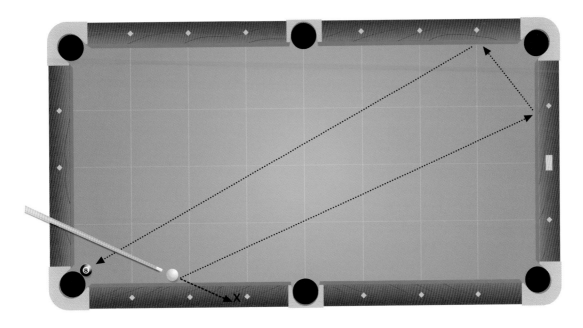

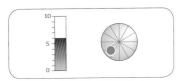

52. THE 8-BALL OFF TWO CUSHIONS

Place the 8-ball on the edge of the corner pocket and freeze the cue ball against the cushion almost opposite the second diamond. Play, applying a lot of 7:30 spin, and aim at the X (see the diagram). The cue ball should strike the two cushions and come back to pocket the 8-ball in the corner. This trick will require a few practice shots, especially if you're not playing on your usual table.

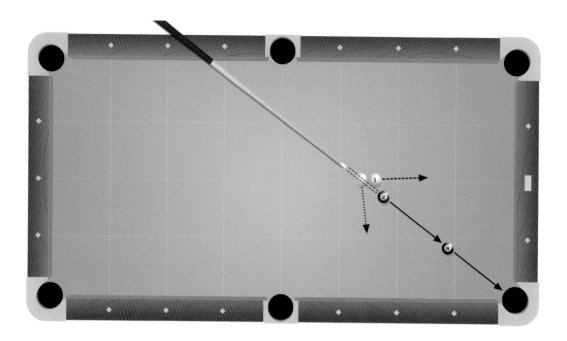

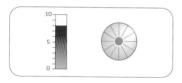

53. THE HAND IS QUICKER THAN THE EYE

This trick was chosen by a participant during the final of a trick world championship broadcast on television in the early 2000s, and he won, since his opponent couldn't do it, although he had the right to try it twice! It's truly incredible when you realize how easy this trick is. Line up the following three balls: the cue ball, the 2-ball and the 8-ball. Ensure that they're perfectly aligned, for doing this trick depends on the precise positioning of the balls at the beginning. Next, place the 1-ball between the cue ball and the 2-ball, but slightly back, to create an obstacle that makes any combination shot impossible. It's possible, however, to pocket the 8-ball in the corner! The secret: place the cue as shown in the illustration

and try to forget about the cue ball and the 1-ball by not looking at them. Hold your cue firmly and play as if these two balls don't exist. Of course, the cue will hit the cue ball as it passes. The cue ball and the 1-ball will each travel along their own side and remove themselves, as shown in the diagram. At the same time, your cue will follow through and strike the 2-ball, which will then be propelled against the 8-ball. The trick is played and the 8-ball is in the pocket. To do this trick in a spectacular way and so the spectators don't see the deception, you have to play fast and hard. When it's done well, it's impossible for an uninformed spectator to understand the trick.

The 1-ball, 2-ball, 3-ball and 4-ball are placed on the edge of two corner pockets. Former world champion James Caras recommends playing this shot by applying a spin high and to the right, while Eddie Parker, a tricks and fancy shots specialist, recommends instead applying a spin high and to the left. Personally, I think this trick is easier to do by applying an 11 o'clock spin. Take care not to raise the butt of your cue, but hold it horizontally. Contrary to what you might think, you don't need to play hard, a moderately hard shot is enough. At any rate, if the curve is too pronounced, play more gently, and vice versa.

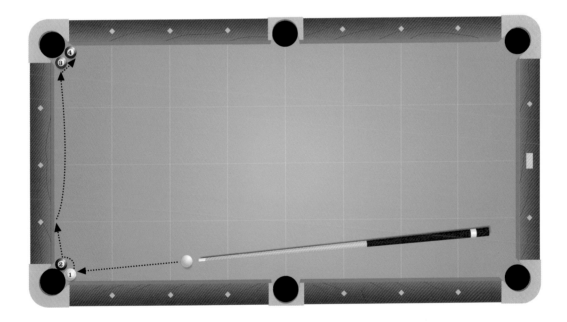

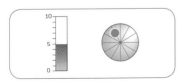

55. FOUR BALLS IN FOUR POCKETS

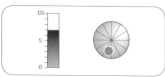

Place all the balls as shown in the diagram. Play with a backspin on the 1-ball by aiming slightly to the left, almost in the center, so that the cue ball reverses to pocket the 4-ball. The 1-ball will push the 3-ball into the opposite corner pocket, the 2-ball will be pocketed in the center, and the 1-ball will come to rest in the pocket at the other end, as shown in the diagram. Compare this trick with trick no. 6: you'll realize that there's some similarity between them, for in both instances, there's a double kiss.

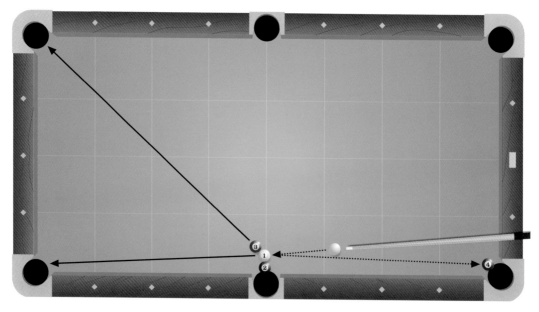

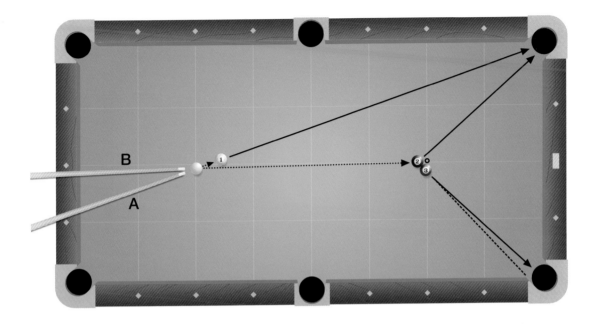

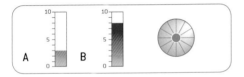

56. THREE BALLS IN TWO SHOTS

Place the 2-ball in front of the head spot and freeze the 3-ball to it by lining it up with the corner of the pocket, as indicated by the dotted line. Then, place the 1-ball at the other end, in the middle of the table, by lining it up directly with the corner pocket, relative to the cue ball. Announce to the spectators that you're going to pocket the 2-ball and the 3-ball first, then the 1-ball, by emphasizing that you'll first play the 1-ball. Then, send the 1-ball toward its pocket gently by striking slightly below center of the cue ball so that it stops immediately after striking the 1-ball. Next, hurry to play hard, striking right in the center of the 2-ball. The 2-ball and the 3-ball will come to a rest in their respective pockets, and the 1-ball will immediately follow the 2-ball.

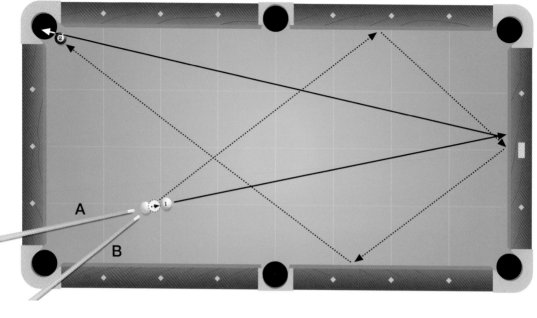

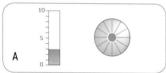

A

B

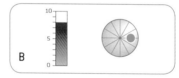

A

B

57. TWO BALLS IN TWO SHOTS

Once again, this is a double play that requires a lot of accuracy. This type of shot is referred to as a timing shot. In fact, you'll have to synchronize things perfectly. Place the balls as shown in the diagram so that the 1-ball is directly lined up for a cross-table shot into the opposite corner. The trick involves opening up a path for the 1-ball by removing the 2-ball before the 1-ball gets there. Play the 1-ball gently in order to stop the cue ball

on the first shot. As soon as the first shot is made, hurry to play again against the cue ball by aiming almost at the diamond in the center of the opposite cushion, applying a 4 o'clock spin. The cue ball will strike three cushions and pocket the 2-ball. The 1-ball will immediately follow and be pocketed in the same pocket. This isn't the easiest trick to do.

58. HOW DO WE GET OUT OF THIS?

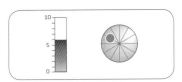

After organizing the 15 balls in the shape of a triangle, remove the first ball and place it behind the pyramid, as shown in the diagram, taking care to freeze it between the second and third balls. Then, place the cue ball on the head spot at the other end, exactly halfway between the two cushions. Ask the spectators if they think it's possible to pocket ball X in the right corner pocket.

The secret: play a "two-cushion" shot first. Aim at a point close to the diamond in the center and apply a 10 o'clock spin. Naturally, this trick requires a few attempts in order to find the precise point to aim at on the cushion and also the right spin to use, for each table has cushions that rebound differently.

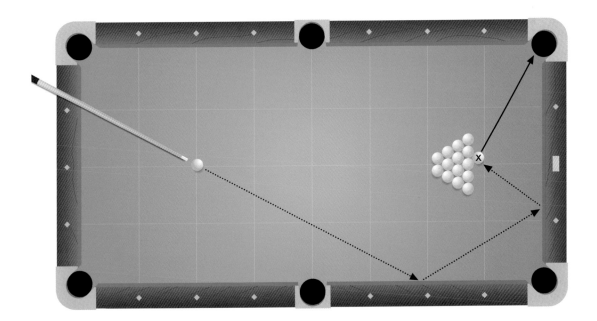

59. CAN YOU GET AROUND THIS OBSTACLE?

Normally, it would be impossible to hit the 1-ball and the 2-ball with a single shot, for the two other balls frozen along the cushion appear to be blocking the path. However, it's possible to get around this obstacle and pocket the 1-ball and the 2-ball in a spectacular way. Play moderately hard and high, with a 1 o'clock spin. The cue ball should strike the 1-ball at approximately 75% on the right side, then will appear to rebound by moving away, but the spin applied with the shot will ensure that the trajectory follows a curve and the cue ball returns to pocket the 2-ball. This trick is difficult to master, but it's worth the trouble to practice it, for it's very impressive.

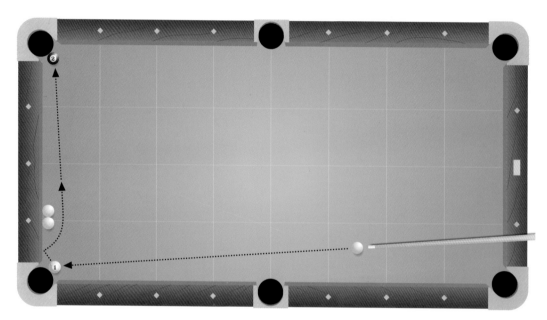

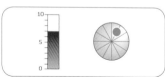

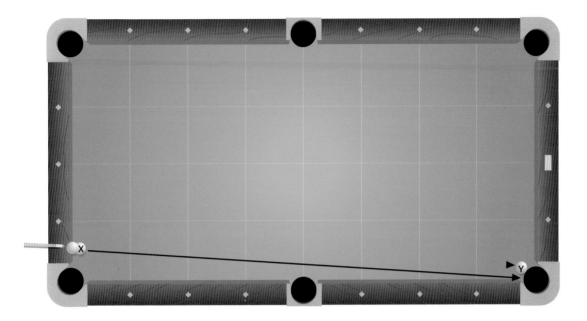

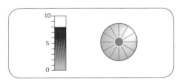

60. THE JUMPING SHEEP PLAY

This is actually a pure trick, for this situation will never occur during a regular game. To start, place the cue ball on top of the cushion, leaning against ball X. If the cloth is brand new, it will take a lot of patience to be able to hold the cue ball in this position. Tell the spectators that you're going to attempt to shoot the two balls by specifying that the Y-ball will be pocketed first. Strike right in the center of the cue ball by aiming at the center of the Y-ball. The cue ball will jump over the X-ball and hit the Y-ball. At the same time, the X-ball will be in motion and follow the Y-ball into the same pocket.

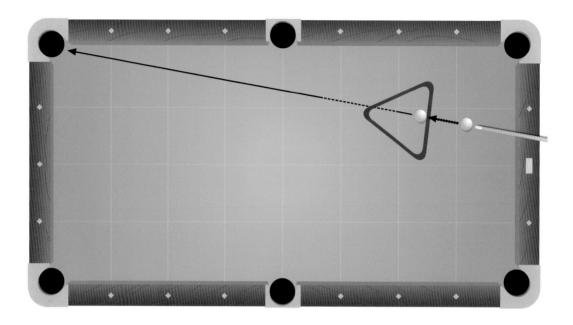

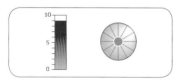

61. A LEAP OUTSIDE THE TRIANGLE

During a television broadcast recorded on February 14, 1978, in the ballroom of the Waldorf Astoria Hotel in New York for ABC (Wide World of Sports), seven-time world champion Irving Crane performed this impressive trick. It was also one of the favorite tricks of Canadian champion Georges Chénier.

Place the numbered ball inside the triangle as shown in the illustration. You will need to use a plastic triangle, which has sides that are thinner than those of a wooden triangle. Raise the butt of your cue and strike the cue ball right in the center. Play hard, aiming to pocket the ball in the opposite corner. The cue ball will rebound over the side of the triangle and hit the top of the numbered ball, which will then leave the triangle and come to rest in the designated pocket. It's a difficult trick that requires a lot of skill. In addition, this shot is hard on the equipment, as much on the tip of your cue as on the cloth of the table.

In this trick and in trick no. 63, the 8-ball, 9-ball and 10-ball are placed in the same position at the start. However, the goal of one is diametrically opposed to the goal of the other. In this case, you have to ensure that only the 8-ball is pocketed. At first glance, it seems inevitable that all three balls will be pocketed. By following the instructions to the letter, you'll be able to pocket the 8-ball only. The cue ball is placed at an angle relative to the 9-ball. The key to success lies in the way the shot is executed. You don't have to do any preparatory back-and-forth motions. On the contrary, press your cue directly against the cue ball, prepare to apply a 9 o'clock spin at the angle indicated in the illustration, then push. The mechanism of the spin, explained in the first part of this book, will ensure that the 9-ball and the 10-ball move away, while the 8-ball travels along the cushion and comes to rest in the pocket. To do this trick, the table must be level.

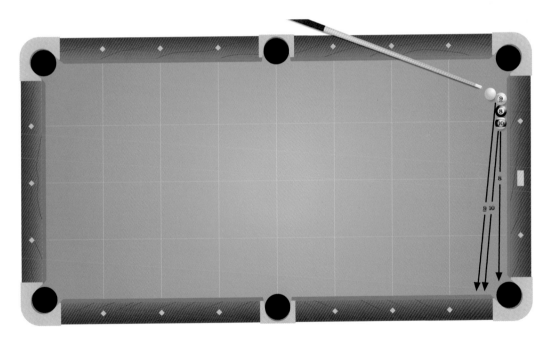

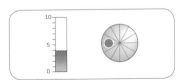

63. THINGS ALWAYS COME IN THREES

You know the expression, "things always come in threes." The goal of this trick is precisely to show that this expression isn't always true. Contrary to trick no. 62, announce that you're going to pocket the 9-ball and the 10-ball, but not the 8-ball. As in trick no. 62, press your cue against the cue ball, prepare to apply a 2 o'clock spin, then push. The 9-ball and the 10-ball will be pocketed, while the cue ball and the 8-ball will move away slightly and remain on the table.

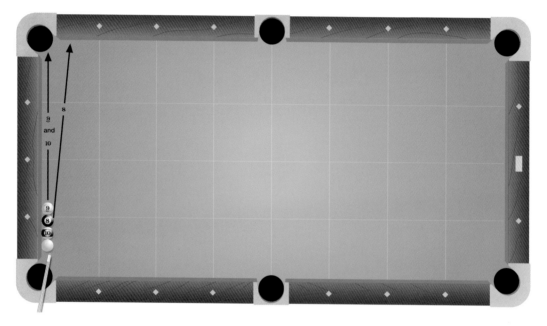

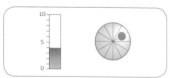

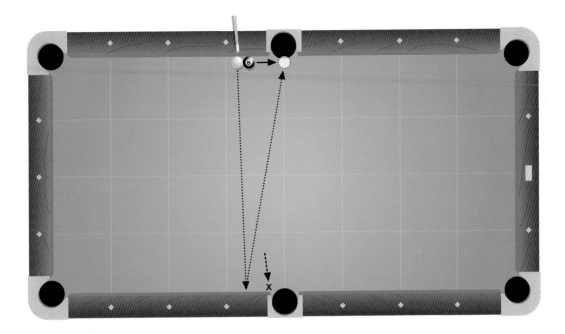

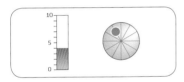

64. DOUBLE IMPACT AGAINST THE 8-BALL

Take great care that the cue ball and the 8-ball are frozen against each other as well as against the cushion. Aim in the direction of the arrow marked with an X, apply an 11 o'clock spin and raise the butt of your cue slightly (approximately 10°). The 8-ball will be moved aside toward the center pocket, while the cue ball will rebound off the opposite cushion and return to hit the 8-ball as it passes in front of the center pocket. You may need to try this a few times before determining the necessary force and spin, but once you have things synchronized, you'll feel a great deal of satisfaction on seeing the 8-ball disappear into the center pocket.

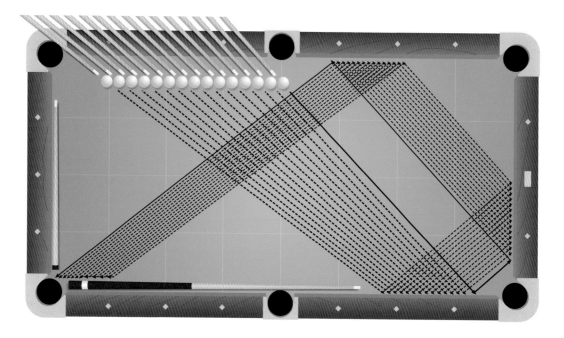

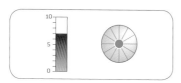

65. MONSTER TRAFFIC JAM

This trick always produces a spectacular effect, even though it's actually easier to do than it appears. Place two cues on the table, the two butts meeting near the same corner, but leave enough space for the balls to pass through. Align all 15 balls in a row approximately 4 in. (10 cm) from the cushion, as shown in the illustration. The idea is to pocket all the balls nonstop in the opposite pocket after touching three cushions. Start with the one that is closest to the center pocket. The attraction of this trick lies in the way the balls cross over in the center of the table.

You'll have to concentrate fully to find the right rhythm and demonstrate that things are smoothly synchronized. To avoid a miscue, strike the balls right in the center and turn your cue before each shot. Of course, on a regular table, you'll be able to strike roughly seven or eight balls only, for the pocket will then be full. It's better to do this trick on a table that has an internal ball-return gutter, i.e. a table that has bottomless pockets, as on commercial tables. The balls move to the inside of the table so that the pocket is never full.

66. FOUR BALLS IN THREE POCKETS

Freeze the 1-ball, 2-ball and 3-ball opposite the center pocket and place the cue ball right in the center of the table. Play fairly hard, with an 8 o'clock spin, while aiming at the left side of the 1-ball. The 2-ball and the 3-ball will disappear into the center pocket, while the 1-ball, kissing off the 2-ball, will be pocketed in the corner indicated in the diagram. During this time, the cue ball will be projected toward the 4-ball. This trick is really easy to do. Don't hesitate to try it in front of your friends, for your chances of succeeding are very high.

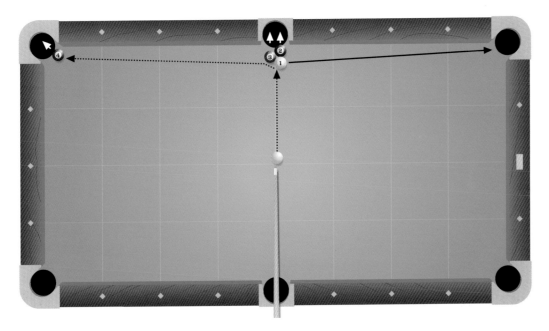

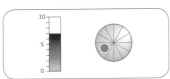

67. MAKE THE CUE BALL DANCE

This game, played with four balls, of which three are near the center at the start, is similar to trick no. 73. The difference is twofold. First, the 1-ball and the 2-ball are positioned differently, so try to place them as shown in the illustration. The second difference is the way the cue is used to do the shot. Apply a 1:30 spin and play hard while aiming fully at the right side of the 1-ball. In fact, you must cut fairly closely. The 2-ball will be the first one pocketed in the center, while the 1-ball will roll along the cushion and end up in the left corner pocket at the foot of the table. At the same time, the cue ball will kiss off the 3-ball, then rebound, with force, one or two times off the cushion toward the 4-ball. The attraction of this trick lies in the erratic trajectory of the cue ball, which will do a few "dance steps" off the cushion after hitting the 3-ball.

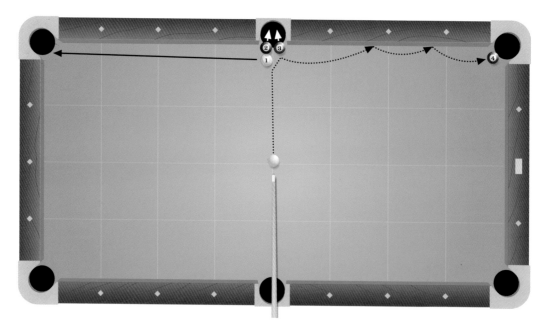

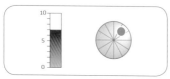

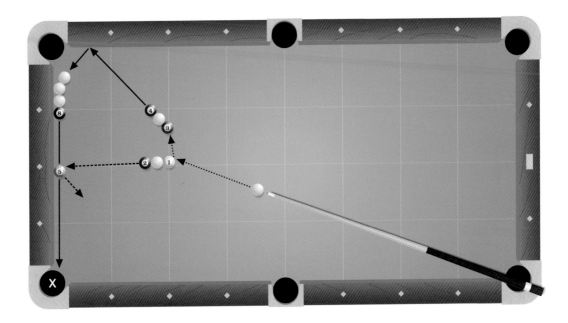

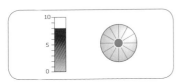

68. DELAYED COMBINATION SHOT

The point here is to pocket the 8-ball in the pocket marked with an X. Of course, you'll first have to ensure that the trajectory of the 8-ball is clear by moving the 5-ball out of the way. Play hard and aim at the right side of the 1-ball. The 2-ball will be the first one put in motion, and it will immediately strike the 5-ball, which will move away in turn. At almost the same moment, the cue ball will continue on its course and hit the 3-ball … You can easily guess the rest. The happy ending should be that the 8-ball comes to a rest in the designated pocket. The secret to doing this trick is to ensure that the row of the first three balls is hit with more force than the other three balls, which you'll be able to do by not cutting the 1-ball too much, but just enough.

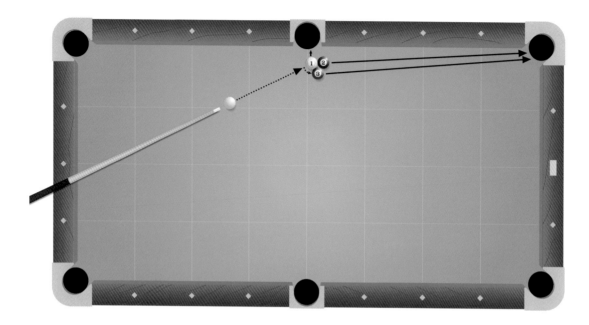

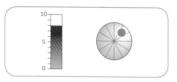

69. THREE BALLS IN TWO POCKETS I

As you place the balls as indicated in the diagram, take care to moisten the point of contact between the 1-ball and the 2-ball. Play fairly hard with a 1:30 spin, while striking the right side of the 1-ball. You'll have to aim almost in the middle between the 1-ball and the 3-ball, but it's essential that the cue ball touch the 1-ball first. The cue ball will rebound immediately off the 3-ball. The 1-ball will be pocketed in the center, while the 2-ball and the 3-ball will drop into the corner pocket.

70. THREE BALLS IN TWO POCKETS II

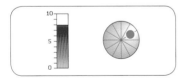

This trick closely resembles the previous one, although it's easier to do. Position the balls as shown in the diagram and play fairly hard with a 2 o'clock spin, while aiming at the left side of the 4-ball. The 4-ball will ricochet off the 5-ball and the 6-ball and drop into the opposite corner pocket. The 5-ball will be projected directly into the pocket located nearby. At the same time, the cue ball will rebound off the 6-ball, which will also be pocketed in the same corner.

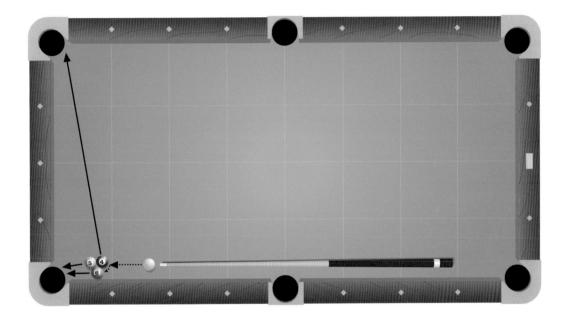

Here's a situation in which you may sometimes find yourself during a game, where the cue ball, whose path is blocked by the corner of the pocket, has no direct access to the 8-ball. However, there are several ways to get out of this impasse. For shot A, you simply aim at the cushion farthest away, almost in the center or slightly to the right of center. Shot B consists of a relatively easy "three-cushion" shot. This shot comes up fairly often during regular games and is used to perform several tricks, so practice it often and learn to master it. Shot C is the most difficult of the four. It is a massé, a shot for which you must raise the butt of your cue almost vertically and aim at the right of the cue ball from above, which will then follow a curve in the direction of the 8-ball. Shot D is the most unusual and therefore the most spectacular. Play the cue ball right against the tip of the opposite cushion and it will rebound while traveling along the cushion. Finally, there are other ways of pocketing the 8-ball in this kind of situation: try to discover them yourself.

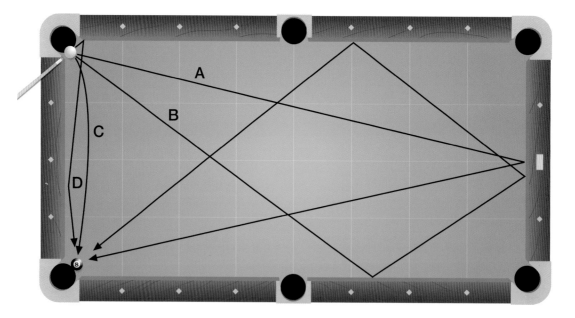

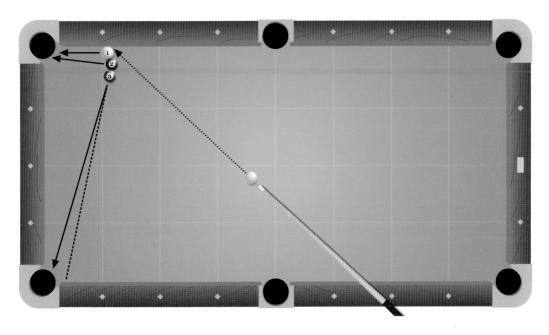

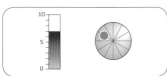

72. A FUNNY TRIO

This trick is one of the easiest in this book, so memorize it and don't hesitate to try it in front of your friends.

Place the three balls as shown in the diagram. The 1-ball is frozen against the cushion, almost opposite the first diamond. The 3-ball is not directly aligned with the opposite corner pocket, but slightly to the side, as shown by the dotted line. Strike the cue ball fairly hard with a 10:30 spin. Aim as if the 2-ball and the 3-ball weren't on the table and as if you wanted to pocket the 1-ball only in the nearest pocket. The two other balls will then be pocketed automatically.

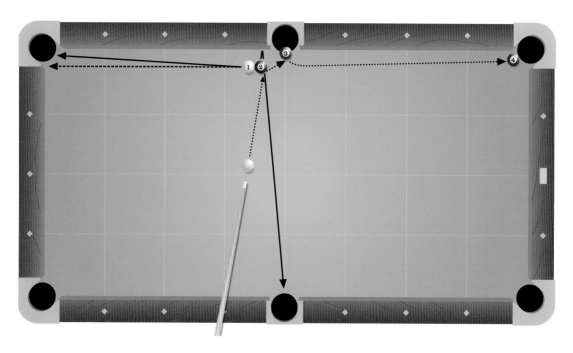

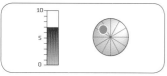

73. FOUR BALLS IN ONE SHOT

This trick and the following one were useful during a commercial simulating a frame of eight-ball. This commercial for a Canadian brewery was shown often on television in 1979. The producers gave me free rein as to the type of plays, specifying nonetheless that I had 17 seconds to end the frame while using as many spectacular shots as possible. At my first appearance at the table

during this frame, after the break, I pocketed four balls with one shot. The 1-ball and 2-ball were frozen parallel to the cushion, so that the 1-ball wasn't lined up directly with the corner pocket, but very closely, as shown in the illustration. Play fairly hard with a 10:30 spin on the cue ball and aim at the right side of the 2-ball. The cue ball strikes the 2-ball, rebounds off the 3-ball and then follows a curve to pocket the 4-ball.

74. FIVE-CUSHION SHOT I

This is the spectacular shot that ended my frame of eight-ball in the famous commercial for O'Keefe. When I designed this five-cushion shot a number of years ago, I was very proud of myself, for I thought I had discovered something truly original. Approximately five years later, I learned that Willie Mosconi had performed such a shot during the final of the world championship in 1946; moreover, it was a shot that allowed him to win against Andrew Ponzi. This fact demonstrates how much Mosconi had an instinct for pool. Place the balls as shown in the diagram and aim diagonally at a point near the last diamond. Depending on the type of table on which you'll be playing, you'll have to apply a 6 o'clock or maybe a 5:30 spin. The trick may even be impossible to do if the cushions are stiff. At any rate, you'll need to do a few practice shots before finding the right place to aim and the right spin to apply.

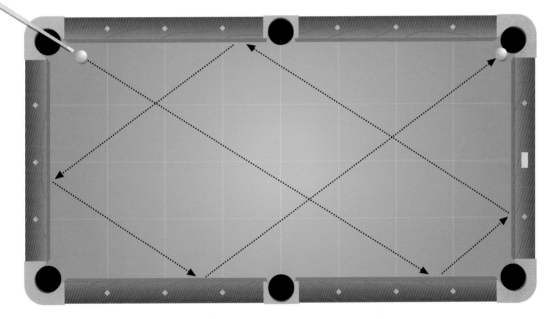

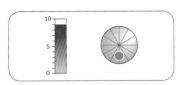

There are a number of options for playing shots off a cushion or several cushions on a pool table. For example, refer to the previous trick. Here's another five-cushion shot that is just as spectacular and perhaps easier to do. Place the cue ball near the head string, approximately 10 in. (25 cm) from the cushion. Aim at the first diamond on the other side of the center pocket while applying a lot of right spin, i.e. a 3:30. Play hard. As with all tricks off a cushion, it will probably take several attempts to do. Don't get discouraged. Persevere, for this shot is easier than it looks.

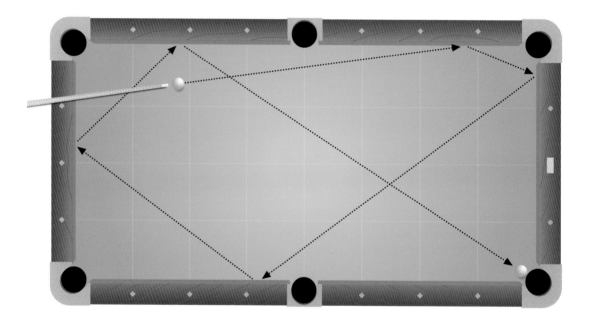

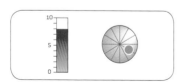

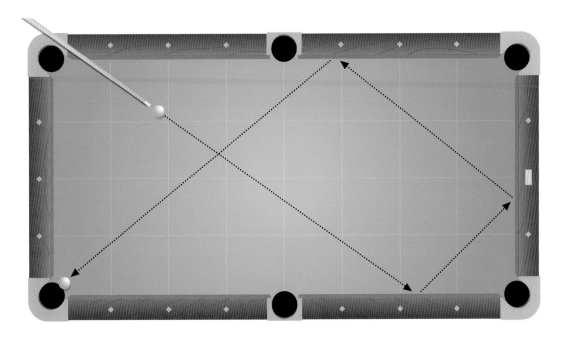

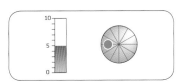

76. THREE-CUSHION SHOT

Here's a trick that any pool amateur with the slightest self-respect ought to know. It's a shot that sometimes arises in pool games, and might therefore be useful to help you get out of a situation. In addition, you'll notice (if you haven't already) that this shot is the basis for several tricks shown in this book. You owe it to yourself

to know it, but also to master it. Play diagonally by aiming almost at the center diamond of the opposite cushion while applying a natural spin, i.e. a spin to the left in this instance. This play is fairly easy to master and can be performed even on a lower-quality table.

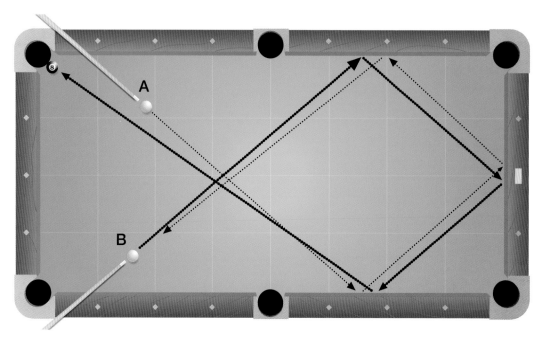

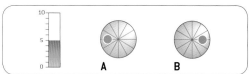

77. SIX-CUSHION SHOT

Is it really possible to pocket a ball off six cushions on a pool table? As incredible as this may seem, the answer is yes. In reality, this play is divided into two steps. In fact, it's a return to trick no. 76, performed two times in one go. You start on the left side of the table as in the previous trick, but as soon as you make your shot, you rush to the other side of the table (the right side), opposite the cue ball, which is coming back toward you after hitting three cushions. The cue ball goes into the right corner at the same time as you, and you'll have to hurry to strike it while it's still moving. This time, apply a right spin and the cue ball will repeat the same trajectory, but in reverse, to pocket the ball waiting at the edge of the left corner pocket.

78. FOUR-CUSHION SHOT

After shooting three-cushion, five-cushion and even six-cushion shots, you're certainly ready for a 4-cushion shot. In fact, this play is a brilliant demonstration of the many possibilities of a sidespin: notice in particular the rebound angle of the cue ball after it hits the first cushion. This deflection is possible only if you apply a lot of left spin to the cue ball. Here is the secret of this trick: play fairly hard with a 9 o'clock spin. How-ever, you might not apply enough spin. If this happens, play your shot, making the following changes to your preparation: raise the butt of the cue until the angle is 30° relative to the horizontal plane of the table. This shows that the intensity of the spin doesn't depend solely on the point of attack against the cue ball, but also on the way you strike with your cue.

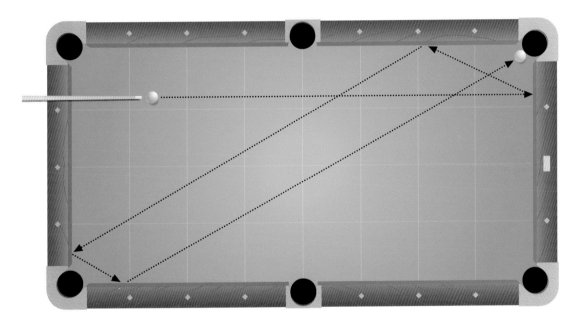

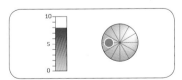

This trick isn't new: it was already done in the 1940s. Willie Jopling reports that world champion Willie Hoppe performed this shot in front of 200 disbelieving scientists at the University of Michigan in 1947. Play hard with a slight 4:30 spin. You'll realize the most difficult part of this trick is to ensure that the cue ball doesn't jump off the table because of the force of the strike. The goal of this trick isn't to pocket ball X, but only to touch it, which is still a remarkable feat. This shot cannot be done on a slower cloth. Mike Massey sug-gests placing a bank note to mark the spot where the ball is supposed to stop, and it if stops there, the trick is even more dramatic! As we saw in the introduction to this part, Larry Grindinger claims to have already done an 11-cushion touch, which appeared in Ripley's *Believe It or Not*. One thing is sure: he had to have done this incredible shot on an exceptionally fast table. Personally, I have not yet seen a table where you can do a touch off more than nine cushions.

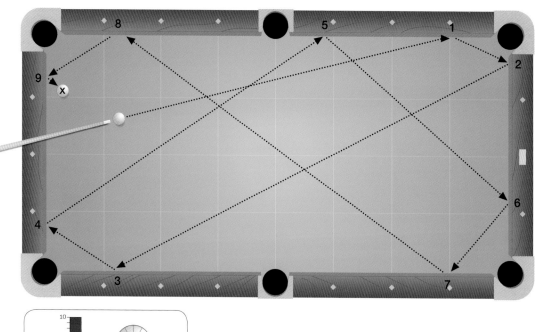

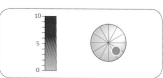

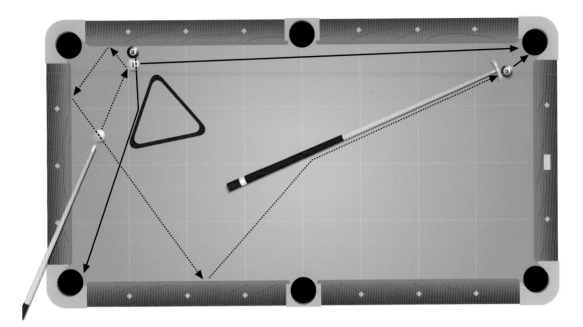

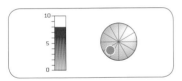

80. TRIANGLE AND RAKE

This trick is especially original, for you use a triangle and a rake to shoot three balls. American Willie Jopling claims to have invented this dramatic shot.

First, freeze the 1-ball and the 2-ball perpendicular to the cushion, almost opposite the first diamond. Next, place the triangle flat on the table so that one of its sides is aligned with the right corner pocket, as shown at the bottom of the diagram. Then, place the rake diagonally so that the head of the rake is near the corner pocket, but leave enough space along the cushion so that the 1-ball can pass through. The 3-ball must be placed very carefully to the right of the head of the rake without touching it, which is critical to performing this shot. Play hard with a 7:30 spin off the cue ball while aiming at the left side of the 1-ball. The 1-ball will travel along the cushion and end up at the pocket in the upper left corner. The 2-ball will rebound perpendicular to the cushion and strike the triangle before rolling into the pocket in the lower right corner. The cue ball will strike three cushions, return to hit the rake, then travel along it right up to the head. The 3-ball will then be projected into the same pocket as the 1-ball.

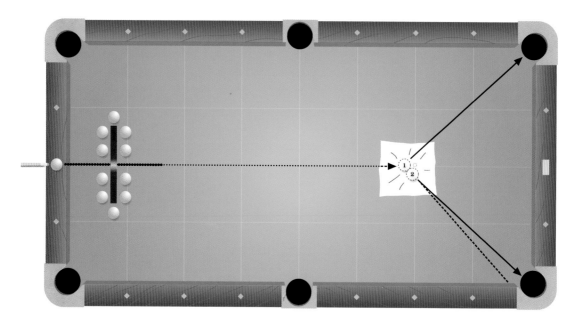

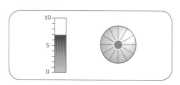

81. A MAGIC TRICK

The magical nature of this trick lies in the fact that you cover the 1-ball and the 2-ball with a paper tissue before making your shot. Place the 1-ball in front of the head spot and freeze the 2-ball there by aligning it with the corner of the pocket, using trick no. 56 as your guide, the trick in which the two balls were positioned in the same manner. Then, stand the triangle upright on one of its sides at the other end of the table at a distance roughly 8–10 in. (20–25 cm) from the cushion. Next, surround the triangle with several balls and, lastly, cover the 1-ball and the 2-ball with paper tissue, taking care not to move them. Announce to your spectators that you're going to attempt to pocket the 1-ball and the 2-ball in a single shot starting from "somewhere behind the triangle." After waiting a few seconds, place the chalk cube upside down on the rail opposite the triangle (see trick no. 38, page 185) and carefully place the cue ball there. Play fairly hard against the cue ball, which will bounce through the triangle and strike the 1-ball. The 1-ball and the 2-ball will be pocketed automatically. By adding a few details to this play, which is simple in itself, you can turn it into a dramatic trick.

82. WHICH ONE WILL DROP FIRST?

This trick is inspired in part by the previous trick, especially with respect to the way the balls are placed on the head spot. The 1-ball and the 2-ball, are frozen on each side of the cue ball and placed slightly ahead of the two center pockets, while lined up with the tip of each center pocket, as shown by the dotted lines. Play fairly hard while applying a 6 o'clock spin and aim at the 3-ball. The 1-ball and the 2-ball will be pocketed in the center, and the 3-ball and the 4-ball will be directed toward their respective corners. This was one of Minnesota Fats' favorite tricks.

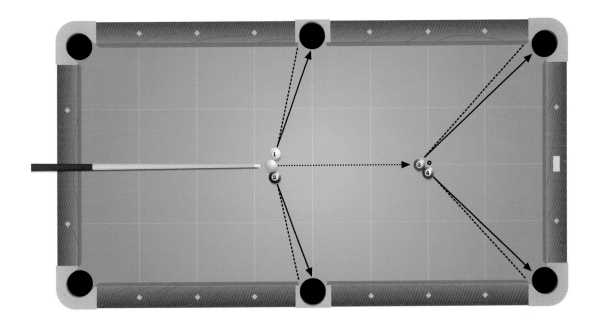

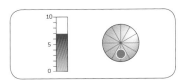

83. THE DISAPPEARING ROW
OF FOUR BALLS

This trick is probably as old as pool tables. Place the four balls in a straight row by positioning the 1-ball very close to the pocket and lining up the other balls with the other center pocket. It's important that the balls are all frozen one against the other. Play hard, while aiming first at the 3-ball, so that the cue ball rebounds immediately off the 2-ball. Apply a 4 o'clock spin.

The 3-ball will move first and, because of the backspin transmitted by the cue ball (see the explanation of how spin works, page 60), it will rebound slightly to the left in the direction of the left corner pocket. The 3-ball is the most difficult to pocket. The three other balls will be pocketed as shown by the arrows in the diagram.

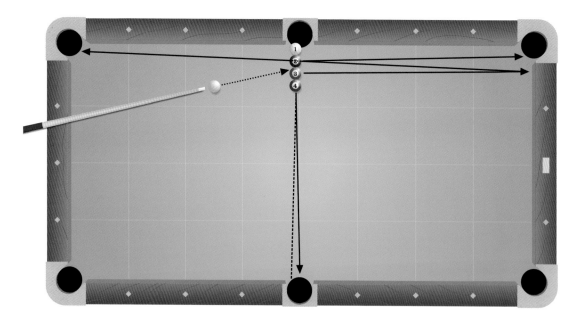

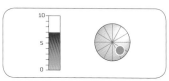

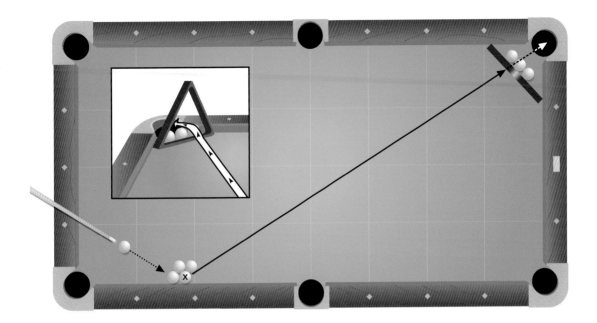

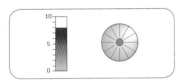

84. TRIANGLE AND SPRINGBOARD

Place three balls near the corner pocket. Next, lay the triangle on its side, opposite the same pocket, its points touching the two cushions. At the other end, near the second diamond, freeze four balls along the cushion at the approximate location indicated in the diagram. You might need to move them forward slightly before finding the spot where the shot becomes possible. Announce to your friends that you're going to attempt to shoot ball X into the opposite corner despite the block. Play hard with no spin, while aiming directly at the first ball. Ball X will be projected toward the

designated pocket, and the base of the triangle will serve as a springboard to help it jump over the three balls and drop right into the pocket. A wooden triangle is better than a plastic one.

Remember that the way balls rebound off a cushion varies from table to table. Therefore, it's strongly recommended that you practice this trick a few times before trying it in public. This way you'll be able to make the necessary adjustments to find the force needed for the cue and the exact spot to place the balls along the cushion.

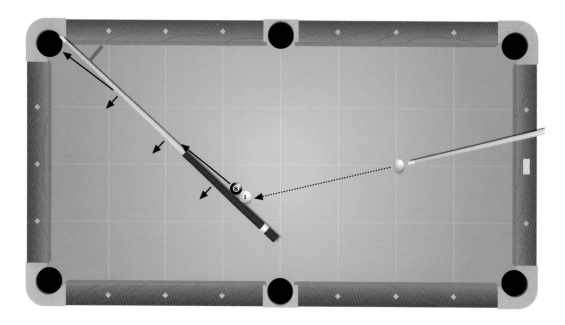

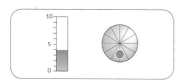

85. IS IT POSSIBLE?

If you're called upon one day to put on a demonstration of tricks in front of several people, it's better to start with a simple shot, a shot that you're sure you can do on the first attempt and one that will give you confidence for the rest of your show. Start with this one.

Place a cue on the table so that the narrowest end is pointing inside the pocket, while the butt is almost in the middle of the table. Freeze the 1-ball and the 8-ball against the butt, as shown in the illustration. Place a cigarette pack near the pocket between the cushion and the cue to serve as an additional obstacle that has to be over-

come. Lastly, place the cue ball on the head spot. Announce to the spectators that you're going to attempt to pocket the 8-ball in the pocket where the cue is, without touching the cigarette pack and without knocking it over. Play fully against the 1-ball, with a 6 o'clock spin, just hard enough so that the backspin will stop the cue ball. The 1-ball will push the cue and the 8-ball at the same time. The cue will roll to the other side of the pocket, thus opening a path for the 8-ball, which will travel along the cue, pass by the cigarette pack and come to a rest in the pocket.

We know that the diameter of a pool ball is 2¼ in. (5.7 cm). Place the 6-ball at a distance of approximately 2 in. (5 cm) from the 7-ball, so that the cue ball doesn't have enough space to pass between the two. In order to show the spectators that the cue ball can't get through, carefully hold it next to the 6-ball and the 7-ball and ask a spectator chosen at random to come and look more closely. When everyone is convinced that the space isn't wide enough, reposition the cue ball approximately 1 ft. (30 cm) from the two

balls. Raise the butt of your cue and play hard. The cue ball will bounce for a fraction of a second and barely pass over the 6-ball and the 7-ball, at a height and a speed such that the jump is imperceptible to those who don't already know this trick. This is what we call a "partial jump," which is described in greater detail in Part 1 (see page 86). It's a perfectly legal shot in a game. If you want your friends to remain surprised, only do the trick once, otherwise they'll quickly discover the deception.

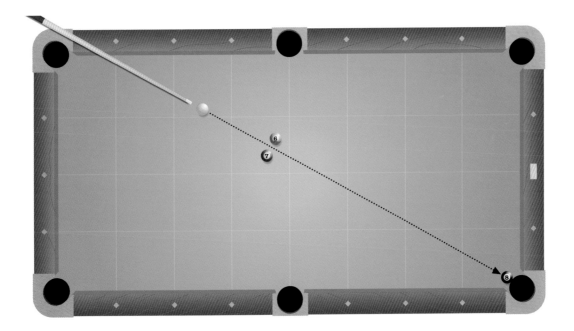

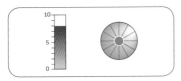

87. THE EVEL KNIEVEL TRICK

When pool professional Alan Hopkins was invited to play against the legendary Mosconi, Minnesota Fats and Steve Mizerak during an American television broadcast, he decided to design a trick that was both dramatic and original.

Create a straight row with 12, 13 or 14 balls frozen against one another in a diagonal line on the table, as shown in the illustration. Place the triangle upright on its side near the center of the table, perpendicular to the row. At the other end of the row, approximately 2–3 in. (5–8 cm) from the last ball, place two chalk cubes one on top of the

other, ensuring that the top one is face up. Carefully perch the 8-ball on top. Then, position the cue ball at the very end, near the pocket.

The secret is to raise the butt of the cue roughly 30°–35° relative to the horizontal plane of the table. Play fairly hard by striking the center and aiming the 8-ball at the pocket indicated. The cue ball will bounce and hit the 8-ball, which will do a perilous jump, like Evel Knievel, over the row of balls, and pass through the triangle to come to a rest in the pocket at the other end.

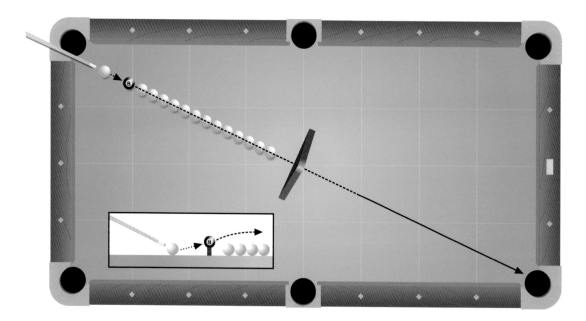

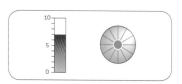

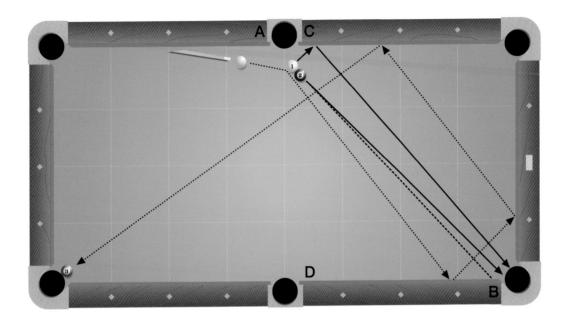

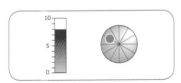

88. THE BUSY INTERSECTION

As this trick needs to be carefully prepared, I indicated some reference points to guide you when placing the balls. The first ball to place is the 2-ball. To find its exact position, draw an imaginary line between corner A and corner B, then another imaginary line between corner C and corner D. The 2-ball must be placed where these two lines intersect near the left center pocket. Then, as you did with the 2-ball, freeze the 1-ball so that the combination is not lined up directly with the opposite pocket, but rather with the corner (B) of this pocket, as shown by the dotted line. The 3-ball is placed on the edge of the other corner

pocket. Play hard with a 10 o'clock spin, while aiming at the right side of the 1-ball. The 1-ball and the 2-ball will be pocketed in the same corner, while the cue ball will strike three cushions before pocketing the 3-ball. When you do it, you'll note with some amusement the traffic around pocket B. Indeed, the 1-ball will go by first, followed immediately by the cue ball, which will pass between the 1-ball and the 2-ball, then the 2-ball which will follow the 1-ball into the same corner. There is a risk they'll collide at that spot but you should be able to pull off this trick from time to time.

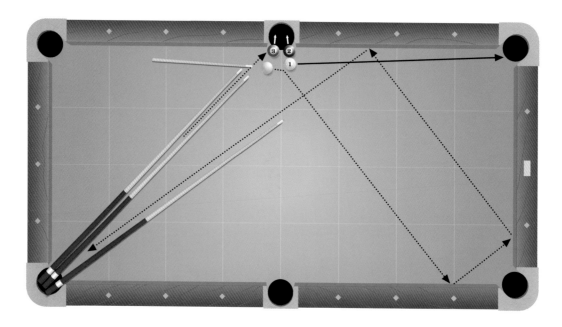

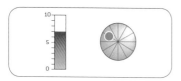

89. THE LITTLE TRAIN

This trick always surprises, because it's simple and clever. It's the favorite of amateurs, the one that people will ask you to repeat the most often. You use accessories known by all players, and you use cues, but in an unusual way. Lay three cues flat on the table, the butt inside the opening in the corner, as shown in the illustration. The shortest of the three must be placed as far out as possible. The cues will act somewhat like the rails of a railroad on which a train rides. Play fairly hard with a 10 o'clock spin while aiming at the right side of the 1-ball. The cue ball will ricochet off the 1-ball, touch three cushions, climb between the

first two cues and come down between the second and third cues to pocket the 3-ball.

Naturally, you'll have to practice a few shots to find the appropriate force. If you play too hard, the cue ball will climb between the first two cues right to their end and be projected off the table. Furthermore, if the cue ball doesn't have enough power, it won't be able to jump over the center cue. If your shot is good, the cue ball, once it reaches the end of the first two cues, will jump over the one in the center to slowly come down the other side toward the 3-ball.

90. CHAIN REACTION

Here's another impressive trick: all the balls are used in an unexpected manner, according to a meticulously planned mechanism. This is a modified version of the football trick (trick no. 99).

Place the balls exactly as shown in the illustration. Note that the first three pairs of balls along the cushion are not positioned perpendicular to the cushion, but at a slight angle. The 3-ball requires a lot of attention during the preparations, for it has to be placed so that it can ricochet off the 4-ball. Once the balls are in the right posi-

tion, announce to the spectators that you're going to attempt to make the 8-ball drop into the center pocket marked with an X. This feat appears impossible, for the 8-ball's trajectory is blocked by six balls grouped in pairs along the cushion. Play hard with a 6:30 spin while aiming right at the center of the 1-ball. A real chain reaction will occur, resulting in the 8-ball traveling along the cushion towards the center, ricocheting off the 9-ball and dropping into the designated pocket.

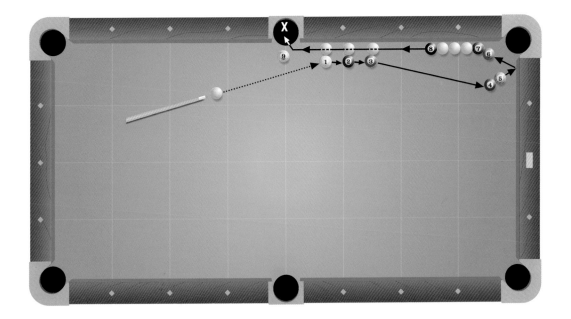

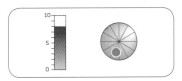

91. AN UNEXPECTED TRAJECTORY

This shot may be useful in a game of eight-ball. In the diagram, you'll notice that the cue ball doesn't have direct access to the 8-ball, which is imprisoned between the opponent's balls. Simulate a frame of eight-ball and announce to the spectators that your opponent has performed a defensive shot and left you this apparently impossible play ... However, tell them that there's a way to hit the center of the 8-ball. Play with a

lot of 4 o'clock spin. The cue ball will hit two cushions and surprise spectators with its erratic behavior. In fact, the last rebound will occur in the direction contrary to the one that would normally be expected, because of the right sidespin.

Note: If you can't apply enough spin, do the same trick again, but raise the butt of your cue approximately 30° relative to the table.

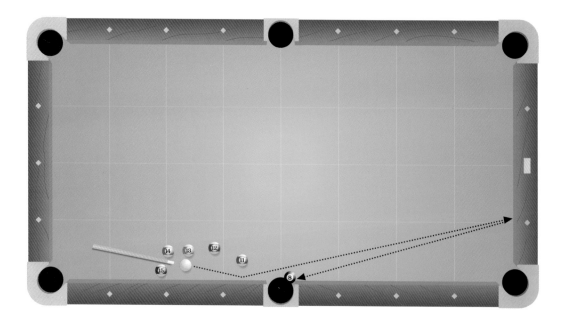

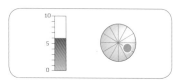

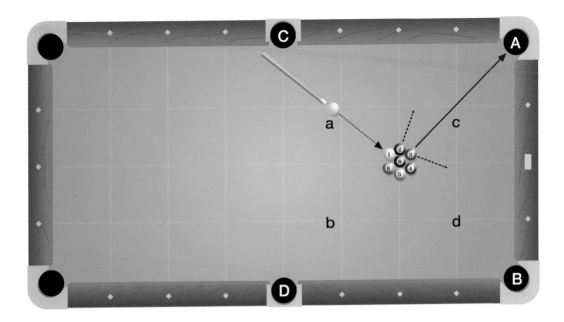

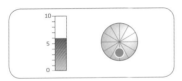

92. TRULY IMPOSSIBLE

I saw this trick for the first time during a 14.1 world tournament that took place at Asbury Park in a suburb of New York a few years ago. Even if I consider myself to be knowledgeable in this field, I must confess that I was dumbfounded when a fellow did this trick on a practice table at the start of the evening. It took me a few hours to understand what really happened when this trick was performed. Truly incredible! The 8-ball, which is placed on the head spot, is surrounded by six numbered balls, so that there's no apparent way to pocket the 8-ball. First, place the 2-ball, the 8-ball and the 5-ball in a straight line. Next, freeze the 1-ball and the 3-ball against the 2-ball, leaving

a space of ³/₈ in. (1 cm) between it and the 8-ball. Lastly, position the 4-ball and the 6-ball the same way, frozen against the 5-ball. The 8-ball can be pocketed in any of the four upper pockets. Ask a spectator to choose the pocket to which they would like the 8-ball to be sent. Depending on the pocket chosen, place the cue ball at the approximate spot designated by a lowercase letter. Each lowercase letter indicates where you should place the cue ball to hit the 8-ball into the pocket that corresponds to the same uppercase letter. Play moderately hard, directly against the ball closest to you.

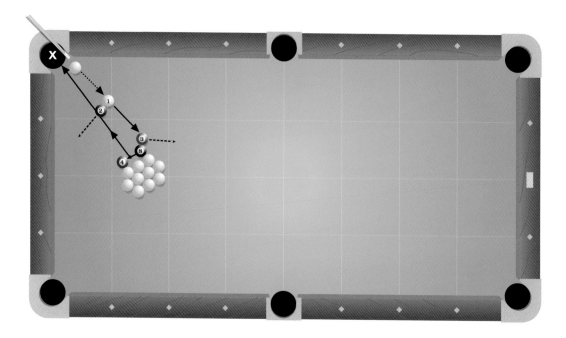

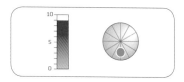

93. MOSCONI'S TRICK

This trick has been around for nearly 100 years, since Ralph Greenleaf routinely performed it during his demonstrations in the 1920s and 1930s. It was made especially popular by Willie Mosconi when he taught Paul Newman to perform it for the film *The Hustler* in 1961. After removing the triangle, place the balls as shown in the illustration. Play hard, with a 6 o'clock spin. Aim at the left side of the 1-ball. It will ricochet off the 2-ball by repelling it and continue on to strike the 3-ball, which will then strike the 8-ball. The compact pack of balls will act as a wall, off which the 8-ball will rebound to head toward the pocket marked with an X.

94. THREE BALLS IN THREE POCKETS

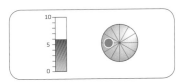

Freeze the 1-ball against the cushion, approximately ¹/₂ in. (12 mm) from the center pocket. Then, freeze the 2-ball against the 1-ball so that it's perpendicular to the cushion. Place the 3-ball facing the opposite corner. Place the cue ball as shown in the illustration, approximately 1¹/₂ in. (4 cm) from the cushion. Strike fairly hard with a 9 o'clock spin. Aim at the right side of the 2-ball to project the cue ball off the opposite cushion, as shown in the diagram. The 1-ball will be pocketed in the opposite center pocket. The 2-ball will travel along the cushion to drop into the corner pocket, while the cue ball will go around the table to strike the 3-ball. Repeat this trick often and learn to master it, for it's the basis of several other tricks. It's also a shot that is both easy and impressive.

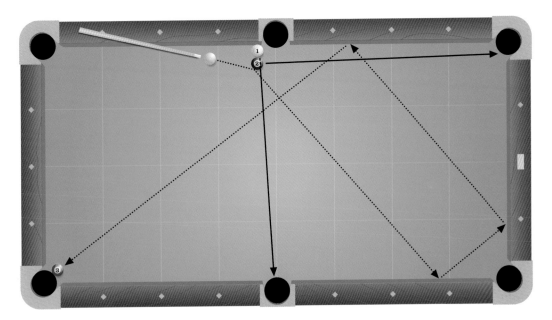

95. SIX BALLS IN FIVE POCKETS

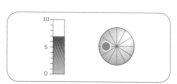

This trick is, in fact, a variation of trick no. 94. You simply add three balls, which makes the trick much more dramatic. Place the 1-ball, 2-ball and 3-ball in the same way and perform the shot the same way. The added balls must be placed very carefully. The 4-ball is positioned opposite the center pocket approximately 1/8 in. (3 mm) from the cushion or, if you prefer, from the imaginary extension of the cushion opposite the center pocket. The 5-ball is frozen against the 4-ball, perpendicular to the cushion. The 6-ball, in turn, is frozen against the 5-ball by lining it up with the opposite corner, not directly with the pocket, but close to it, as shown in the diagram. The 2-ball will strike the 5-ball, thus putting in motion the 4-ball, the 5-ball and the 6-ball. The 1-ball will be projected into the opposite pocket in the center, the 2-ball and the 4-ball into the nearest center pocket, the 5-ball into the corner pocket farthest away, and the 6-ball into the right corner. As for the 3-ball, it will fall into the nearest pocket. This trick was the subject of a popular commercial on American television in the late 1970s. The star of the commercial was a member of the BCA Hall of Fame, Steve Mizerak, and he needed 191 retakes before the producer was satisfied with the way it was done. If a champion needed that many attempts, don't become discouraged if it also takes you a lot of attempts to be able to do it!

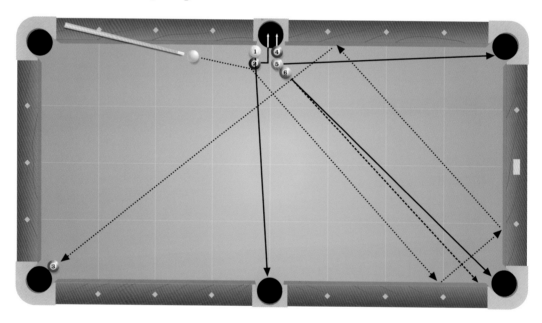

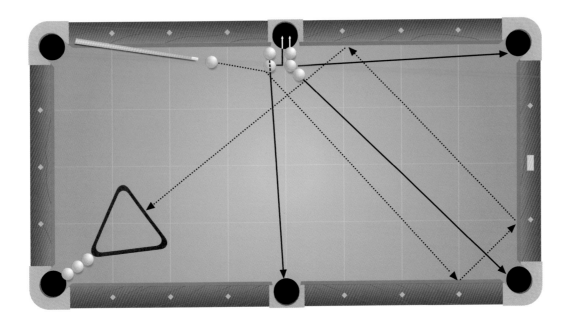

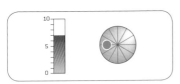

96. EIGHT BALLS IN FIVE POCKETS

This trick is an adaptation of tricks no. 94 and no. 95, and it seems even more dramatic. In reality, this one is easier than the previous one, for the margin of error is larger. You simply add two balls that you freeze in a straight line with the one in the corner, then you place the triangle on the table so that the point is frozen against a third ball, as shown in the illustration. The cue ball, after hitting three cushions, will return to hit the triangle, pushing the last three balls into the pocket at the same time. This trick was shown on television several times during trick shots championships over several years. Always spectacular, it never fails to impress the crowds.

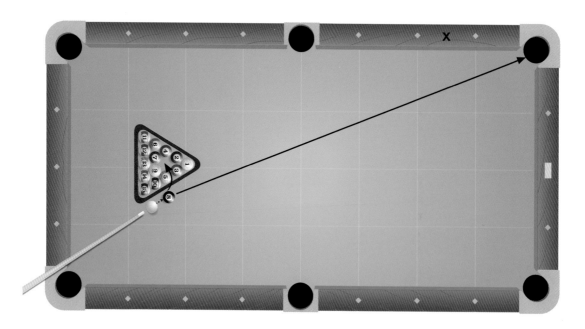

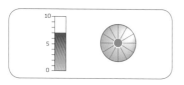

97. THE PERILOUS LEAP

Put all the balls inside the triangle, placing the 8-ball in the center. Next, remove the 8-ball and place it approximately 2 in. (5 cm) from the pyramid, along the extension of an imaginary line located between the second and third rows of balls. Place the cue ball at a slight angle by lining up the 8-ball with the X on the left cushion. The secret is to raise the butt of the cue approxi-mately 30° relative to the horizontal plane of the table. Play fairly hard right in the center of the cue ball to pocket the 8-ball at the other end. If you find the appropriate force, the cue ball will jump and rebound directly into the empty space in the center of the pyramid. Spectators are always surprised.

98. DROP THE TRIANGLE

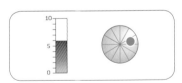

Place the 15 balls inside the triangle in the usual spot. Raise the point of the triangle and carefully remove the first ball, placing it slightly to the left. Next, lay the triangle on top as shown in the illustration. The cue ball is positioned to the right of the triangle. Play a shot moderately hard and with a 2:30 spin diagonally to the second diamond of the opposite rail. The cue ball will touch three cushions to remove the ball supporting the triangle, which will be knocked to the outside. After ricocheting off this ball, the cue ball will rebound inside the triangle, which, by falling, will then hold it prisoner. The final result: you'll have 15 balls perfectly positioned inside the triangle.

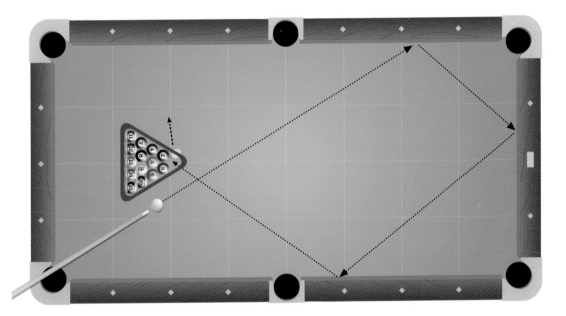

99. THE FOOTBALL TRICK

Group 12 balls into pairs in a row starting at the center pocket and moving back toward the center of the table. Each pair is frozen, at a slight angle. Next, place the last three balls so that the 8-ball is aligned with the extension of the center of the row. The cue ball is placed farther back, roughly at the spot shown in the illustration. Be very careful to place the balls as shown in the illustration, for their position will determine whether the shot succeeds or not. Play hard with an 11 o'clock spin between the 1-ball and the 8-ball, but first touching the 1-ball. Remember this detail, for it's critical. As in football, all the balls will move apart to allow the one that could be called the receiver, i.e. the 8-ball, to be pocketed in the center. This is one of the most spectacular tricks.

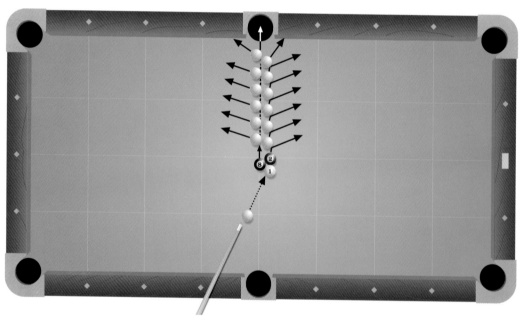

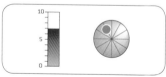

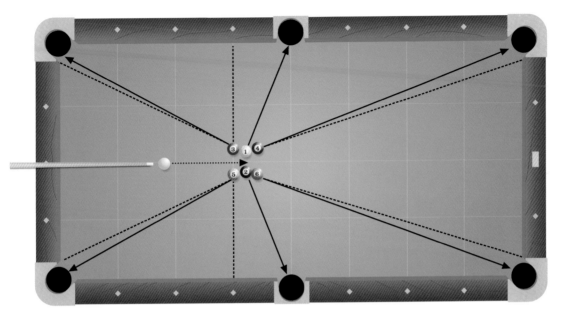

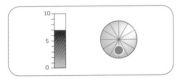

100. SIX IN SIX

To do this trick, the most important thing is to place the balls in the right spot. Use the illustration to help you line up the two center balls, not in the middle of the table, but almost opposite the spot shown. To help you find the exact position, a dotted line indicates the position of the two outside balls that will be placed almost opposite the diamonds adjacent to the two center pockets. The 1-ball and the 2-ball must be approximately 1¹/₂ in. (4 cm) apart. It's critical that the 3-ball, the 4-ball and the 5-ball are aligned, not directly with the center of the pocket, but slightly to the side, with the inside corner, as shown in the diagram. Play hard with a 6 o'clock spin. The secret of this trick is the exact placement of the balls. Once these are correctly positioned, anyone can do this trick if they're told where to strike. This is why this trick is performed by the actor Jerry Lewis in one of his films. If this clown could do this trick, persevere in your attempts and you'll certainly be able to do it!

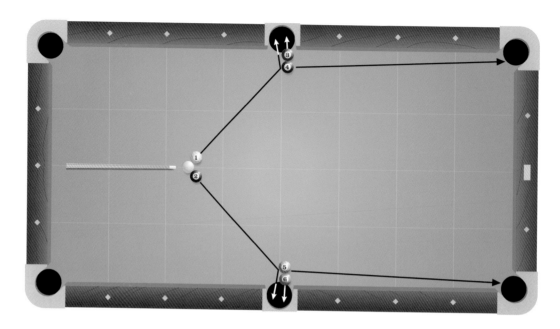

101. SIX BALLS IN FOUR POCKETS

Place the cue ball close to the head spot, in the middle of the table. Next, freeze the cue ball against the 1-ball and the 2-ball, not directly with the 4-ball and 5-ball, but rather with the two balls closest to the center pockets, i.e. the 3-ball and the 6-ball. Play hard with no spin, between the 1-ball and the 2-ball. Because of the slight deflection caused by the strike, the 1-ball and the 2-ball will hit the 4-ball and the 5-ball and ricochet into the center pocket. At the same time, the 3-ball and the 6-ball will be pushed toward the center, while the 4-ball and the 5-ball will ricochet toward the two corner pockets.

Warning: Without a doubt, you'll make several fruitless attempts before finding the exact direction in which the 1-ball and the 2-ball must be lined up. Persevere, for even the great experts were forced to practice this trick.

102. FIFTEEN BALLS IN ONE SHOT

Look closely at the position of the balls and you'll discover that this is essentially a combination of tricks no. 100 and no. 101, to which three balls have simply been added. In my opinion, this is the most dramatic play there is. The fellow that designed it had a stroke of genius. I was taught this trick for the first time in a practice room in the Biltmore Hotel in New York during the 1978 world tournament. It was the expert Willie Jopling himself, the creator of a collection of pool tricks, who explained it to me. However, in 1908, Joe Hood had already shown it in his book of tricks! I never try this trick during my public demonstrations, though, for it takes 15 minutes to place the balls correctly, which bores the spectators.

First, place the six balls in the center with care, then place the six other balls as shown in the diagram for trick no. 101. Lastly, add the last three balls near the three corner pockets. The trick is performed in one motion, but can be divided into two steps. First, the two balls frozen against the cue ball are projected toward the center pockets and open up the path. While this is happening, the cue ball continues on its trajectory and sets the six balls in the center in motion. As for the rest, see the trajectory of each ball as shown in the diagram. Be patient and good luck.

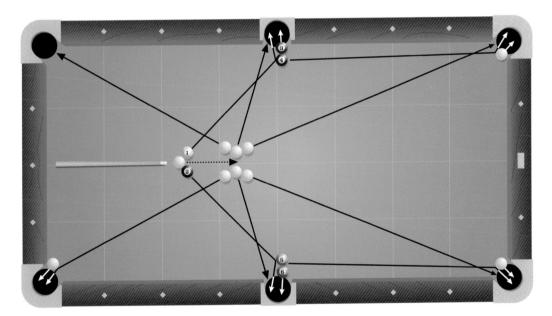

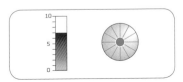

103. THE ROBERT BYRNE TRICK

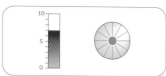

The engineer Robert Byrne is a fan of pool. He's published 21 books, of which six are on this topic. In 2001, he was elected to the BCA Hall of Fame. One of his books, published in 1982, is entitled *Byrne's Treasury of Trick Shots in Pools and Billiards*. This book took eight months of full-time work, for the author wanted to publish the greatest number of original tricks possible, but also to find the real inventors. His research covered a period going back to 1810.

This play is easy to do and is very dramatic. Use two cylinders of different lengths, the shortest one 2$\frac{1}{2}$–3 in. (6.5–8 cm) high, and the other one, approximately 4$\frac{1}{2}$ in. (11.5 cm) high. Use a cigar tube, coin containers or create your own cylinders using thin cardboard and tape. You can also use a cigarette pack for the first pillar and a cigar pack for the second. Place a ball on each of the cylinders in the middle of the table, exactly in a straight line between the two center pockets. Place the cylinders very close to each other, as shown in the illustration. Say that you're going to pocket the three balls in the center pockets with only one shot. Play fairly hard while aiming at the opposite center pocket, hitting in passing the two pillars, which will move apart. The two balls that were in the air will drop to the table one on top of the other, and be projected into the two center pockets. Everyone can do this simple trick, and your chance of succeeding is 90%.

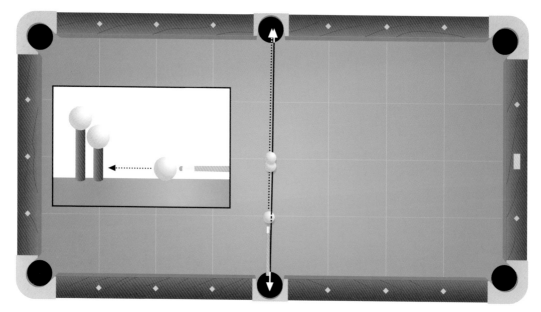

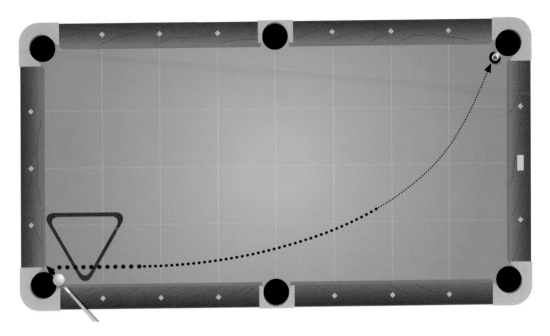

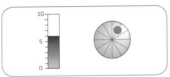

104. THE SLALOM JUMP

A slalom is a winding route that includes obstacles. And this is what we have here! Believe it or not, this trick appeared in a book on pool in 1827, written by Frenchman François Mingaud. Position the 8-ball near the corner pocket and place the cue ball at the far end of the pocket chute in the opposite corner, frozen to the angle formed by the cushion (see the illustration). Then, lay the triangle flat on the table to block the path of the cue ball to the 8-ball. Tell the audience that it's possible to pocket the 8-ball, which is at the other end of the table, using a perfectly legal shot. To do it, you'll have to make the cue ball bounce over the obstacle. To do this, position yourself to play,

raise the butt of your cue approximately 20° (you'll have no other choice but to play off the top of the cue ball, for you don't have access to the bottom, which is hidden by the cushion). Play moderately hard with a 1 o'clock spin. Make sure you aim at the corner or the tip of the opposite cushion. If you strike at the right spot, the cue ball will take off, drop on the other side of the triangle, travel along the cushion toward the center pocket, then turn off toward the 8-ball. You'll need to try it a few times to find the right height to raise the butt of your cue and the exact spot on the opposite cushion to send the cue ball off, but with perseverence, you'll get it.

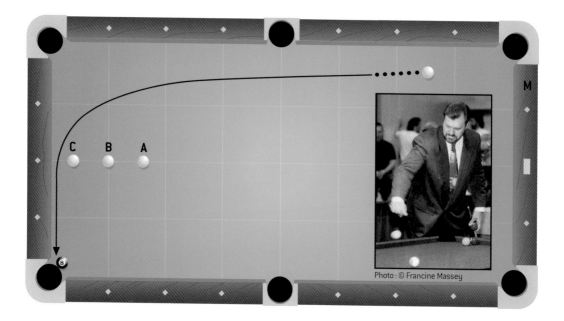

Photo : © Francine Massey

105. FINGER POOL

 5

This is a trick that uses a variety of incredible shots performed without a cue, where the cue ball is projected using only your fingers! The champion at this is none other than the famous Mike Massey, who performs extraordinary feats with disconcerting skill: the cue ball follows curves that are unheard of. You have to see it to believe it. So, if you really want to have a clear idea, don't hesitate to watch a few demonstrations on YouTube. One important point: you must have large hands to do this kind of trick. Massey is 6 ft. 4 in. (1.9 m) tall and he has enormous hands and very long fingers. The M indicates the spot where Mike stands to perform this trick. He explains what he does: "I stand where shown (see letter M on the rail) and face the table with

my right hand in front of my chest. I sling the ball out to my right and snap my fingers. My thumb faces down and my knuckles are angled anywhere from 50° to 80°..." He confirms that to do these tricks, you have to be able to pivot the cue ball on itself for at least 15–20 seconds. In the situation shown, which he baptized "the limbo," Mike starts by getting around the ball located at A to pocket the 8-ball. Then, with the next throw, he moves the ball roughly 6 in. (15 cm) to B. And he ends by moving the blocking ball again another 6 in. (15 cm) to C, only two ball widths from the cushion, so that the cue ball follows a curve toward the left (trajectory shown) that's almost 90°! This is only one sensational shot, for he performs many other similar ones.

106. CHINESE BILLIARDS

While in the previous trick you didn't use a cue, here, on the contrary, you'll need two of them! Since a picture is worth a thousand words, I refer you to the photos. Hold the cues in two hands: the rear hand on top and the forward hand underneath. The index finger of each hand is placed between the cues. You hold the cues closer together than the width of the ball and, lowering them, you pass them over the cue ball that you want to pick up and capture between the cues. Then, you raise the cues, slowly rolling the cue ball toward you while you line yourself up in front of the ball you want to pocket. Last step: you lower the cues in the direction of the spot you want the cue ball to go, and strike the one you've chosen by hitting it at the required angle: the cue ball will drop down between the cues like a train rolling along the tracks. When I do this demonstration of Chinese billiards, I say the following just before starting: "Recently, I traveled in China and I noticed that not only do they eat with cues, but they also play pool using two cues ..." Your show will be even better if you use a little humor.

CONCLUSION

I hope you found in this book everything you need to enjoy pool, whether it's the technical aspects, in order to discover and master the principles of this game, which is not as simple as it appears when you see others play, or its lighter side, made up of all the tricks that, paradoxically, seem so astonishing but aren't as complicated as you might think. In short, the book serves to pass the time as you discover and learn everything about this exciting game. You'll understand that pool is not just glossy balls on a green baize. Beyond this basic image, you'll discover a fascinating history of a game that evolved as society evolved over several centuries. Over time, what was once considered a basic pastime has become a structured recreational activity adopted by all social classes, regardless of age, gender or race. It's really an ideal pastime for everyone. Its history is sprinkled with surprising and colorful anecdotes. Once you know the game's secrets, you'll no longer look at these focused champions in the same way, as they battle hotly contested matches. As with all other sports or recreational activities, we realize that excellence isn't the product of chance, but the result of intense learning and the desire to excel against all opponents. Naturally, we can't all become champions, and at any rate, there's no need to be an expert to enjoy playing pool. Whether you see it as a simple pastime or as an extremely competitive activity, it will be highly entertaining, offering an infinite number of possibilities. A few years before the death of Luther Lassiter (many times world champion in the 1960s), he was asked why he still spent many hours practicing, since he must know all the secrets behind the science of this game to which he had devoted his life. Lassiter replied that, even after all these years, he was still discovering new things and there were shots that he had forgotten that he would remember when he practiced!

What is the future of pool? At a time when people are quitting violent sports in favor of team sports and family activities, pool is certainly well positioned to continue to benefit from the wave of popularity it currently enjoys. It's the ultimate universal leisure activity, popular around the world. Good luck to all readers. I wish you as much pleasure playing pool as I've had writing this book.

GLOSSARY

BACKSPIN: Backward spin.

BAIZE: Cloth that covers the pool table (see *cloth*).

BALK: Areas drawn on the cloth for different games in European billiards.

BANK SHOT: Synonym for *cross-table shot*.

BREAK: The first shot played at the start of each frame, with the objective of breaking the pyramid (or the diamond, in a game of nine-ball) and to scatter the balls.

BREAK BALL: The ball off which the cue ball ricochets to break the group of balls.

BREAK BOX: The space located at the head of the table, where the player places the cue ball at the start of a game.

BRICOLE: A shot where the cue ball strikes a cushion before touching the desired ball.

BRIDGE: A support formed by the hand and on which the cue glides to play.

BUMPER: The piece of rubber attached to the end of the butt of the cue to protect the end and absorb any shock.

CAROM: When the cue ball hits the first ball before striking the desired ball. The carom is the basis of European billiards.

CHALK: An abrasive in the form of a cube, most often blue, used to coat the tip to avoid a miscue.

CLOTH: Wool cloth (or a combination of wool and nylon) covering the slate and the cushions.

COMBINATION: A shot where the cue ball strikes one or several intermediate balls that will themselves rebound off the designated ball.

CONTINUOUS (14.1): A variation of pool in which the balls are returned to the triangle each time that only one (apart from the cue ball) remains on the table. It was the game played during professional competitions in the United States until 1990.

CROSS-TABLE SHOT: A shot where the object ball is projected off a cushion to rebound into the opposite pocket.

CUE (or pool cue): Word commonly used for the thin wooden stick used in pool to hit the cue ball.

CUE BALL: The white ball, i.e. the one which the player strikes directly with his cue.

CUSHION: A rubber strip, attached to the rail, used to ensure the balls rebound.

DIAMOND: Small white spots embedded in the top

of the rail at regular intervals, which, while marking the break box, are used as reference points to prepare some shots. On older tables, the diamonds were sometimes in the shape of a rhomboid.

DIRECT HIT: A player takes a direct hit when the cue ball has direct access (not hidden by any other ball) to the object ball.

FERRULE: The little cylinder around the end of the shaft used as the base of the tip.

FILING: The back-and-forth motion made with the arm to prepare each shot.

FOOT OF THE TABLE: The end of the table opposite the cushion on which the manufacturer's plate is attached.

FREE ZONE: The space opposite the break box.

FROZEN BALL: A ball stuck to the cushion or another ball.

HEAD OF THE TABLE: The part of the table where the break box is found, determined by the manufacturer's plate attached to the edge of the rail.

INTERFERENCE: The action, by a player, a spectator or a piece of equipment, of moving one or several balls accidentally or deliberately.

JOINT: The joint between the shaft and the butt on jointed cues.

JUMP SHOT: A shot that forces the cue ball to leave the bed of the table and to rise slightly over a short distance while traveling along its trajectory.

KEY BALL: In continuous pool (14.1), the second-last ball.

KISS: A word commonly used as a synonym of ricochet, is a shot where the cue ball rebounds off another ball before hitting the object ball, or where an object ball rebounds off another ball before being pocketed.

LAG: A process used to decide the order of the players at the beginning of a match.

LINE-UP POOL: A type of pool game in which the balls after each round are returned to the head spot and lined up along the foot of the table.

MASSÉ: A shot played so that the cue ball follows a curve before hitting the object ball.

MISCUE: A player performs a miscue when the tip slides or skids off the cue ball.

POCKET: The chute placed at each of the six openings on a pool table.

POCKET, TO: The action of projecting a ball into a pocket.

PUSH SHOT: To push the cue ball and the object ball using the same stroke.

PYRAMID: The shape of the balls grouped together after the triangle is removed.

RAIL: The edge of the table, which defines the playing surface.

RAKE: An instrument consisting of a handle and a head in the shape of a rake, used to support the cue when you want to reach balls that are impossible to reach normally.

RICOCHET: See kiss.

ROUND: A round lasts as long as the player continues to score points and it ends when the player misses.

SHAFT: The narrowest part of the jointed cue, at the opposite end from the butt.

SPIN (more commonly called "English"): The rotation of the cue ball on itself, which varies according to the point of attack and changes the ball's final trajectory.

SPOT: Little black disks or dots attached to the table at different locations and used as a guide for placing the balls.

THREE-CUSHIONS: A type of carom billiard game where a carom shot is performed in which the cue ball must touch at least three cushions before striking the second ball.

TIP: The little leather disk attached to the end of the shaft on a pool cue or cue.

TOPSPIN: A forward spin.

TRIANGLE: A wooden or plastic frame in the shape of an equilateral triangle, used to correctly position the balls at the start of a game.

WHITE BALL: Another name for the cue ball.

ACKNOWLEDGMENTS

The author would like to thank all those who helped him to publish this work, in particular Luc Morin of Studio Tango, for the color photographs in the technical section. He would also like to thank Michael E. Panozzo, publisher of *Billiards Digest* in Chicago, Billie Billing of Southern Exposure in New York, and Francine Massey for the photo of Mike Massey.

He would also like to thank Sylvain Delage of the luxurious pool hall, Dooly's, in Longueuil, Quebec, for allowing him to use the establishment free of charge to take the photographs for the technical section.